Apprentices of War
Memoir of a Marine Grunt

Gary L. Tornes

ISBN 0-9752600-0-6
No part of this book may be used or reproduced in any manner whatsoever without
written permission except in the case of brief quotations embodied in critical articles
or book reviews.

Library of Congress Control Number: 2004105803
Library of Congress in Publication Data
Summary: [1. Vietnam War 2. Military History 3. Autobiography 4. Gary Tornes
5. Apprentices of War 6. Tornes 7. War]

Printed by:
MK Publishing
420 E. St. Germain
St. Cloud, MN 56303
www.yourbookpublisher.net
800-551-1023

Distributed by:
A.O.W. LLC
3301 E. Northshore Blvd. #142
Appleton, WI 54915

Printed in the United States of America

For:
The grunts, corpsmen, medics,
and the 58,235 names on the Wall.

They are heroes of a war that few wanted.

And for:

James "Doc" Clopton, HM2/USN
who gave it his all trying
to save so many.

Acknowledgements

Writing a memoir is an individual activity, but the actual writing is the only part that is a solitary event. Many people have contributed to this book.

My editor was Donna Peterson, a special friend of 35 years and an early supporter of the concept of the book. She meticulously edited and re-edited the manuscript and came up with ideas to make the book better.

Two years ago I stored the 150 pages I had written on a floppy disk. One morning I turned on my computer and there was nothing where the budding manuscript had been. I was told by the head of our IS Department that all of it probably was lost. I agonized over this and doubted I could reproduce what I had written. I was, in a word, devastated.

Jayne Spielvogel was assigned the task of data recovery. She worked for several weeks and was only able to recover the text in a printed version. Everything was out of sequence and very little made sense, but she continued with quiet determination. About a week later she handed me my 150 pages. Not only had she retrieved the lost data, but she put it in order and retyped it on her own time. Thank you, Jayne. Without your phenomenal effort, the book would not exist.

Tim Sloat, Platoon Commander of Delta Company's First Platoon, was an early supporter of my mission. He was an excellent advisor on terminology and Marine procedures. He was totally unselfish with his time reading many of my early drafts. His input and support meant more to me than he will ever realize.

Doc Clopton was with me in the field and is one of a kind. He spent a week with me in the early stages and reviewed a partial draft. He filled in parts I had forgotten and added a different perspective to the story. I will always be grateful for his personal friendship as well as his contributions to the book.

I enlisted a number of people to read the fifth draft of the book. I asked them to forget that they knew me and read it critically. Special thanks go to Paul Reiser, Stephanie Jack, Dick Alberts and Bonny Fetch for their helpful comments.

I also want to thank Pike Military Research for the fine job they did collecting two volumes of the actual battlefield orders and chronological details of the Battalion during the period of July 66 through August 67. It made my job so much easier.

Finally, I must thank Mike (Monk) McNally, a character in the book and still a character in life. Mike kept the eighteen letters I wrote him while I was in the Marine Corps and later sent copies of them to me. These letters along with the material from Pike Military Research made it possible to create a timeline of my tour. Mike, a professional photographer, also took the pictures of my jungle boots and dog tags that appear on the cover of the book. Thanks, Mike.

Table of Contents

Introduction

For me, Vietnam was thirty-seven years ago, but it was also yesterday. During the last three decades, hardly a day has passed without a thought or reminder of those months of my life trying to stay alive.

Initially, I had planned to write a brief personal narrative about my Vietnam experience for my teenage son. My intention was to give him a better understanding of both that war and his father. But as this project developed, it evolved into a much fuller account.

The enlisted field troops and junior grade officers are the apprentices of all wars. Most are facing combat for the first time and ultimately end up doing the majority of the fighting and the dying. They don't consider themselves heroes, yet they perform acts of valor daily without regarding that as special. Typically they neither expect, nor do they receive medals or special recognition for their actions. They do the job they were trained to do. Their apprenticeships are usually short, intense and violent.

I have written what I remember about the war and my personal battlefield as seen through the eyes of a nineteen-year-old, high-school-educated, Marine grunt.

This book is not meant to be a chronologically accurate history of Delta Company, 1st Battalion, 1st Marines during the years 1966 and 1967. I have carefully researched unit histories to establish chronology and big picture facts, but the book is based primarily on my recollection of what happened to me and to those special Marines in my fire-team, squad and platoon.

Over the years I might have forgotten certain names and dates, but my memory of events has remained clear. I treasure and fear those memories. They have influenced many decisions in my life – both good and bad.

I have heard it said that Vietnam produced no heroes. I have a different view. We had 58,235 of them. Their names are permanently engraved in the black granite of the Vietnam Veterans Memorial Wall. Whether they died performing heroic acts or were simply in the wrong place at the wrong time, they are, in my opinion, the heroes of the Vietnam War.

Da Nang / Hoi An T.A.O.R. July 1966 - July 1967

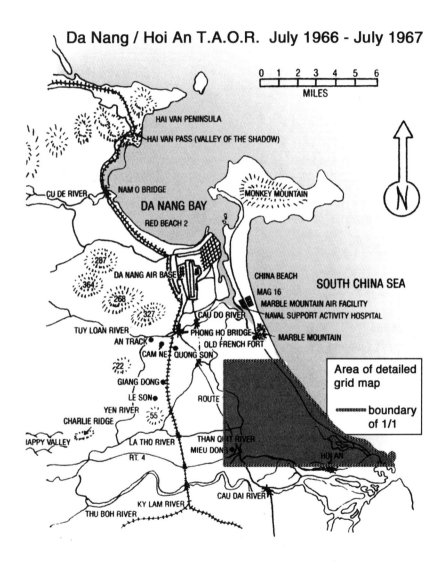

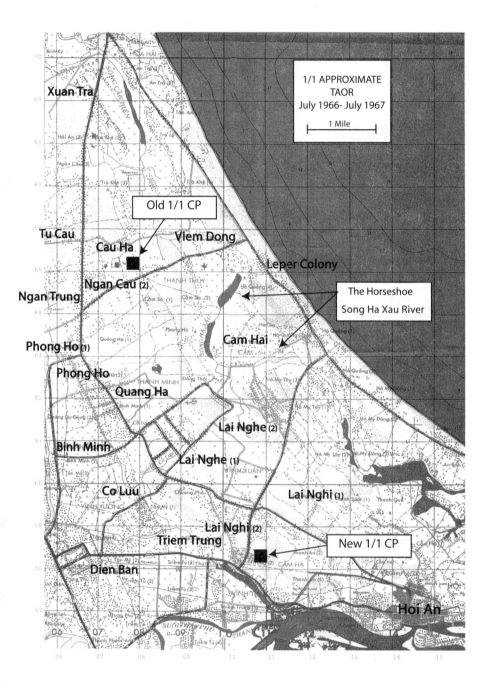

1/1 APPROXIMATE
TAOR
July 1966- July 1967

1 Mile

Old 1/1 CP

The Horseshoe
Song Ha Xau River

New 1/1 CP

Apprentices of War
Memoir of a Marine Grunt

Chapter 1

No Trophy Today

The old Winchester Model 94 fired once, twice, three times. The buck kept running. I could feel my heart pounding in my chest. My hands were sweating inside red jersey gloves. My jaw was clenched and my whole body was trembling.

"Think I hit him, Dad?"

"Don't know, Son. Didn't see him flinch. Might have shot over him."

It was November 10, 1965—the opening day of deer hunting season in Northern Minnesota. The deer herd had been hurt by the past few years of harsh winters—too much snow, extremely cold temperatures or both. You could go for days and not see a deer. We were hunting on Barney Cox's farm, eighteen miles west of International Falls. This was one of the many sub-marginal farms along the Canadian border. The land was more hospitable to deer and wild blueberries than it was for Holsteins and wheat.

As we walked to the middle of the narrow hay field to check for blood that would confirm my marksmanship, I was overwhelmed by the anticipation of experiencing the kill. My first deer, and it was a buck. We approached the middle of the field where the deer had crossed. I saw the tracks. They were huge. This was a trophy buck. Maybe I could mount the head and hang it in my bedroom. That option seemed remote because I knew Mom wouldn't allow it in the house.

"Don't see any blood, Son."

"There has to be blood," I insisted. "I know I hit it. I *know* I did."

Fervently, we searched the snow for any sign of blood. We found none. I was devastated. I felt as bad as a teenager from Northern Minnesota could possibly feel on opening day. I would never again have an opportunity like this—the chance for three, unobstructed shots at a trophy. But I was wrong. About a year later I was successful. The target had been running in a straight line across the field. My first two shots were high, just like last year. My third shot, however, hit. Down it went. Unlike last year, we wouldn't have to look for a blood trail. It wasn't moving.

"Good shot," said Langley. This year, Langley was with me instead of Dad.

"Did you see that third shot"? I said. "Flipped him right over, he ain't moving."

As we walked to the center of the field toward the downed trophy, I experienced the same physical sensations as last year. I could feel my heart pounding. My hands were sweaty; my jaw was clenched. It was warmer this year, so I wasn't wearing gloves. Langley and I reached the trophy at the same time. Blood was everywhere. Langley unceremoniously kicked the trophy over.

"It's a little girl, not a Viet Cong," he stammered, almost whispering.

"Shit!" I exploded.

As I looked down at the young Vietnamese girl floating in two feet of tepid rice paddy water, I felt no remorse or guilt. I had just taken the life of an innocent, teenage girl and my only regret was that it hadn't been a North Vietnamese Army (NVA) or Viet Cong (VC) kill. Once again, I had missed a trophy.

In the course of a year, my definition of trophy had changed from a whitetail buck to a human being. Shooting a pre-pubescent girl instead of a VC or NVA was like shooting a fawn.

Langley, a young PFC from Texas, had recently been assigned to my squad. He was nineteen years old, considerably younger than I. He looked like an innocent teen on a Norman Rockwell poster. I was twenty years old and had been with the 1st Platoon of Delta Company, 1st Battalion, 1st Marines for nearly four months. In those few months I had been promoted once. I was now a lance corporal and the leader of the 1st squad. I hadn't done anything spectacular to earn the promotion. My main achievement had been staying alive.

What had happened in the course of a year that had so dramatically changed my perspective on life and death? A year ago I had only a vague idea where Vietnam was and I had a negative opinion of military personnel. I was convinced that the smartest American youth were attending college—trying their best to avoid the draft.

The girl lying face up in the water was about the age of my sister, Debbie. If she had started loading the oriental vegetables, that were now floating around her body, into her shoulder-pole baskets two minutes sooner, she would be alive. If the Viet Cong had waited until she had crossed the dike before firing at us, she would be alive. If Shively hadn't had to stop and take a shit earlier in the patrol, she would have made it to her destination.

If, if. If I hadn't joined the Marine Corps, she probably would have grown up, married, had children and lived her life in one of the many bamboo-walled, thatched huts that dotted the countryside. A miserable existence by our standards, but she still would be alive.

We left the young body floating in the flooded rice paddy, then carefully made our way across the narrow dike to a water-encircled Vietnamese village.

"Check the hooches for VC signs," I directed.

The squad responded by unceremoniously emptying all the large storage baskets of rice and cautiously examining several reinforced shelters connected to the larger huts.

I stooped to enter one of the smaller huts next to a muddy fish-pond. Many Vietnamese farmers had small fishponds adjacent to their hooches where they raised a species of carp for food. The hut's interior was identical to hundreds of structures I had seen during my tour. It resembled a miniature pole barn—the kind you find on midwestern farms. Other than size, the major difference between the huts and pole barns was the building materials. Instead of steel and concrete, the huts were made of bamboo and thatch.

The hooch's floor was petrified mud and as hard as slate. Generations of padding bare feet had polished its surface to a glossy sheen. Against one wall was a Buddhist shrine with incense sticks and a meager offering of small greenish bananas. Almost every Vietnamese home, regardless of status or size, had some form of religious shrine. We ate the bananas.

Two bamboo beds were pushed together in one corner. Each had small blocks of well-worn wood that functioned as pillows. A small lean-to attached to the main room was the cooking area. It reminded me of the summer kitchen attached to my grandparents' farmhouse. The design was the same, but in Vietnam it felt like it was always summer.

I continued to search the small hut and found a trunk under one of the beds. Inside the trunk was a neatly folded Viet Cong flag. Among troops in the field, an enemy flag was a valued war trophy. It didn't have the status of a captured AK-47, but it was a prize.

We searched the other huts without finding anything of military value. The flag was our only booty. I called the squad together and told them we would take a short break before continuing on. Hicks, my radioman, approached me and asked what he should do about calling to report the friendly kill.

"Call Delta One and report that we took enemy fire from a tree line and returned fire. One Viet Cong confirmed kill," I replied.

"But that little girl wasn't a VC." Hicks responded.

"How the fuck do you know? We found a VC flag in the hut she was running to, didn't we? Call it in as a VC confirmed kill."

I took my helmet off, lit a cigarette and sat down, leaning against an overturned earthen vat. The cigarette tasted good. I was exhausted. We had been on an extended squad patrol for the last five hours. It seemed like I was always exhausted, thirsty and wet. As I took another drag on the Salem, I glanced down at my helmet.

The camo covering was caked with dried mud and ripped in several places. The helmet had been with me since I arrived in Vietnam. It felt like part of my body. Most field troops used a black grease pen to write a name or message on their camo covers. Usually it was their nickname or the name of their girlfriend or wife. Sometimes it was a Bible quote or a more macho phrase like "Fuck Ho Chi Minh."

As I looked at what I had written, I realized that it was incomplete and then I remembered why. Three months ago, I had started to write on my helmet. Only three months. I couldn't believe it. It seemed so much longer.

It was mid-August 1966, and our undermanned platoon was on an extended search-and-destroy patrol. These patrols often lasted several days. At night we would set up a perimeter of two-man fighting holes around a village and that would be our campsite. Usually, the temporary platoon headquarters would be located in a larger building near the center of the perimeter.

I was teamed with Pat Connors and he was furtively trying to dig a fighting hole that would accommodate both of us. Because of the high water table, our depth was limited to several feet. If you dug deeper, you would be flooded. Digging was also hindered by surface root systems.

Pat was a twenty-one year old PFC from Michigan who had been in-country three months. Most Marines his age were unmarried, but not Pat. He had married his childhood sweetheart during boot camp leave.

Although I was born and raised in Minnesota, Alaska was my adopted state. I left for Alaska three days after graduating from International Falls High School. Since I'd spent more than thirteen months in Alaska, I considered myself an Alaskan.

Being from Minnesota seemed so ordinary and bland, but being from Alaska was different and exciting. I wanted something on my helmet that would let everyone know I was Alaskan. With a grease pen in hand, I almost completed my helmet signature when it started.

The late afternoon quiet was interrupted by the throaty rattle of an M-60 machine gun and a popping .30 caliber carbine. On the opposite side of the perimeter, grenades exploded. Bullets tore through the dense jungle foliage. The smell of cordite wafted across our half-completed fighting hole. Pat and I tried to crawl farther into our hole than he had dug.

One VC round found its mark that day. The platoon sergeant was killed. My personal signature on the helmet would never be completed. As the weeks and months went by, being from Alaska seemed less and less important.

I gazed at my tattered camo helmet cover and I mentally completed what I had started: A-L-A-S-K-A-N K-I-D.

Chapter 2
The Alaskan Kid

Alaska was created for adventurers and seventeen-year old boys. I traveled there twice—in June 1964 and March 1965. Both times I failed to find fortune but I did experience adventure that teenage boys usually only find in books. It was a combination of *Treasure Island* and *Call of the Wild*.

In the early 1960's, Alaska was the closest thing to a true frontier America offered. It had been a state for only five years in 1964. The massive earthquake that hit on Good Friday, along with the consequent tidal wave, added confusion and destruction to Alaska's personality. This was the Alaska we found when we arrived in Anchorage on June 6, 1964.

Melvin Gushulak, a high school friend, was my traveling partner. Our planning for the trip started two years earlier, long before the quake.

Three days after graduating from high school, we headed north in our co-owned 1954 red and white Buick Century. The car had been cheap, only $175. It was a masculine looking car—big, strong and, most importantly, the radio worked. There were other things that didn't work, but they were minor. First gear slipped—but you really didn't need it, you could start in second. Reverse worked, sometimes—but we were going forward not backward. It had a broken window on the rider's side, but a double layer of cardboard solved that problem. We were confidant not concerned. It was Alaska or bust.

I had already said goodbye to my family. Mom, of course, cried. Dad was his stoic, Norwegian self. My three sisters actually seemed excited to see me go. It introduced some adventure into their small town lives.

We had grown up in International Falls, the northernmost major town in Minnesota. The town's centerpiece was a large paper mill owned by the Minnesota and Ontario Paper Company. If you lived in International Falls, you worked for the paper mill, the railroad, or you owned a business. There wasn't anything else. My Dad worked in the mill. Melvin's father worked on the railroad.

After saying our good-byes, we traveled west, past the high school onto U.S. Highway 11. We reminisced as we drove by the small gas station and beer joint called The Junction. We had spent many school nights there, smoking and playing pool rather than studying at the library.

Our first stop was my grandmother's house in Thief River Falls, my birthplace. Dad had owned a farm fifty-five miles north, on the edge of one of the largest and most sparsely populated areas in the state, the Beltrami Island National Wildlife Refuge.

The most recent immigrants to Minnesota ended up with the least desirable land. My grandfather had received the homestead deed for his 160 acres in 1915. After clearing eighty acres of virgin white pine, he was ready to farm. He and my grandmother scratched out a living, raising one daughter and three sons on that homestead. Before emigrating from Norway, Grandpa had been trained as a carpenter. He knew nothing about farming. My father, the oldest of the three sons, was my grandfather's primary helper during those early homesteading years.

Dad loved farming and when he returned from WWII, he purchased 160 acres across from the home place. Mom lasted five years. In 1950, after the birth of my sister, Sandra, Mom gave Dad a choice—her or the farm. She couldn't endure the social isolation.

That her closest neighbor was her mother-in-law didn't make things easier.

Dad gave in. He sold the farm and we moved to International Falls in the spring of 1951. Dad never enjoyed another day's work in his life.

We parked the big Buick on Red Lake Boulevard in front of the house my grandparents bought when they moved off the farm in 1952. Two years later Grandpa died of a stroke and Grandma lived alone ever since.

I entered the house without knocking. This was familiar territory, and I had a special bond with Grandma. Not only was I her first grandchild, I had spent much of my first five years with her. Now she was busy in the kitchen preparing our meal. She was bent over the sink peeling potatoes when I embraced her and gave her a loving hug.

Grandma was a tough Norwegian—stubborn, opinionated and independent. Our family's only claim to fame was that Grandma's uncle, Martin Ronne, my great-great uncle, had been with Amundsen on his first voyage to the South Pole in 1911. Martin Ronne's son, Finn, was the leader of the last privately funded exploration of Antarctica. During that expedition, he mapped a large portion of a previously unmapped ice shelf. He named it in honor of his wife, Edith, who was the first woman to spend the winter on that frozen continent.

Grandma taught Grandpa how to farm. Although he had a European high-school education and she had only finished third grade, she had been the teacher—he the student.

"I wish you weren't going to Alaska. I hear that it is not such a good place," she said. "People have not had it good in Alaska since the big earthquake."

"Don't worry, Gram, there are lots of good jobs up there. We'll be okay."

We enjoyed what would be our last home-cooked meal for many months. Grandma was a Scandinavian stoic, but when she hugged me goodbye, I heard a sniffle. She also embraced Melvin and wished him well. As I opened the door, Grandma grabbed my hand and palmed me a neatly folded bill. I thanked her without looking at what she had given me.

Mel fired up the Buick and we headed south on Red Lake Boulevard. I opened my hand and saw that the neatly folded gift was a fifty-dollar bill. Grandma certainly couldn't afford it, but she was always generous. I felt rich with one hundred and thirty-nine dollars in my wallet. Mel had ninety. Together we had two hundred and twenty nine dollars. We were optimistic and naïve—necessary ingredients for youthful adventure.

The old Buick made the 3500 mile trip without incident. More than half our combined assets had been spent during the trip—but we didn't worry. We were confident that jobs paying big bucks were out there just waiting for us.

Melvin and I were only seventeen years old, too young to apply for most jobs. We also had few marketable skills. Our naiveté and honesty didn't help our job-hunting efforts. We eventually learned to be creative when filling out employment applications and interviewing for jobs. Since we had little to offer employers, we more or less invented the education and experience sections. Usually the only true fact once we completed an application was the name.

After learning to play the game, we managed to get a variety of jobs. It was amazing how far a good line of bullshit, a positive attitude, and a tolerant, easy-going manner could take you. Some of the jobs were good; most were not. I worked in a salmon cannery, was a roofer, drove a Good Humor Ice Cream truck, crawled sewer lines and bartended on the Alaskan Railroad. My most enjoyable job was as a temporary desk clerk at the Armed Forces YMCA in Anchorage.

Although I managed to work enough to survive, my jobs were short lived and for most of 1964, I was unemployed, broke, and homeless. Melvin and I spent many nights sleeping on church altars and in parks. We weren't alone. A number of indigents frequented the YMCA, and a brotherhood of unemployed, homeless youth flourished.

Melvin and I decided to see what Fairbanks had to offer. After living six weeks in a Salvation Army shelter and city campground, we returned to Anchorage.

In November, Mel and I hitchhiked back to Minnesota, but by the following April, I was back in Anchorage. I had less money in my pocket than my first trip, but I knew it would be different this year. This time I knew the rules of the game.

September 1965

The letter Monk brought me had been sent to my old address at the YMCA in Anchorage. I met Monk the previous summer when we were both unemployed and living at the Y. His real name was Mike McNally, but everyone called him Monk. He really *did* look like a Trappist monk with his full beard and Salvation Army clothes.

In May, Monk and I moved into a small house on L Street in Anchorage. This was not a typical rental. In fact, it wasn't a rental at all, but one of several adjacent houses that had been condemned after the earthquake in 1964. It was free—illegal, but free. Usually, we would abandon the house during the day, fearing that neighbors would report us to the police.

It was about 10:15 PM and we were almost asleep when the door of the forty-year old house was kicked open.

"What the hell are you guys doing here? These houses are condemned. Didn't you see the no trespassing signs?"

We didn't have a good response to his tirade. We were guilty, and we knew it. The man screaming at us with his hands on his hips was Ted Wright, the owner of four condemned houses on the block.

We tried to play the naïve teenager role but he didn't buy it. We tried the homeless victim role but he didn't buy that either. Finally, we tried the young-and-willing-to-work-for-almost-anything role. He bought that. Ted was the owner of a successful small construction company, and you could see the wheels turning in his head as he physically surveyed us.

"What's your name?" he demanded.

"Tornes," I said. "Gary Tornes."

"You?" he stared at Monk.

"Mike McNally."

"You guys play football in high school?" He scowled, staring at us.

We both nodded.

"So you think you're pretty strong, huh?"

We didn't respond, wondering what this guy was after. There was a long pause, then he said, "Okay, here's the deal. I'll pay you $500 for each house you tear down. The city has given me until September 15th to demolish and remove three of the four condemned houses on this block. The log cabin on the corner is considered a historical dwelling, and I'm donating it to the city. They will take care of that. I will sign the other three houses over to you, and you'll be responsible for removing them by the deadline. In the meantime, you can live in the abandoned house next to my home. It doesn't have water, heat or electricity, but it's not condemned. The house is full of stainless-steel coffin liners, but there's still plenty of room."

It was a deal too good to be true. We would be demolition contractors and have free housing. We accepted the offer immediately.

Ted knew we had no choice. He also knew that he would make money on the deal. It would cost him much more to have a legitimate contractor do the work. We started demolition the next day. Ted let us use the tools that we needed to tear down the houses. He also let us use one of his pick-ups to haul the wood and debris away.

We felt like real contractors. We had a truck, a contract, and even a payroll to meet. We hired several unemployed friends to help us complete our work. We were kept busy most of the summer.

We were half way through demolishing the second condemned house when I found it.

It was shining up at me from its long-hidden location between the hardboard sheeting of an inner wall. Almost delicately, I picked it up and held it between my thumb and forefinger. It was a quarter unlike any quarter I had seen before. The date on the coin said 1881.

"Monk, Monk, get over here, you're not going to believe what I've found!" My wavering octave-higher voice got Monk's attention and he hustled to my side.

"Look at this, Monk. Just look at this! This is our ticket, Man, we hit the big one. This quarter has to be worth thousands."

"Holy shit, it's almost a hundred years old. You're right. It's worth thousands," Monk was euphoric. "We can tell Ted to get fucked, split the money and go to Mexico."

Our work came to a halt as we mentally spent our newly found fortune on beautiful women and beer on a beach somewhere warm. We only had one problem: we had to find somebody to buy the quarter.

We decided to take the quarter to the Book Cache. Not only was it the largest bookstore in Anchorage, but it also had a rare coin and gold nugget shop. If anyone in Anchorage knew what the quarter was worth, it had to be an employee at the Book Cache.

We pulled Ted's blue Ford pickup into an open parking spot on Fifth Avenue directly in front of a dentist's office I had walked by hundreds of times. The only unusual thing about it was the name of the dentist: Dr. Payne.

We swaggered into the Book Cache. We had to walk down book-lined aisles to get to the coin shop in the back of the store. The shop was next to the cocktail lounge. The Book Cache was the only bookstore I had seen with its own bar.

The guy sitting behind the coin-filled glass display case had a monocle eye-piece strapped to his head. He seemed to be examining a gemstone in the grip of a strange looking tweezers. He ignored us. We leaned on the display case, waiting for him to acknowledge our presence. He continued to ignore us.

Monk finally said, "Hey, Buddy, we got something here that I know you will like."

The man looked up, not bothering to remove his eyepiece.

"So what exactly do you have for me today?" There was bored sarcasm in his voice.

"Here, take a look at this," Monk said, as he laid the coin on the display case.

The guy didn't even stand-up. He just pushed himself around on his wheeled chair. Appearing professional, he carefully examined the old quarter. After turning it over several times and running his finger around the coin's edge, he opened a large book that looked like a dictionary. He flipped about an inch of pages until he got where he wanted to be. His finger traced the margin of the page until it was almost at the bottom—then it stopped. He was too far away for either of us to see what he was reading.

"What's it worth?" Monk was leaning over the counter.

The guy finally stood up. He held our quarter in his hand. As he started to talk, I detected a faint smirk.

"Well, it is old and in very good condition."

"What's it worth?" Monk was getting spastic.

"I would say about six-dollars and sixty cents."

"What? You have to be kidding me. I know it's worth thousands." Monk was struggling.

The man gave Monk a superior stare as he placed the coin on the counter. Then he sat down and turned back to the gem he'd been examining when we walked in.

For about a minute, we said nothing. We just continued to look at the 1881 quarter on the counter.

We had spent the last hour in our own little paradise. Now we were back in reality. We returned to our partially demolished house and smashed the boards with feeling.

The Letter

"It's a letter from Uncle," Monk chortled as he handed me the envelope. The letter *was* from Uncle. I had received my second notice from the draft board in International Falls.

My first draft notice arrived about six weeks earlier. I was selfishly anti-military. The last thing I wanted to do was waste two years in the army. I wasn't against our involvement in Vietnam. In fact, I knew nothing about what we were doing over there. I wasn't even against war in general. The reason that I didn't want to spend two years in the army was simple. It would be more fun, and less dangerous, to drink beer and cavort with co-eds than march to cadence, spit-shine boots, and slog around in the jungle dodging bullets.

My first draft notice instructed me to show up at the Federal Building in Anchorage. There, a bus would take me to a medical facility on Elmendorf Air Base for the actual physical. About thirty potential draftees boarded the bus that drove to the base and dropped us off at a drab gray building.

Once in the building, a wimpy-looking airman escorted us into a large locker room where we registered, disrobed and filled out a medical history form. We were then split up into three groups, each with its own air force escort. Our group started with the lab portion of the physical—urinalysis and blood work. After we had completed the required lab activities, we were herded back to the holding area. I looked around and didn't like what I saw. I decided then and there that military life wasn't for me. I excused myself, went back to the locker room, dressed, and quietly walked out of the clinic.

Once outside I walked to a bus stop three blocks away and caught a city transit bus that was going into Anchorage. I got off at the Y and walked the seven blocks to our house. It was noon and Monk was sitting on a crate of casket liners eating a sandwich. He was surprised to see me since I thought I was going to be gone most of the day.

"What are you doing back so soon? Did they flunk you on sight? They should have told you about the butt-ugly-face test *before* the physical." He laughed loudly and smiled.

"Couldn't handle it, Monk. Looked around and saw all these dipshit airmen and all this military spit-and-polish-bureaucratic bullshit. Just couldn't handle it."

"What did you do?"

"I walked out. Took a bus back to town."

"You what???"

"I walked out. I had completed the lab portion and I didn't bother with the rest. I voted with my feet."

"No shit!" Monk stood up and shook his head. "You just walked out? Didn't anyone try to stop you?"

"No. Either no one saw me or they figured whatever I was doing was legitimate."

He slapped me on the shoulder. "You just walked out! You out-foxed Uncle. I'll drink to that, my man!" He pulled out two Buds and we each opened one.

"Here is to the Fox! He snookered Uncle!!"

We raised out beers high and clinked the cans in a toast. After that my moniker was "The Fox".

What I thought was a brilliant shell game bought me only an additional six weeks of freedom. The government couldn't find the other two sections of my physical. They had me registered and completing the lab portion of the physical, but that's all. I learned that missing paperwork confuses any government agency.

The second letter from my draft board arrived much faster than I had expected. The language of this notice was neither friendly nor ambiguous. SECOND NOTICE was stamped in red ink at the top of the page. The bottom of the page had both the threat and the remedy, "If you fail to report as required, you may be subject to a $5,000 fine, 10 years in prison, or both." Two days later, I was on a flight to Minnesota.

Christmas Day, 1965

At 8:30 AM, the Greyhound Bus pulled away from the International Falls bus depot located in the Rex Hotel. It was 34 degrees below zero.

In my wallet I had the ticket-stub for a one-way trip to Minneapolis, a government meal voucher for $1.25, and a hotel voucher for $5.25. I had a reservation at the Pick Wick Hotel in downtown Minneapolis. I looked out the window at my family waving good-bye and saw my Mom dabbing her eyes with a handkerchief.

I had been home for three months. Rather than be drafted into the army, I signed up for the Marine Corps whose two-year enlistment had no active reserve obligation. If I were drafted into the army, I would have to serve two years active duty and two years active reserve. That, of course, meant one weekend meeting a month and two weeks active duty every summer. Also weighing in on my decision to enlist in the Marines was the Corps' stellar – almost mythical – reputation.

Sgt. Geronimo, the Marine recruiter based in Duluth, called me the same day I was notified that I passed the induction physical. I had tried hard to flunk it by staying awake all night, drinking coffee and eating No-Doz pills. Maybe if I got enough caffeine in my system, my blood pressure would exceed the acceptable limit. It didn't work. My blood pressure was 138/82. It needed to get to 140.

After spending an hour at lunch with Sgt. Geronimo, I would have followed him up San Juan Hill carrying the Marine Corps banner. My Marine orientation, or as some would say – brainwashing – had begun.

The next day, December 26, 1965, Vice President Hubert H. Humphrey swore me into the Marine Corps. I was a member of the Viking Platoon that consisted of eighty-four Marine enlistees from Minnesota, the Dakotas and Western Wisconsin. We had one minority, Private Yellowbird, a Sioux from South Dakota.

The plane ride to San Diego was a red-eye charter. We arrived at 1:30 AM. Few of us slept on the plane. We smoked, bullshitted about our hometowns and girlfriends and wondered what Marine Corps boot camp would be like. None of us thought it would be as tough as we had heard. Many had been through high school football camps. It certainly couldn't be much more demanding than that.

As we walked down the steps from the plane to the tarmac, the smell of eucalyptus tantalized our nostrils. It was a new smell for most of us and it was exotic. Our anticipation grew.

A yellow and black bus pulled up next to the plane. We were standing on the runway, milling around, talking and smoking cigarettes. The sound of nervous laughter was everywhere. The door of the bus opened and two sharply dressed Marines jumped out. They looked like you expected Marines to look: tall, tan and physically superior.

"Put out those cigarettes, Assholes! Do you want to kill us all?" they shouted. I thought that it was a safety concern that had triggered their outrage. We quickly complied with their order.

"Get into the bus, now!" they screamed. We obeyed their order and boarded the bus.

The ride to Marine Corps Recruit Depot was brief, since MCRD is adjacent to the San Diego International Airport. The bus drove under a masonry white and pink arch to enter the base. The buildings on both sides of the bus were Spanish-style, painted white with orange tile roofs. From what I could see of the base, it resembled a large Mexican hacienda or resort.

The bus stopped in what seemed to be a large parking lot. From the window of the bus I could see yellow spots leading from the bus to the large Spanish-style building. This was really nice.

The door to the bus opened. A tall, bronze, muscular drill instructor wearing a Smokey Bear hat entered. He serenely surveyed the bus full of half-awake recruits, a faint smile on his face. He looked like a nice guy.

"GET THE FUCK OFF MY BUS, NOW!" he screamed.

His eyes had become wild and spittle flew from his mouth. The seats of the bus emptied. Everyone was trying to get to the aisle and out the door at the same time. Some recruits fell, and in the process and were trampled by their seatmates. We poured out of the bus onto the cement parking lot.

"GET ON THOSE YELLOW FOOTPRINTS, YOU FUCKING MAGGOTS!"

"YOU'RE GOING TOO SLOW, GIRLS. . ."

"FASTER, FASTER. . . . . YOU SLIMEY PIECES OF CIVILIAN SHIT!"

We couldn't believe what was happening. Were these guys crazy? At that moment, I'm sure all of us believed that we had made a monumental mistake enlisting in the Marine Corps.

The yellow spots that I had seen from the safety of the bus were actually yellow footprints painted on the pavement and leading to the large Spanish-style building.

Pushing a smaller recruit aside, I quickly claimed my set of yellow footprints, trying carefully to keep my shoes within the boundary of the outline. I glanced to my side to look at one of the strutting, maniacal drill instructors without realizing I had just committed the mother of all recruit sins—I had looked directly at a drill instructor. In less than a second, he was three inches from my face. I could smell his breath.

"YOU FOUR-EYED FUCK. ARE YOU QUEER FOR ME?" he shrieked.

"No Sir," I replied. "I just glanced at you."

Unknowingly, I had committed yet another mortal recruit sin— I had used a personal pronoun when referring to a drill instructor. I used the word "you."

"EWE, EWE, do I look like a female sheep?"

"No Sir!"

"DO YOU WANT TO FUCK ME"?

"No Sir," I stammered.

My Marine Corps training had begun.

Chapter 3
Flying Fish And Typhoons

The breeze that usually blew across the San Diego harbor had stopped. The sun was directly overhead and it was Southern California hot – dry and windless. The USS *Gordon*, a WWII vintage troopship was tied to the moorings with huge chains and ropes as big as my torso. I would be traveling across the Pacific in this massive floating barracks. It was July 6, 1966.

I was now a Marine. I had made it through boot camp, advanced infantry training, and staging battalion. I felt I had received the best training in the world. It had been physically demanding, but it also tested your mental and emotional stability. The mental and emotional aspects were actually more challenging and in many respects more important for survival on the battlefield.

I was a Marine and I was prepared to perform whatever task I was asked to do. I was ready for war, or at least I thought I was. I had been assigned a military occupational specialty (MOS) of 0311/0351, an infantry MOS. I would be a grunt, but not a rifleman. The 0351 designation was a specialty infantry designation. I had received specific training in 106 recoilless rockets, the 3.5-inch shoulder fired rocket launcher (the bazooka of WWII), and the flame-thrower. I would have been disappointed with anything less than an infantry MOS. During boot camp our drill instructors said that if we were assigned an 0300 MOS, our odds of being killed were one out of four and our odds of getting wounded were fifty-fifty.

The last six weeks had been spent in staging battalion at Camp Pendleton. This was the final combat training all Marines completed before being assigned to Vietnam. Everyone had to go through the training including forty-year old 1st sergeants that had been sitting on their asses for ten years. I felt sorry for some of the old Marines. When we went on our full-gear-and-pack conditioning runs over the Pendleton hills, a military ambulance followed us. By the end of the run, the ambulance was full of those older Marines who couldn't make it. If you failed the training you repeated it until you passed.

We were allowed liberty on weekends during staging battalion—unlike boot camp and advanced infantry training. I became good friends with four other Marines in the training battalion. One of them, John R. Williams, was born and raised in California and his home was in Santa Monica. John's father worked for the Federal Aviation Administration, and his mother was a night supervisor at a Santa Monica hospital. Every Friday afternoon we would manage to get a ride into Santa Monica and stay at John's house. It is hard to describe how much these weekend visits meant to me. It was one more chance to experience a family setting before leaving for war. It was overwhelming how both of John's parents catered to us. Mrs. Williams would wash our dirty laundry and neatly fold it so it would be ready to pack when we returned to base Sunday night. John had three brothers: one was a pharmacist in Los Angeles, one a senior in high school, and the youngest was in middle school.

Our weekends were spent primarily on Santa Monica Beach. There, we would lounge around on the sand, drink beer and lustily eyeball the bikini-clad girls. We looked out of place with short military haircuts, PX clothes, and farmer tans. I am sure everyone on the beach knew we were servicemen. The bikini-clad girls ignored us. The female bartenders working the variety of small beach cabanas served us without a smile. Nevertheless, we enjoyed ourselves. We spent hours talking about our pasts and what we thought our futures held.

One weekend stands out, not only for the setting and the players, but because it was the first time we realized how different we were from other people our age.

John's oldest brother, the pharmacist, was married to a beautiful California girl whose father worked in the Hollywood entertainment industry. They had invited us over for drinks and dinner, and without our knowledge had also invited four young USC co-eds. It was the first time I had ever been in such an opulent house—located in Westwood, a neighborhood abutting Beverly Hills. The appetizers were mysterious, but good. The conversation between the Marines and the co-eds was either stilted or nonexistent as we realized that we were in different worlds.

I felt sorry for John's brother and sister-in-law. Their hearts had been in the right place, but their matchmaking failed miserably. Nevertheless, the food was the best I had tasted since I left home, and the beer was free. As we left the party, we thanked our hosts for their hospitality. The four USC debutantes barely acknowledged our departure.

The weeks of training passed quickly and the wonderful weekends on Santa Monica beach passed even faster. Our physical conditioning, our education on Vietnamese history and culture, and our introduction to VC tactics and weapons had reached the point of diminishing returns. Staging battalion was over. Our training was cut short as the demand for troops rapidly increased with the war's escalation. We were warm, willing bodies. The war needed us.

About 600 Marines carrying seabags were assembled in loose formations on the docks. The steel ramp abridging the dock and the USS Gordon was still gated. We were waiting. We had already become familiar with the military tradition of hurry-up-and-wait.

It was normal to receive a thirty-day leave after boot camp, but because of the rapid build-up of American troops in Vietnam, our thirty-day leave had been reduced to three weeks. I spent them visiting friends and relatives in Minnesota.

During my leave, I shared many twelve-packs of Hamm's Big Sixteens with my old friend Tom Edens as we watched the Rainy River flow on its journey from Lake of the Woods to Rainy Lake. I confided to Tom that I was fatalistic about my Vietnam assignment. In my heart, I felt that I would never return. He said that I would make it and insisted I was being melodramatic.

We usually went to a lightly used park on the river between the forgotten logging towns of Indus and Birchdale. There, we would sit on the weathered, partially-rotten picnic table, look at the river, drink beer, and bullshit for hours. Since we were both under the legal drinking age of twenty-one, our beer drinking had to be secretive. I was about to go into combat for my country, but I still could not drink a legal beer.

My final farewell was the hardest. Mom cried world-class sobs. Dad shook my hand. My hand is large but it was lost in Dad's massive, calloused hand. His handshake was unusually strong and lengthy. Mom clung to me, sobbing on my shoulder. I had said goodbye to my sisters the night before. They were too young to really know what was happening, but they knew it was bad because Mom had been crying for three weeks.

I checked my seabag as luggage. The only thing I carried was a large brown envelope containing my orders. I had been instructed not to lose the envelope, and I wouldn't. Horror stories about Marines who had lost their orders were legendary.

As I walked across the cracked concrete tarmac toward the twin-engined DC-8, I felt sad—this might be the last time I would see my parents—and excited—I was about to start a new chapter of my life.

The North Central Airlines DC-8 took off to the north and circled east before heading to Minneapolis. I looked out the window at my childhood below. We lived half a mile from the airport, and the flight path went directly over our house. I recognized familiar landmarks of my youth—the woods where I used to play cowboys and Indians with Tom Denny and Jerry Sullivan, the old barn where Rod Olson and I drank a twelve-pack of warm Schmitt's beer and threw-up, my old paper route, the Airport Grocery and Café where Millie would let me charge gas and cigarettes, the drive-in theater where we would sneak in without paying, and the cemetery at the end of our road. The cemetery was divided into three sections, Protestant, Catholic, and veterans. Apparently veterans could be buried together but nonveteran Catholics and Protestants couldn't.

Life on the USS *Gordon*

The steel gate that blocked our entry to the ship was removed. Six hundred Marines, each carrying an eighty-pound seabag, slowly started up the ramp into their new home. Four thousand army troops had already boarded the USS *Gordon*. I didn't know where or when they had boarded, but their destination was the same as ours: Vietnam.

The ship was huge, longer than two football fields, and as tall as some of the hotels near the waterfront. It was old but clean and well maintained. It looked just like the troopships I had seen in WWII movies.

Since we were the last to board, we got the least desirable accommodations, deep within the bowels of the ship. To get there, we had to navigate steel grated circular stairwells while balancing our seabags on our shoulders. After descending four levels, we reached what would be our home for twenty-three days. The bunks were in tiers, four high. The aisles between the bunks were wide enough to accommodate only one person walking sideways. Each Marine was assigned a bunk, with the most desirable being the bottom level. I was assigned a bunk on the second level.

Not only did the bunk serve as the bed, it was also the storage area. We had not been assigned lockers, so we each shared the bunk with our seabag. The short distance between bunk levels made it impossible to turn over without your shoulder hitting the bunk above you.

The head was small, but functional. To better use space, everything in the head was reduced in size. The toilets were small, the urinals smaller, and the showers were built for midgets.

We had been at sea for a few days, when differences between Marines and army personnel emerged. The most noticeable was in personal grooming and attire. The Marines wore clean, sharply pressed utilities, appropriately buttoned, bloused trousers and polished boots. Our covers (caps) were worn with the brim facing forward and we removed them when we entered an enclosure.

The majority of army troops aboard ship didn't follow the same dress code. Even more amazing was the dress and demeanor of the army officers. It was often impossible to distinguish enlisted men from officers. Army officers looked disheveled and unkempt. Many wore their caps at jaunty angles, or even backward. Their trousers were rarely bloused. If it hadn't been for the gold or silver lieutenant bars on their collars, we wouldn't have been able to identify them as officers.

Most of the army enlisted men did not salute their officers, and the officers didn't seem to care. Another difference between the Marines and army troops was what they did with their time. The Marines conducted shipboard classes in military tactics and survival techniques. The army troops lounged on deck, read magazines, ate candy and smoked cigarettes. Often we would be jeered by groups of ragtag looking soldiers as we conducted our twice-daily PT routines. I was now sure that I made the right choice when I enlisted in the Marine Corps.

Life aboard ship really evolved around one activity—eating. The food was very good and well prepared by navy cooks and

Philippino kitchen helpers. Since there were almost 5000 total personnel aboard, serving three meals was a daylong event. There were several galleys (eating areas) on the ship for the enlisted men and two officers' dining quarters. Because the number of troops eating was so large, the galleys served meals from 5:00 AM until 6:30 PM.

Each section of the ship had a designated time for breakfast, lunch and dinner. This was the time your unit was expected to start standing in line. Usually, the minimum amount of time you stood in line before eating was an hour. When you finally reached the eating area, you picked up a tray, went through the serving line and then searched for a space at one of the circular, chest high tables. All meals were eaten standing up except in the officers' dining quarters. You were expected to eat as quickly as you could without choking to death. When you finished, you would go out on deck, have a smoke, look at the ocean and get ready to repeat the entire process in about two hours.

There was very little recreation available for anyone, enlisted or officer. The ship had been retrofitted to increase the number of troops it could carry. Space that previously had been used as recreation rooms and lounge areas had been remodeled to accommodate bunks and equipment. The ship had one small movie theater with one show at 7:00 PM. Since the theater was extremely tiny, you had to start standing in line at about 5:00 PM to get standing room to watch the show. Your scheduled mealtime determined whether or not you would be able to see a movie. I did manage to see one movie during the trip. It was Lolita. I can't remember much about the film other than it was about a young teenage sexpot and an older guy. I was in the back of the theater and could hardly see the screen through the cigarette smoke.

The lack of recreation didn't seem to bother most of us. I felt fortunate that two of my closest friends from staging battalion, John Williams and Arturo Villarreal, were on board. John, the native Californian, had been my guide and host in Los Angeles and Santa Monica. Arturo was an extremely intelligent and witty Hispanic from El Paso. He was also the only member of my second boot camp training platoon who had been with me continuously—for over six months.

I had started boot camp with the Viking Platoon but I hadn't finished with it. An infected abrasion on my knee put me in the Naval hospital for two weeks. The Viking Platoon continued their training schedule without me. When discharged from the hospital, I immediately became one of the lowest forms of life in a recruit training company—a pick-up.

Pick-ups were recruits who hadn't completed training with their original units. They had been dropped and this meant that they had spent time in the motivational platoon, the fat farm, correctional custody, or in my case, the hospital. When discharged from one of the above, you were picked up by a new recruit platoon. The objective was to try to place pick-ups with a platoon that was at the same stage of training that your original platoon was at when you were dropped.

The Viking Platoon had been all white guys with the exception of Private Yellowbird. Everyone had at least a high school diploma. Many had attended college and several had graduated with four-year degrees. This was not the case in the platoon that picked me up. The only similarity between the two platoons was that they both contained Marine Corps recruits.

I was a double minority in my second recruit platoon. Whites were a plurality in the platoon, and I was a minority among the white recruits. Only two recruits were from north of the Mason Dixon Line—Private Rafferty and me. Rafferty was also from Minnesota, but he wasn't a pick-up. You couldn't drop any lower than me. I was a white, Yankee, pick-up in a platoon that was mixed race and redneck.

The platoon consisted of Blacks, Hispanics, Whites, Guamanians, Puerto Ricans, and four Peruvian Marine trainees. Spanish was spoken as much as English, and only Rafferty and I knew the difference between a piece of lefse and a tortilla. Everyone in the Viking Platoon had enlisted in the Marine Corps. My pick-up platoon was primarily draftees. Many had not graduated from high school and nobody had attended college. Although it was a major culture shock, I learned and adapted.

I had joined the Marine Corps with a high school friend and we were both proud members of the Viking Platoon. Unlike me, he completed his entire boot camp with the platoon. Years later he told me that although most members of the Viking Platoon had ended up in Vietnam, only two had received an infantry MOS. In my new platoon, *everyone* got an infantry MOS. We would all be grunts.

Most of our free time on the USS *Gordon* was spent on deck looking across the endless expanse of the Pacific. We told each other about our hometowns, girlfriends, high school activities and the good times we had. We shared our fears and doubts. We talked about what we wanted to do if we made it through our tour alive. Since we all had an infantry MOS, we knew that combat was a certainty, not a possibility.

Our favorite place was on the top deck at the very back of the ship—aft in navy terminology. Once there, we would lean against the metal guardrail and look backward at the boiling wake left by the massive metal hull. About an hour before sunset, you could usually see several schools of flying fish following the boat. From our perch high above the water, the angle of the late afternoon sun made the fish look like delicate, silver flecks being tossed out of the ocean. The fish would be airborne for a short time before re–entering the water. Their exotic performance was fascinating and unreal. The fish seemed to be dancing and playing to entertain only us. We continued to believe we were getting a private showing until someone told us that the reason the fish were following the boat was because of the jettisoned food waste. Like us, they were just trying to survive.

Typhoon

Originally, the USS Gordon was scheduled to stop in Hawaii. At least that was the scuttlebutt. Everyone eagerly anticipated a Hawaiian liberty. If we had actually stopped in Hawaii, liberty for the entire ship would have been highly improbable, but we enjoyed fantasizing nevertheless. Our route took us within 300 miles of the islands. Our illusions of a luau vanished.

As we approached the International Date Line, preparations began for a crossing-the-line party to celebrate the moment the ship went over the imaginary line. I don't know where the ship's crew managed to come up with such exceptional talent. Naval personnel staged a hilarious King Neptune skit. The audience demonstrated appreciation with spontaneous and frequent applause. Everyone enjoyed the show. At the exact moment the ship crossed the line, a huge bell was banged with a mallet. A spectacular fireworks display ended the ceremony. Marines and soldiers cheered wildly.

Two days after crossing the International Date Line, we received the weather alert. The ship's daily one-page mimeographed newsletter warned us that a large tropical storm system was building in an area of the Pacific that we were about to enter. They said that it was possible that the storm could reach typhoon intensity.

Most of the young Marines didn't comprehend the seriousness of the alert. I, for one, had no idea what a typhoon was. My exposure to inclement weather was limited to midwestern thunderstorms, tornado warnings and blizzards. I had experienced several earthquakes while living in Alaska, but they had all been less than 5.0 on the Richter Scale. In a strange way, I was looking forward to experiencing a tropical storm.

Late that night I was awakened from a deep sleep by a loud noise. The sea bag belonging to a Marine in the top bunk of our tier had crashed to the deck next to my head. The noise of the falling sea bag woke most of us. The violent pitching of the ship that caused the bag to fall kept us from getting back to sleep.

At 0600 hours, we started cleaning up and dressing for breakfast. The head was full of Marines shaving, shitting and showering. It was becoming rough and hard to maintain your balance. To shave we had to secure our position and balance with one hand while trying to shave with the other. The initial damage of the storm was visible on the faces of a number of Marines.

Our climb up the circular steel stairway toward the hatch that led to the deck was more than a minor challenge. To keep from falling, we had to use both hands—one to grip the outer guardrail and the other to grasp the round center pole. Finally, we reached the hatch and pushed it open. We were unprepared for what greeted us.

The deck was awash with ocean water pouring over the guardrail. The wind's ferocity was driving bullet-like rain into our faces. Several Marines fell and were pushed across the water-slicked deck by the force of the wind. By the time we reached our designated chow line position, we were soaked and bruised. The good part was that the line was shorter this morning.

Eating was an adventure. Since you ate standing up, you secured your food tray by pressing your body against the tray's outer edge which forced the inside edge against the center pole of the kiosk. One hand gripped the center pole for balance while the other was used for eating. This tactic was semi-successful, though the punctuation of food trays hitting the deck was not uncommon. When we left the galley, the floor was covered with scrambled eggs and biscuits.

Slipping and sliding, we returned to our quarters. On-deck activities were canceled until further notice.

The heat and humidity added to our below-deck discomfort. Our quarters had air-conditioning, but it had not been turned on. Senior Marine commanders felt that sleeping in a non-air-conditioned environment would acclimatize us. The army had turned on their air-conditioning units the day we left San Diego. It was the only time I can remember that I wished I were in the army. The Marine Corps strategy made sense, but considering the present conditions of heat, humidity and the nauseatingly constant movement, we didn't agree with it.

As time passed, the number of Marines exhibiting full-blown seasickness multiplied. Supposedly, the best antidote is to eat. Medically, this may be correct, but realistically, the last thing you want to do when you're seasick is eat. Consequently, many sick Marines skipped meals. For the rest of us, the process of eating was much easier. The lines got shorter as the storm continued. Also, the quantity and choices increased.

I felt queasy, but I never vomited. Most men spent more time in the head than anywhere else. Many were unable to make it that far so the deck was covered with puke. Our head was like a set from a horror movie: the floor was covered with two inches of sloshing vomit. Since nearly everyone was sick, there weren't enough healthy men to clean the floors. The vomit would flow back and forth across the deck of the head synchronized with the rolling and tossing of the ship. The stench was unbelievable. Those of us who had not become sick had lost our appetites. As the days passed, few troops on the ship were eating.

The storm ended as quickly as it had started. The sun reappeared and the sea returned to its mesmerizing beauty. It took almost two days to clean up the mess.

Land Ahoy!

We had one scheduled stop before Vietnam and this was in Okinawa to pick up some military equipment. Nobody knew exactly what the cargo was. The USS *Gordon* stopped offshore. Apparently they didn't have room in the harbor for the ship. Everyone aboard was positioned along the guardrails looking toward the large island.

From a distance, the island resembled an idyllic Pacific paradise. Twenty-one years earlier it had been the scene of one of the bloodiest Marine battles of WWII. Today, Japan was our ally and several large U.S. military bases were located in Okinawa.

A small naval craft approached the *Gordon* and a minor amount of material was loaded into the hold by the onboard crane. From where we stood, we couldn't see what it was. Everyone continued to wait for larger vessels to deliver the equipment we had heard was supposed to be picked up. They never came. We later learned that the small amount of material we had taken delivery of was parachutes. Most of us thought it was a waste of time to make the stop.

Vietnam

Two days before our scheduled arrival in Vietnam, the ship's newspaper ran a headline article on a major Marine Corps battle called Operation Hastings. The action was located near the demilitarized zone (DMZ) along the northern border of South Vietnam. The operation involved nine battalions of Marines fighting an equally large number of North Vietnamese troops.

This was significant because it was the war's first large scale battle between Marines and large units of NVA regulars. It was also the first incursion into the DMZ. Apparently, the term "demilitarized" was no longer appropriate. Every Marine aboard eagerly read the battle reports. Those of us with an infantry MOS read the articles many times.

We wondered if ultimately we would be involved in Operation Hastings. Maybe it would be over by the time we got to our units? Maybe our battalion wasn't involved? We really knew nothing about what to expect. Speculation was rampant.

It was dark when we approached the landmass of Asia. The deck was full of Marines anxiously looking toward shore. Men were crammed elbow to elbow at the guardrails on the middle and upper decks. Hundreds of glowing cigarette butts illuminated intense young faces. Conversation was hushed and anxious.

Special effects consisted of red-orange explosions flashing randomly on the distant mountains. There was a time lapse before we heard the explosions. The noise carried for miles across the quiet South China Sea. A Marine next to us said the explosions were naval gunfire bombarding suspected enemy locations in the mountains southwest of Da Nang. He seemed to know much more than we did and we suspected he had been here before.

We went to bed late that night after the fireworks stopped. The next morning the sun was bright and the heat was suffocating. The Marines all wanted to believe that the heat affected army personnel more than us.

The first wave of landing craft approached the ship from the Da Nang harbor. Rope debarkation nets were dropped from the second deck to the landing craft bobbing below in the water. A 1st sergeant who had probably made many amphibious assaults during WWII directed the process. He ran the show with confident efficiency. We had practiced climbing and descending rope netting in boot camp and Infantry Training Regiment (ITR). The one instruction that was reiterated over and over was: hands on the vertical, feet on the horizontal. The reason for this is simple—if you were to grab the horizontal ropes, the Marine descending above you could step on your fingers.

I descended to the waiting landing craft without incident. When the craft reached capacity, it headed for shore. The trip was short but choppy. Nobody puked. I felt the landing craft hit the hard-packed, sand shore. The ramp dropped and we spilled out.

It wasn't a typical Marine amphibious landing. There was no gunfire, no blood, no dead bodies floating in the water and no fear. Also, we had no weapons. I casually walked down the ramp and took my first step into Vietnam.

The convoy drove through the middle of Da Nang. We passed
it appeared to be a major governmental building that was pro-
ted by guards and flying the South Vietnamese flag. I
embered reading about a group of Buddhist monks who had
nolated themselves in Da Nang. I had seen pictures in *Life* mag-
e of monks dressed in saffron robes, sitting cross-legged,
ulfed in flames. I vaguely remembered they had committed
r act in front of the regional capitol in Da Nang. Was this the
e?

Ve headed for the Headquarters (HQ) of the 1st Marine
iment. Everything looked temporary as we entered the main
—sandbagged bunkers around the perimeter, tents with wood-
floors and a few larger structures built with wood and
anized metal sheets. Maybe they didn't expect the war to last
long.

Ve split up here. A small group of us was directed to three
ed trucks. Most remained, waiting for a convoy that would
them to the 26th Marines. Others had been told that they
ld be going south to Chu Lai. Seabags first, bodies second, we
bed into the back of the waiting trucks. Our visit to Regiment
been a brief fifteen minutes.

owly, the three six-bys with their young cargo headed west.
didn't know where we were going, as would typically be the
in the future. We passed a large tree-covered mountain that
ared to erupt from the flat, sea level terrain. It was really more
a huge rock at least 1000 feet high with narrow trails hugging
uter edges and spiraling upward. Near the summit we could
white pagoda built into the side of the mountain. Later we
d learn that this was called Marble Mountain and the pagoda
major Buddhist temple. We would also hear rumors that the
ple and the mountain's labyrinth of caves and shrines were
ious hiding places for Viet Cong insurgents. The VC knew it

Chapter 4
Assignment

The only thing our amphibious landing had in
the famous Marine Corps beach assaults of the past
As we trotted down the ramps of the landing ship t
didn't know where we were supposed to go. We h
landing crafts randomly, and our debarkation was to
milling around on the beach we began to organi
bunching together about fifty yards from the water
gunnery sergeant took command.

It took several hours to shuttle the 600 Marin
peaceful but now chaotic shores of Red Beach
arrived last, and the process of matching sea bags
another hour.

A nearby convoy of six-by trucks was ready
began. Each truck could hold only twenty men
the process was destined to be slow. I was lucky t
wave.

The trucks crept through Da Nang, careful no
Vietnamese on the road. I hadn't expected to be s
landing, but I thought I would see some local
knew where they were—here on the road, the
Motorbikes and motor scooters were everywher
young men who did not appear to be in the Vie
If their country was at war, and we were here t
were they riding around on Hondas with girlf
their waists? We were riding into combat.
going?

was American policy not to attack or bomb religious or cultural sites. Consequently, they used them as areas of safe refuge.

Our intermediate destination was the command post for the 3rd Battalion, 1st Marine Regiment, 1st Marine Division. Once again, the size of our convoy decreased. Two trucks stayed at the 3-1 Battalion base. The truck that I shared with John, Arturo, and about thirteen other Marines continued. I was excited that the three of us were still together.

Twenty minutes later we arrived at the base that would be home for several months. Coils of concertina and tangle-foot barbed-wire surrounded the command post for the 1st Battalion, 1st Marine Regiment, which was located near the small ville of Cau Ha. Inside the protective outer perimeter was an elevated circular berm of sand and fortified bunkers. The buildings inside the perimeter were either tents with wood floors or wood and metal structures. Our truck stopped in front of the Battalion HQ. We were home.

"Get your bags and into formation over there," ordered a corporal, pointing to an open area next to a tent.

We followed his directions and got into loose formation, sea bags by our sides, orders in hand. A young captain came out of the HQ with a clipboard in his hand.

"Anderson, Boyinton, Baxley, Ellison, you're in Alpha Company. Report to their company command office, over there," he said, pointing to a nearby tent.

"Goodhope, Gullespie, Hernandez, Johnson. Bravo Company, over there," he repeated, pointing to a different tent.

"Leon, Olson, Perez, Richter. Charlie Company, over there."

"Tornes, Villarreal, Williams, Zuiga, Delta Company, over there." We had lucked out. We were going to be in the same company simply because our last names started with letters near the end of the alphabet.

Seabags on our shoulders, we shuffled toward Delta Company's command tent.

"Where is everybody?" Arturo asked.

"Maybe they're out on an operation or something," John responded.

The base seemed abandoned. The anxious activity that we had observed at the other bases seemed to be missing. We entered Delta Company's tent and presented our orders to the scholarly looking PFC manning the reception desk.

"Where is everyone?" I asked.

"Well, I just suppose they must be up north kicking ass," the PFC answered. He had an attitude that immediately pissed me off.

A salty, old 1st sergeant, with sweat rings under his arms, came out of an office in the back of the tent and greeted us.

"Welcome to Delta Company." His greeting seemed friendly but impersonal. He looked like my Uncle Norman.

"We need replacements," he continued. We're severely under-staffed, and you troops will help. Hopefully, we can get you some gear and send you up to join the company tomorrow."

"Where's the company?" I asked.

"Up north on Operation Hastings," he answered.

We were going to join the battle that we had read about in the USS *Gordon's* newsletter. At that time we joked about the possibility of ending up on Operation Hastings, but none of us really thought it would happen.

We completed the process of checking in by giving the nerdy looking PFC the orders that we had guarded with our lives for almost a month. He checked our names off a list and told us to report to the company supply tent for 782 gear and to the armory for an M-14. I informed him that I had an 0351 MOS (3.5 rocket launcher, flame thrower and 106 recoilless). He said it didn't make any difference, we were now all 0311's—ordinary grunts, riflemen.

As we left the Company HQ tent, the 1st sergeant (Top) wished us well. He pointed to a nearby tent that would be our temporary living quarters. Since we were scheduled to leave the next morning, our stay would be brief.

The company supply tent was behind the HQ building. It consisted of two, large, connected tents. The wood-framed entrance had a hand painted sign over the door identifying the tent as Delta Company Supply.

We entered the supply tent where a young corporal was busily inventorying the contents of several sea bags.

"Top sent us over to pick up our gear," I said.

"Don't know if we got enough on hand to give you all a complete issue," he responded. "We had to give everybody that went up on Operation Hastings a complete issue, and that included the HQ personnel. Might be short of some stuff. You guys supposed to go up north tomorrow?"

"That's what Top said," we replied, nodding our heads.

"Some bad shit up there, real bad shit. Heard this morning that they can't even find Bravo Company. Been out of contact with everyone for three days. See those sea bags I been going through?" he said, pointing to the huge pile of bags on the floor. "Those are all bags of guys who were killed on Hastings, and I expect lots more."

It was a sobering sight. I could see some of the names that had been written on the bags. I'm sure they didn't think they would be dead within a year. Or maybe they did. I couldn't be the only Marine who thought he never would return from the war.

Corporal Briggs, the supply clerk, informed us that he didn't have enough canteens, e-tools or jungle boots to completely outfit us. He also said that they were out of jungle utilities and ponchos. He suggested that we go to the armory and get our weapons while he continued to look for additional equipment and clothing. Before we left the supply tent he made one more comment.

"Hope you guys don't mind wearing clothes or boots that belonged to some of these KIA's, cause that's where most of your stuff'll come from. We've been so short of jungle boots and utilities that most of the recent stuff I issued belonged to dead Marines. That's why I've been going through these sea bags to see if there's any stuff in there I can re-issue. I know it probably ain't right, but I don't have a choice. I never touch the personal stuff; that'll get sent back to regiment."

The armory was unusual because it was a wood building, not a tent. It supported the entire battalion, not just Delta Company. Inside the building, three Marines were busy working on a variety of weapons: mortar tubes, M-60 machine guns and M-79 grenade launchers. The building was filled with wooden racks holding M-14s and cases of ammunition. One of the Marines looked up from his workbench where he was repairing an M-60 machine gun and asked us what we wanted.

"The 1st sergeant at Delta Company sent us over to get our M-14's. We're supposed to join the Company tomorrow up north on Hastings," I answered.

"You guys ain't going nowhere tomorrow, cause the battalion is coming back here," he said. "I heard that a platoon from Delta Company got ambushed and when the shit stopped only 19 out of 40 were left. All the rest were either dead or wounded."

"Here you go," he said, as he handed us our rifles. We're short on magazines so I can only give each of you one."

Although I didn't have all my gear, I had enough to make me feel like a warrior—a rifle, a bayonet and one magazine. I didn't, however, have any ammunition.

My M-14 was used, not new. The color of my wood stock was lighter than either John's or Arturo's. It was tan, almost the same color as my first gun, a three shot, bolt action, full choke Mossberg .410. Oh, how I had loved that gun. I didn't feel the same way about my M-14, yet.

The three of us headed toward the tent where Top said we could stay. The battalion base camp was eerily quiet. With few exceptions, everyone was on Operation Hastings. One platoon and part of H&S Company remained behind to guard the perimeter of the base. Since the artillery unit attached to 1-1 was not entirely mobile, elements of it also stayed behind. The mess hall was operational and the motor transport contained trucks, so the personnel assigned to those areas were still here.

Arturo pulled aside half the end flap that covered the entrance to our tent. Inside, the air was moist and still. Canvas drop curtains covered the screen netting around the walls. They had probably been in the down position since the company left eight days ago. It took several minutes for our eyes to adjust to the darkness of the tent. We each found what appeared to be a vacant cot. The cots were made of canvas and wood and resembled the army cots I had slept on at Lake Vermillion Bible Camp.

We threw our seabags onto our cots and left the stagnant air for the blinding brightness outside. The reflection of the intense sun off the white sand left us temporarily sightless as we emerged from the tent. The battalion base camp was built on world-class sand— white, fine, and not quite ankle deep.

The few remaining Marines that were not on perimeter guard were concentrated in the middle of the compound, in and around a tent that functioned as the battalion's Enlisted Men's Club. The club was small and spartan. A sign over the door stated that the hours were from 1600 to 2100 daily. The beer was cool and cheap. We had been required to convert our dollars to military payment currency (MPC) at the regimental headquarters. This was the first time I had a chance to spend it. Beer was fifteen cents a can. Although it was only cool, not cold, it tasted good. It was my first beer in nineteen days. I ordered a second.

There were more Marines than chairs in the small club. Since we were the new guys, we kept our mouths shut and listened to the macho banter among the veterans. The three of us had claimed our space near the door where we stood, sober and subdued.

"The NVA had goddamn tanks up on Hastings."

"Tanks?"

"No shit, tanks!"

"Gooks don't have no fuckin tanks."

"I heard we kicked the shit out of the gooks."

"Charlie Company got mortared for three hours straight, lost forty guys."

"That ain't what I heard. I heard Charlie Company captured three Red Chinese Officers."

"Someone said the NVA had some kind of Chicom Chopper."

"That's a bunch of shit. The gooks don't have no choppers."

"That's what I heard. Ain't shitting you."

"Fuck it, fuck everything. Give me another beer."

"Goddamn Korean beer."

"Who ever heard of Crown beer? Why can't they get some real beer? Where the fuck's the Bud?"

We drank a couple beers and left the club. We really couldn't identify with what was said. We didn't know what was true and what was bullshit.

It was almost 2100 and we were exhausted. We had been in Vietnam for 14 hours, only 376 days to go. One advantage of going to Vietnam by ship was the credit you received for the trip. Every day on ship counted as a day in Vietnam. We headed back to our tent, not knowing whether we would be going into combat in the morning or not. We had heard many conflicting stories about what was happening. Nobody seemed to know what the straight scoop was. We certainly didn't. We slept soundly and woke up with only 374 days and a wake-up left.

After finishing breakfast, the trucks started rolling in. The battalion was returning. We would not be going into combat today. I felt both relieved and, in a strange way, deprived. I had missed the largest Marine Corps battle of the war to date, and the test of my personal reaction to combat would have to wait.

The wait wouldn't be long. The company had called a formation in front of the headquarters tent. The three of us joined the seasoned veterans from Operation Hastings. We felt out of place. The talk was boisterous and loud with stories of both heroic valor and tragic death. The remnants of Delta Company numbered fewer than eighty, a little over half of a full company size.

The commanding officer (CO) of Delta Company had been medevaced during Hastings, and the acting CO, Lieutenant Megal, addressed the assembled Marines in a sober but supportive manner. He told them that they had fought well and that they were a credit to the Marine Corps. Once he finished, the company 1st sergeant addressed the still assembled troops. He said that the battalion was going to move its HQ about twelve miles south, near the city of Hoi An. The new battalion base was almost completed and was scheduled to be operational September 1st. He also said that the company had received three replacements and would be assigned to platoons according to need and current strength.

"Tornes," he shouted.

"Yes, Sir," I responded. Although he was not an officer, I called him sir out of respect.

"Find the 1st platoon sergeant; that's where you'll be assigned."

"Villarreal, report to the weapons platoon."

"Williams, you're in the 3rd Platoon, report to Sergeant Jacobson."

Our comfortable little unit of three was being split up. Although we would be in the same company, we would not be together as we had been for many months. All of a sudden I felt alone. Now I would have to start over. I was the fucking new guy (FNG). The rest of the 1st platoon was battle-seasoned veterans. They had proved their worth. I would have to prove mine.

I found the platoon sergeant. He pointed to a large raw-boned Marine wearing an olive green boonie hat. "That's Corporal McGougin, 1st Squad. Report to him."

Corporal McGougin was concentrating on some papers that had just been handed to him. I didn't know if I should interrupt him or not. Finally, I said, "Corporal McGougin?" He slowly looked up.

"I'm PFC Tornes. I was told to report to your squad for assignment."

"Torns?" he asked.

"No, Sir. Tore-ness," I stressed the second syllable.

He looked me over closely, squinting his eyes and tilting his head to one side. He didn't say anything for about ten seconds, then he said, "Call me Mac." His accent was deep south and his handshake firm and friendly.

"This squad's way under strength. Only have seven men; supposed to have thirteen. You'll be with Connors, Cullens and Rosser in the 1st fire team."

I had received my first assignment in the Marine Corps.

Chapter 5
Search And Destroy

The platoon was moving to a new forward base of operation about 3000 meters southwest of the battalion command post (CP) near the village of Quang Ha. My day at the battalion had been a learning experience.

I had been assigned to the 1st Squad, and since I was the FNG, my assignment would be rifleman. Everyone is basically a rifleman in the Marine Corps, but in the organizational structure of a Marine squad, the designation "rifleman" is at the bottom of the career ladder. A fully staffed squad consists of three fire teams, a squad leader (usually a sergeant E-5), maybe an M-79 grenadier, and any temporary additions from the weapons squad (M-60 machine gun, 3.5 rocket launcher or flame thrower). If available, a navy corpsman would be assigned to most squad sized patrols. The fire teams consisted of four Marines: a fire-team leader, an automatic rifleman and two riflemen.

Before leaving the battalion CP, I managed to get some essential gear – jungle boots, an additional magazine and another canteen. The only pair of jungle boots available was a slightly used pair of size tens. My normal size was eleven, but it was either take what was available or continue to wear my standard issue leather boots. As I crammed my feet into the undersized jungle boots, I wondered who the original owner had been and what had happened. Had he been killed or had he been lucky?

The decision to go with a size ten instead of waiting as long as necessary for an eleven was my first mistake in a combat zone. I would make many more, but this mistake would affect me for months. The heel bone in my right foot would become inflamed and ulcerated making every step a painful reminder of the bad choice. After three months in the field and miles of trudging through jungles, the boots and my feet would finally mold to each other and the pain would disappear.

On August 1, 1966, the first platoon of Delta Company was assigned to a new forward patrol base. The new location was about three clicks (kilometers) from the battalion CP. Our severely undermanned platoon rode to the new base on top of two amtracs. Since we would usually walk wherever we went, we quickly learned to appreciate the luxury of an amtrac ride.

The drive to our new base camp was my first real exposure to an enemy-controlled area. Although traditional front lines didn't exist in Vietnam, I had felt secure in Da Nang and at battalion. The trip was short—about ten minutes by trac. The temperature was over 100 degrees, and since it was the dry season, clouds of sand and dust swirled around us as we tore through the sand.

Our route took us through, not by, several small villages. The bamboo and thatch hooches in the villes made the tarpaper shacks on the Red Lake Indian Reservation look like mansions. From our perch atop our mechanized elephants, we could see the residents of the villages doing everyday tasks. Children were playing and women were doing household chores. The only man I saw looked like Ho Chi Minh. Where were all the men? They couldn't be working at factories; there weren't any. The rice paddies were almost dry and I hadn't seen any field workers. The absence of men or teenage boys was obvious, even to an FNG.

I couldn't believe it. Here I was, sitting on top of an amtrac riding into combat. One year ago I was living in Alaska with my old friend, Monk, and having lots of fun. I was skillfully managing to avoid the draft, oblivious of what was happening in Vietnam.

Monk and I were living in a house that didn't have water or electricity and was full of casket liners. A local undertaker had apparently expected a larger earthquake death toll and had ordered too many. They were packed in six-foot cardboard boxes and stacked throughout the house. They functioned quite adequately as our beds, our table and our chairs.

The only similarity between last year and this year was the music. A year ago I remember listening to the Rolling Stones singing "Satisfaction" as we split a twelve pack of Bud in our condemned quarters. This year, I had also heard Mick wailing that he "couldn't get any," but the setting was quite different. I was in the battalion Enlisted Men's club drinking Korean beer.

The amtrac's sudden halt brought me back to reality. We had stopped in front of a six-foot protective sand berm encircling two large tents. A tank guarded the backside and several Marines were setting up a mortar pit. An advance party from battalion had brought the basics for our temporary camp—water, C-rations and ammo.

We hopped off the amtracs into the soft sand that cushioned our eight-foot jump. Sergeant McGougin called the squad together. (Mac had just been promoted to sergeant yesterday.)

I was assigned to the 1st Fire Team as an automatic rifleman and was issued a bipod for my M-14. The automatic rifleman designation was outdated—a carry-over from WWII days when the standard issue rifles did not have an automatic fire option. Now, most troops on patrol selected the automatic fire option for their M-14s. But the Marine Corps had structure and tradition. A fire team included a fire team leader, one automatic rifleman and two riflemen. Marine tradition is as hard to change as the Constitution.

As I scrutinized the members of my fire team, none looked like highly trained killers. They looked more like the backfield of a high school football team. We were a microcosm of America. Maybe some people back in the States didn't consider us the best and the brightest, but we knew the truth. We were the best-trained, most motivated fighting force in the world. That is what the Marine Corps told us, and that is what we believed.

Gary Rosser was the fire team leader. He looked younger than his nineteen years. Maybe it was the freckles that were splattered across his face or his Dennis-the-Menace smile that made him seem so boyish. Gary was a hillbilly with attitude from the southern hills of Ohio. He spoke with an accent not heard in northern Minnesota.

The senior rifleman was Pat Connors. Although Pat was from Michigan, his accent was almost east coast. He looked and sounded like my old Alaskan buddy and Philadelphia native, Monk. Pat's resemblance to Monk was uncanny. I asked him if he had any relatives from Philly that had worked in Alaska, but he said no. Pat, like Rosser, had been tested by combat.

Joe Cullens was the other rifleman in our fire team. His heavy Brooklyn accent made him sound like a two-bit gangster in a B-movie. Joe's accent was as thick as his black bushy eyebrows that would have shielded his nose if it hadn't been so large. It wasn't an ugly nose. It was a dominant and strong nose. Joe didn't walk—he shuffled. When he shuffled, his head was down, but his eyes were up. Joe had been on Operation Hastings. He, too, had proved himself. I liked him immediately.

Sgt. McGougin made team assignments for our sector of the perimeter. I was happy when he teamed me with Joe.

"The two of you set up here," he said, pointing to an area next to the perimeter's sand berm.

"Don't really have to dig much cause you all got the berm for protection. Make sure you coordinate your fields of fire with the positions on your flanks. Your fields of fire should overlap."

A clump of trees adjoined our assigned area. Three trunks grew out of the ground together, then went their separate ways toward the sky. If the bark on the trees had been white, the tree grouping could have passed for a perfect white birch clump, but the bark wasn't white, and I had no idea what kind of tree it was. It provided us with welcome shade that now was moving outside the perimeter as the sun reached its midday peak.

We decided to make our own shade by constructing a primitive lean-to from a poncho. One side of the lean-to was attached to the birch-like clump of trees. The other was anchored to the ground by our backpacks. The sand berm blocked the sun from the west and the poncho functioned as the roof.

Rosser walked by to check our position and field of fire.

"We're supposed to go on patrol at 1400 but I won't be going out," he said.

"Where you going?" Joe asked

"Have to go back to battalion and fill out some paperwork on that NVA map case I got off a dead gook on Hastings," he said. "Erickson, a fire team leader from second squad will be with you guys. He doesn't have a fire team anymore, lost them all up north."

We watched as he climbed aboard one of the amtracs that had dropped us off less than an hour ago. Both tracs departed leaving behind a cloud of diesel exhaust and sand.

"Where are we going on patrol?" I asked Joe.

"Don't really know," he said. "Usually we go out for four to five hours and have three or four checkpoints where we call in our position to Delta One. We just look for gooks and gook shit. Usually, they find us first. We are kind of like live bait. The only way we find them is to have them shoot at us first. Kind of fucked-up, but that's the way it is."

Joe sounded like he knew what was going on. I felt safe being with someone who knew more about war than I did. I didn't know shit.

Joe also said that we usually had nightly ambushes. We would leave the perimeter after dark and move quietly to the ambush site. The location of ambushes varied from several hundred meters outside the perimeter to several miles away. The ambush team was small, usually no more than six. If a corpsman were available, he would accompany the ambush team. Most ambushes were set up on well-traveled trails. The most common type was an L ambush. Trip flares would be set on the trail and claymore mines would be pointed toward the most probable approach routes.

Joe's description of night patrols continued. "Ambushes really aren't too bad. Its cooler than walking through the jungle during the day, and you get some sleep. Half the team sleeps, and the other half is awake; we take turns. We just sit quietly in our ambush and wait for some slope to come dittybopping down the trail and then we blow him away."

"Do you kill a lot of Cong on ambushes?" I asked.

"Nah, Joe replied. They're not that dumb. We get a few once in a while. Most are probably sleeping or bedded down with their gook honey somewhere--while we're sitting out in the jungle swatting mosquitoes."

"Get ready to go!" The command came from our temporary fire team leader, Erickson.

The patrol was a daytime search-and-destroy mission and my first venture into the combat arena. We filled our canteens with warm water, grabbed an extra bandolier of ammo, splashed on some bug juice and headed out. It was a squad patrol, or at least it was supposed to be. The first squad was down to seven men, six short of a full squad. Phil Parsaghien took point. Mac had us in a single-file patrol formation. We were told to keep at least twenty meters apart. Slowly, the patrol snaked away from the perimeter.

I couldn't believe how little information I had. I didn't know where we were going, didn't have a map, didn't know half the guys in the squad—I didn't know shit. My life was in the hands of a sergeant that I had spoken to twice. Amazingly, I was not uneasy about entrusting my fate to this stranger. I had confidence in Mac's technical combat skills and leadership abilities. He exuded a quiet, confident strength. I also had confidence in the Marine Corps and they had demonstrated their confidence in Mac by promoting him to sergeant.

The pace of the patrol seemed much too fast. The area was supposedly heavily booby-trapped and we were walking down trails like we were in some park back in the States.

Our first checkpoint was about 2000 meters from the patrol base, near the village of Cam Sa. Kranz, who was carrying the PRC25 radio, called Delta One to verify our position and status. Other than the suffocating heat and pesky flies, the patrol had been uneventful. Most of the villages and hooches looked alike. Occasionally, we would see a building that looked like a real house. These upscale homes were the result of the nearly one hundred years of French occupation. Pat said they were the homes of former French landowners. The houses were faded shades of pastel colors with masonry walls and tiled roofs. Most had large courtyards surrounded by overgrown, untrimmed hedges. Now that the French were gone, they were occupied by Vietnamese.

We continued on to the second checkpoint—a room-sized Buddhist pagoda perched on a hill overlooking a dry rice paddy. Mac warned us to stay out of the pagoda because it might be booby-trapped. Kranz called in to update Delta One. We trudged on, walking on top of a two-foot dike that crossed an irrigated rice paddy. The dike separated two fields connecting a small village to the jungle in front of us.

Pat, who was in front of me, turned and pointed across the paddy to our left front. "That's Phong Ho, the French ville," he said.

Phong Ho was about 600 meters away. The foliage seemed a much darker green than other tree lines. I assumed that was because the vegetation was thicker and better watered than other areas. Phong Ho meant nothing to me. It was just another Vietnamese village with a strange sounding name. I didn't know it at that time, but I would get to know Phong Ho very well.

We were nearing the tree line on the far side of the paddy. The point and two other Marines had already entered the jungle. I was about fifty meters from the trees when the firing started. At first I couldn't tell where the shots were coming from or who was firing. I heard one of the Marines in front of me returning fire, but I couldn't see him.

I finally realized that the shooting was directed at those of us exposed in the middle of the paddy, so I dove headfirst behind the mud dike. I snapped the bipod on my M-14 into the down position, anchoring the pods on top of the mud walkway. I could hear the firing coming from the tree line about 100 meters to my left front, but I couldn't see any movement. The front element of our patrol was somewhere in the jungle—exactly where, I didn't know.

The tree line continued to fire and .30 caliber rounds were chewing off chunks of the dike. Still, I couldn't locate a target in the tree line. Momentarily, I hesitated, wondering if I should shoot into the tree line or wait for a clear target. I chose to shoot.

I fired three controlled bursts into the trees. The twenty-round magazine was spent in seconds. I quickly replaced it. Behind me I heard the pop of an M-79 grenade launcher. Several seconds later I saw an explosion near the source of the hostile fire. Mac, who carried an M-79, was lobbing 40mm projectiles into the tree line with confident precision. I emptied the second magazine into my faceless target with increased confidence. Ahead, I could hear Marines shouting. Three had made it into the jungle before the attack had started.

"Try to make it to the tree line," Mac yelled.

In a low crouch, I ran toward the trees. The shooting had momentarily stopped. The temporary silence was shattered by a loud explosion, screams, and the chilling call of "Corpsman up!"

I had reached the safety of the trees, but still could not see anyone. Jim "Doc" Clopton, the navy corpsman assigned to our patrol, ran by clutching his field medical bag in one hand and a .45 pistol in the other. Doc was running upright, seemingly oblivious to danger. He ran toward the area where the distress call had come from.

Mac approached my position on a dead run.

"What happened?" he shouted.

"Someone got hit," I responded.

"Who?"

"Don't know."

"You and Cullens set up an LZ perimeter in case we need a medevac," Mac ordered. He then followed Doc's trail into the jungle.

"What do we do now Joe?"

"We have to establish a secure landing zone before we can call in a medevac chopper," Joe said. "We should probably set-up in that open area over there." He pointed to a piece of ground that looked like a large vegetable garden. We moved quickly to establish the first two positions of the LZ perimeter.

Mac emerged from the jungle followed by two Marines carrying a body in a poncho. He acknowledged that we had selected an appropriate LZ location for the medevac. Other members of the patrol were positioned around the hastily constructed landing zone. We were instructed to lie on our stomachs, facing outward, our weapons at the ready.

"Who got hit, Mac?" I asked.

"Erickson. Stepped into a foot-trap rigged with a grenade—blew his foot off."

I had only spoken to Erickson once. He was from Rochester, Minnesota—my home state. That was all I knew about him.

Mac called Delta One, gave them our coordinates and a medevac chopper was dispatched from the hospital (NSA) in Da Nang.

We remained in our defensive positions until after the chopper had picked up Erickson and safely departed. The experience of my first medevac created an indelible memory. I would always associate the sound of rotating chopper blades with dying or maimed Marines.

Somebody must have felt sorry for us because amtracs were sent to bring us back to the platoon base camp. The remaining portion of our patrol was canceled.

It all seemed so impersonal. I didn't even know Erickson's first name. I wondered if they had found his foot and sent it back in the chopper. They surely wouldn't leave it in the jungle.

I reflected on my reactions today and I felt satisfied: I didn't freeze up, I returned fire, I followed orders, and I didn't get killed. I had won the first battle – the battle of uncertainty and self-doubt.

Chapter 6
The Pagoda

Flies woke me up at about 0500 on my second day in the field. They were crawling around my nose and lips. The ones on my lips created a tickling sensation that almost felt good. I had expected the mosquitoes to be worse, but the military-issue bug juice actually worked. The sand that had served as my mattress had been quite comfortable. It was possible to make indentations in the sand for your hips and shoulders. The ground then followed the contour of your body.

Joe and I shared perimeter watch during the night—two hours on, two hours off. The night was uneventful and black. I was amazed at how quickly it got dark. There wasn't a midwestern twilight to ease you into darkness. When the sun dropped over the horizon, the lights went out.

From my prone position under our makeshift shelter, I could see Joe scanning the rice paddy and hedgerows in front of our position. I again felt lucky to be teamed-up with him. He had been on watch since 0400 and had one hour left on his shift. I felt rested and decided to relieve Joe early.

"Hey Joe, any action?"

"Naw, pretty quiet."

Joe was frugal with words, only saying what needed to be said. Before relieving him, I needed to "shit, shower and shave." Only one of the famous three would be accomplished this morning. I looked for an appropriate place to dig a cat hole. I had to stay inside the perimeter, but not in our living room. I found a spot against the sand berm about ten meters from our shelter half. With one swing of my E-tool I instantly created the perfect cat hole. I squatted over the hole and fertilized Vietnam.

Breakfast consisted of C-ration crackers with cheddar cheese spread and a cup of C-rat instant coffee. I used a C-ration can stove fueled by a heat tab to warm water for my coffee. For the next six months, this would be my method of cooking. The only change would be my heat source. I quickly learned that a small gob of C-4 (plastic explosive) would burn faster and hotter than the regulation issue heat tablets. C-4 became my fuel of choice.

I lit a cigarette and took my first drag of the day. It doesn't get much better than the taste of your first cigarette with your first cup of coffee.

Joe gladly accepted my offer of early relief, crawled under the lean-to and quickly fell asleep. The flies were happy to have another immobile target.

At 0800 Mac approached us. He was checking the perimeter positions of the 1st squad.

"Y'all get ready to head out in an hour," he said. His Alabama accent massaged the words. We would be leaving at 0900 on a platoon patrol. The patrol would be reinforced with an M-60 gun team and two German Shepherd dogs with their handlers. Joe said he had heard about dog teams accompanying other patrols, but this was the first time they had been assigned to us. Supposedly, the dogs were good at detecting VC caves and tunnels.

I was eager to see the dogs. I had owned three dogs in my life and they had all been Labradors. The two dog teams arrived with our re-supply convoy. Once again, the tracs were proving their worth. They were an extremely versatile vehicle for this type of war and terrain. In addition to the dog teams, the convoy brought WWII vintage Jerry cans filled with water, as well as mail, beer and soda.

We received a daily ration of two beers and two sodas. I was amazed at the large number of young Marines who didn't drink beer. It was easy to find someone who would trade beers for sodas. The only item on a re-supply convoy that ranked higher than beer or soda was mail. Since I had been on the ship for almost a month and in the field less than a week, I didn't expect to receive mail for a while. In fact, I hadn't received mail for almost six weeks.

Realizing that my parents didn't have my new address, I retrieved some Marine Corps logo stationery from my backpack and quickly wrote them a note. I kept the letter short and uninformative. I told them I was healthy (true), hot (true), and safe (untrue). I could always write about the weather and I knew they would find it interesting. Mom and Dad had both been born and raised on Minnesota farms where the weather was an important and acceptable topic for conversation. Farmers could talk about the weather for hours without becoming bored.

Writing about the weather allowed me to bulk-up my letters. Since I never told my parents what was really going on in Vietnam, without the weather, my letters would have been extremely short. Mom and Dad worried enough. The truth would have only made it worse. I finished my letter and took it to the command tent. The mail would be sent with the tracs when they returned to the battalion.

As I left the tent I spotted the two handlers with their dogs. They were talking to the platoon commander and Sgt. McGougin, probably about the planned patrol. The dogs were more of an attraction for me than the handlers who were corporals based out of regimental headquarters in Da Nang. Both humans and animals were hot. The corporals were sweating and the dogs were panting. Everyone was uncomfortable in the 100+ degree heat.

I dropped to one knee in front of the dogs and started scratching their ears. Both dogs enjoyed the attention. They pushed their heads against my knuckles rotating inside their ears. When I stopped moving my knuckles, they would push their heads toward my hand. They didn't want me to stop the pleasurable ear massages. If I had a choice, I would have continued petting the two German Shepherds for the rest of my tour. Hell, if I were a dog handler, I'd be a lifer.

At 0900, the larger than normal patrol left the perimeter. We had a weapons team, another squad, and the dog teams.

"Where are we going today?" I asked Joe.

"Probably to the same area as yesterday."

Once again, I really didn't know a hell of a lot. The closer you are to the bottom of the Marine Corps ladder, the fewer details you know. You were not expected to see the forest; you were only expected to see the trees. Staff officers and senior NCOs were responsible for big picture strategic planning whereas junior officers and enlisted Marines at the squad and fire team levels did the work.

Since the patrol was larger than the day before, we were moving much more slowly. Another contributing factor to our more cautious pace was the realization, through Erickson's missing foot, that the area was heavily booby-trapped.

The dogs were allowed to snoop and smell as we moved along the patrol route. Our fire team was in the middle of the patrol and I could see the dogs stopping every ten meters to investigate some unusual scent. Although the dogs were hot, they were obviously enjoying their assignment. Their wagging tails were held high and their ears were up and alert.

The patrol moved forward at a leisurely pace, stopping and starting to accommodate the sniffing dogs. I had no idea where we were, but it looked similar to the area we patrolled yesterday. Most villages looked alike so you had to search for specific landmarks to distinguish one from another.

We had one map in the squad and Sgt. McGougin carried it. Actually, Mac had two maps, but one was an old French map that was issued to him when he first got to Vietnam. A perk that came with being a squad leader was a map that gave you some idea where you were and where you were going.

Pat said we were headed for Ngan Trung. The name meant nothing to me. As we emerged from the shaded environs of one of the many nameless hamlets, I recognized several landmarks from the day before. We were moving west on a well-used trail following a curving tree line. The trail turned sharply to the left before it straightened out and headed for a large hill.

The hill looked man-made, but it wasn't. It rose from the flat, near sea level elevation to a height of about twenty meters. The hill was about seventy-five meters long, fifty meters wide and devoid of vegetation. Basically, it was a large pile of hardened sand. As I followed the trail around the south edge of the hill, I saw the small Buddhist pagoda we passed yesterday. It looked like a concrete outhouse with four masonry pillars supporting an orange tiled roof. Its faded walls with tints of blue and pink looked out of place on the small hill.

The patrol stopped; everyone was ready for a break. A pre-monsoon cloudburst started dumping rain on us. I moved off the trail, found an umbrella-like tree to sit under, lit a cigarette and gulped down some ninety degree water. I relaxed as much as the situation would allow. The other Marines in the patrol did the same.

I could see the two dog teams and the platoon sergeant looking at a map and pointing to various positions in front of us. Two other Marines joined the group and discussions continued. One of the group pointed to the small pagoda that was located above them on the side of the hill. Shortly after, they started climbing up the hill moving toward the small Buddhist shrine. They, too, were seeking cover from the rain.

The dogs, still leashed and controlled by the handlers, enthusiastically headed for high ground. As the small group of Marines and dogs approached the pagoda, they hesitated briefly before entering. As I watched them enter the shrine, I remembered Sgt. McGougin's warning from the day before.

I lit another smoke and had another shot of warm water. The cigarette tasted better than the water. I could see Joe about twenty meters ahead of me wiping sweat from his face with the sleeve of his shirt. Since Joe didn't smoke, his only pleasures were warm water and rest.

I had turned my head toward the pagoda when it disintegrated in front of my eyes. I felt the concussion and heard the blast. The air was filled with small pieces of concrete and dust. Screams of "Corpsman up!" came from several locations. Then I realized that I, too, was screaming "Corpsman up!"

I didn't know what to do. My first reaction was total disbelief followed instinctively by an urge to help those who had been injured by the blast. I was halfway up the hill when I was stopped in my tracks by an order from Sgt. McGougin.

"Stay away from the pagoda, it could still be booby trapped!" he screamed. "Go back to where you were and set up in a defensive perimeter around the hill."

It all seemed like a rerun of yesterday–like dreaming the same bad dream two nights in a row–booby traps exploding, corpsmen running, secured LZs, defensive perimeters and medevac choppers. I ran back to the trail and dropped to one knee. I didn't know what the casualty count would be, but I knew it would be bad. I had counted five Marines and two dogs in or very close to the pagoda before the explosion.

I turned to look at the devastated shrine. It was still partially intact, but the entire front half had been turned into crushed rock and cement dust. Once again, I saw Doc Clopton running toward what was certain to be a scene of death. Although we had been instructed to stay away from the site of the explosion, the same precautions didn't apply to corpsmen. They went where they were needed—safe or unsafe.

Another corpsman had joined Doc in his valiant but futile attempt to bring life back to motionless bodies. Several minutes later, word spread that both dog handlers and the platoon sergeant had been killed. Two other Marines had suffered serious injuries. Miraculously, the two dogs were alive.

I didn't know the name of the platoon sergeant or the two Marines who had been killed. I felt empty, but not really sad. It all seemed so impersonal. I felt closer to the two dogs than the three Marines. I had met the dogs and knew their names.

The routine for evacuating the dead and wounded was the same as the day before. A secure LZ perimeter was established for the medevac chopper dispatched from NSA. The casualties were loaded into the chopper and it departed leaving in its wake a cloud of sand and cement dust. Although it had seemed like hours, the entire event from explosion to dust off had taken only thirty minutes.

Unlike the day before, amtracs were not sent to give the remaining members of the patrol a ride back to base. The usual bullshit between Marines was absent. Everyone was silent and expressionless on the trek back to camp.

Chapter 7
County Fair

I had been in the field for two and a half weeks when I heard our platoon was going to participate in a county fair. I associated the phrase with arcade games, tilt-a-whirls, and grandstand shows. I would soon learn that the Marine Corps definition of a county fair differed greatly from mine.

During my first month in Vietnam, everything that happened was new to me. The conditions I lived in, the combat situations I experienced, and my thoughts and emotions were all new. Every Marine who went to Vietnam had a learning curve. For those assigned to field combat units, the curve was short and steep. You accepted, improvised and adapted or you didn't survive. You usually didn't have the luxury of a concerned mentor, so the bulk of your learning was by yourself and on the job.

The county fair we were supporting was designated County Fair 1-10. The first phase of a Marine Corps county fair is to swiftly and secretly cordon off a strategically selected Vietnamese village. This was done at night or in the early morning hours. After the cordon was in place (usually not swiftly or secretly), a unit of Army of the Republic of Vietnam (ARVN) troops, often supported by local militia (Popular Forces) would enter the village. Once inside, they would herd all the women, children, and elderly into several tents that had been erected outside the security cordon.

The tents were manned with navy medical personnel—doctors and corpsmen—to treat the sick and injured. Medicine would be dispensed, and with the assistance of Vietnamese interpreters, medical advice would be given to those who requested it. Food and drink were also available to the temporarily displaced villagers. Additional foodstuffs, such as rice, flour, dry soup, canned meat, dry milk, and salt would also be distributed to them.

When available, clothing would be given to the locals. It was not unusual to see a small Vietnamese child in the middle of nowhere, wearing a UCLA t-shirt. Most of the clothing was used but in good repair, probably donated by an American charity. The item that seemed most out of place was a basketball. I never figured out why basketballs were given to villagers who would never see a basketball hoop in their lifetime. Although the Vietnamese were very clever at improvising, I never saw them use a basketball for anything.

While the women, children, and elders were being fed, clothed, and treated, the ARVN troops searched the vacated ville for Viet Cong and sympathizers. Usually they were very thorough, and some county fairs resulted in substantial enemy kills.

From our perimeter positions, we could hear sporadic shooting and grenade explosions coming from inside the village. Our assignment was to block the exit of any Viet Cong who tried to flee the village. I found out that the name of this village was Thanh Thuy. As the weeks and months passed, I would begin to associate village names with firefights, ambushes and casualties. I can't remember the name of any village that was linked to a positive event.

Although there were two platoons of Marines and a number of tanks and amtracs in the perimeter around Thanh Thuy, our positions were still more than fifty meters apart. The dense jungle made it impossible to see the Marines on our flanks. I was teamed up with Gordon Wilson, a black PFC who had recently been transferred to our squad. Wilson had been with the platoon for three months and had previously been assigned to the third squad.

As it had been with Joe, I liked Wilson immediately. He was from the Bedford Stuyvesant section of Brooklyn, New York, and like me, had enlisted in the Marine Corps for two years rather than be drafted into the army.

We didn't attempt to dig a fighting hole in the root-infested jungle floor. Instead, we found a large tree with tentacled, mangrove-like roots to sit behind. The above ground root systems provided us with more than psychological protection, and it divided our area of responsibility in half. Wilson was responsible for the right flank and I was responsible for the left. We could barely see five meters into the dense undergrowth, yet we remained in constant voice contact with the positions on both sides of us.

The adjacent position on Wilson's side consisted of two Marines from the first squad. My side was considerably different. One of the tracs supporting the operation was set into a blocking position in a small clearing about half a football field to my left. The trac team consisted of three Marines: a driver/operator, an assistant operator, and a gunner for the .30 caliber machine gun mounted on top of the trac.

The firing inside the village had almost stopped. We could hear two Marines from the amtrac position calling out the name, Jim. The intensity and volume of their shouts increased. We heard the sounds of someone crashing through the jungle approaching our position from the direction of the trac.

A frantic, young PFC stumbled into our position and gasped, "Any of you guys see Jim?"

"Who's Jim?" I responded.

"He's the assistant trac operator. Went to take a piss and never came back."

"How long ago?" I asked.

"About a half hour."

"You should tell the major in charge of the county fair so he can put together a search party," I suggested.

"Yeah, think that's what I'll do. Can't believe Jim vanished into thin air. Maybe he found some little slope to pork."

The Marine from the amtrac turned and trotted in the direction of the command tent for the operation. I said I'd go with him and told Wilson that I would be back in about fifteen minutes.

The command tent was located near the orientation and medical assistance tents. The orientation tents were currently being used to interrogate Viet Cong and Viet Cong suspects. A temporary holding area for suspects had been established outside the tents. Several young Viet Cong suspects had been blindfolded and tied together back to back. They were sitting with their arms pulled behind them in awkward angles.

These were the first real VC I had seen. They didn't look like clever and courageous champions of liberation to me. They looked like scared and confused Vietnamese teenagers. The Marine from the trac went into the command tent and emerged quickly, accompanied by several officers and a gunny sergeant. A search party was quickly mobilized and ordered to conduct a detailed search of the area where the missing Marine was last seen.

Although I was not part of the search party, I followed the hastily formed group back toward the trac's position, and then returned to where I had left Wilson. It was 1700 hours and would be dark soon. They had to locate the missing Marine quickly because it would be next to impossible to conduct a thorough search at night.

The blocking position that Wilson and I were manning had been quiet all day. We heard shooting and explosions earlier, but the action was away from our position. In a way we felt cheated— like playing shortstop in a baseball game when all the hits are toward first base or into the outfield. You don't get a chance to show what you can do. We had been trained to kill the enemy, but we hadn't had the opportunity to use that training.

Since the firing from inside the village had stopped, we assumed that the Viet Cong and Viet Cong suspects were all either dead, captured, or fugitives. The operation was scheduled to terminate at 1900 hours when amtracs were supposed to transport us back to the Platoon base.

At about 1800 hours we heard activity and loud voices coming from the area where the search party had entered the village. We remained in position, but our attention was directed toward the trac's position where something obviously was happening.

We heard them before we saw them. The team that had been searching for the missing Marine was coming in our direction. Several minutes later, they were directly behind our position, moving in single file toward the operation command tent. Two members of the search team were carrying an apparently heavy poncho. The others were walking slowly and quietly behind them. Near the end of the column, an attractive Vietnamese woman was tethered to a rope that was held by another Marine.

The woman didn't look like she belonged in a rice-farming village. Her teeth were white and straight, not blackened from years of betel nut abuse. Her skin was clear and smooth, not rough and weathered from overexposure to the elements. She looked smart and arrogant, even though she was being led like a dog through the jungle. The Marine behind her kept his M-14 pointed at her head.

Wilson and I left our position to watch the procession. The search team consisted of about fifteen Marines and a corpsman. I approached the last person in the column, a black lance corporal.

"What happened? Who's the woman?" I asked.

"Fuckin' VC cunt," he answered. "Cut the dick and balls off the dude in the poncho."

"What?"

"Yeah, no fuckin' shit. Cut 'em off and stuck 'em in his mouth."

"Did you see him like that"? I asked.

"Nah, I didn't find him. Some other dudes found him. But that's what they said."

I felt queasy in my stomach. Having your dick and nuts cut off and stuffed in your mouth seemed worse than death itself. Getting shot was one thing, but having your cock cut off was unimaginable.

They didn't have to call a medevac chopper in this time. The wandering Marine was definitely dead. He had been shot thirteen times with a small caliber weapon.

They found him in a hooch about 200 meters from the trac. He was naked from the waist down with thirteen bullet holes in his torso. The Vietnamese female suspect was captured in a nearby hut, hiding in a large earthen vat usually used to store rice. She was an immediate suspect because her appearance didn't match the profile of a typical female villager. We also heard that they found some intelligence documents on her.

It seemed ironic that this woman would be going back to battalion headquarters on the same amtrac as the dead Marine. She would then be sent to ARVN headquarters in Hoi An for interrogation. The Marine would be going to Graves Registration in Da Nang.

Chapter 8

The Birthday Gift

It was August 17, 1966. I was 11,000 miles from home, and it was my birthday. It seemed unreal that so much could happen in such a short time. A year ago Monk and I celebrated my birthday in Alaska by drinking two cold six-packs of Budweiser. This year, I would celebrate my birthday with Joe. We would each have two warm cans of Falstaff beer.

Our family had always celebrated birthdays in a big way. My mother would bake a cake from scratch and poke little wax candles in the top. She always baked my favorite cake, German Sweet Chocolate. When I celebrated my 19th birthday in Alaska, she baked me a cake and airmailed it to Anchorage. This would be the first year of my life that I would be celebrating my birthday without a cake baked by Mom.

I decided to answer the letter that I had received from Monk earlier in the week. Monk had been drafted into the army. He completed boot camp, then spent his leave with family and friends in Philadelphia. Instead of flying back to the army base, he decided to drive his motorcycle.

The trip back to base was at night and the blacktop was wet from rain. He was traveling too fast on a strange road and lost the bike in a sharp right turn. The big Harley hit the pavement and spun down the road, eventually flipping over a steep embankment. Monk was thrown from the bike and ended up on the edge of a pasture.

He didn't know how long he was unconscious, but when he came to, he couldn't move. Because he had been driving on lightly traveled secondary roads, it was several hours before a motorist discovered him. Luckily, he wasn't bleeding badly and his neck wasn't broken. An ambulance finally transported him to the nearest hospital.

Monk suffered severe damage to his legs and knees. It wasn't bad enough to put him in a wheel chair, but it was enough to keep him out of the army. He received a medical discharge and an automatic extension of life. He too, had received an infantry MOS, and was scheduled to go to Vietnam.

As I started writing the letter, I found it hard to explain what I was doing and experiencing. Although we were close friends and could always relate to each other, it was different now.

Dear Monk,

In case I didn't tell you before, I am not an 0351 like I had trained for (rockets, flame throwers, etc.) I am an Automatic Rifleman and I walk point every third day. Let me tell you, it is nerve-wracking as hell. You never know when you will step on a land mine or get ambushed. Since you are the first man, you're usually the first to get it. I feel like I walk with death daily.

I have been in some mean-assed combat in the last three weeks. The VC failed to hit us only three days in the last twenty-two. In our platoon, five Marines have been killed, four have been wounded and two have come down with malaria. Our platoon has been hit harder than any other platoon in our company.

You were right in saying that a person should live every day as his last and have direction, but not definite plans. That is why I try to savor the small luxuries—like the two beers we receive every day.

I hope you're impressing the doctors with your ability to heal rapidly. You have my hopes for a speedy recovery.

We have a patrol in about twenty minutes, so I have to go. Write soon and take it easy.

The Fox

I had received few letters since arriving in Vietnam. My parents had written twice, and then there was the one from Monk. I hadn't been involved seriously with any girl before joining the Corps, so I didn't get any perfumed love letters. It was amazing how much mail some guys got. Their wives or girlfriends would write them a daily four-page letter. To write that much, you would have to describe the minutiae of daily life over and over again. There didn't seem to be that many ways to say, "I miss you and I love you."

In some ways I envied those who received daily mail from their wives or sweethearts. In other ways, I felt sorry for them. Those who were married, and especially those who had children often seemed like their minds were 11,000 miles away. Walking around the jungle thinking about your wife and kids instead of concentrating on the details of a patrol or ambush could be fatal.

As I smoked my second cigarette of the day, I could see Joe heating up some C-rat eggs and ham. I wasn't hungry yet, but I was thirsty. It seemed like you were always hot, sweaty, and thirsty. I hadn't had anything cool to drink in almost a month. The water was always hot, our beer ration was hot, and the sodas that we received were hot. After a while you became accustomed to drinking everything warm or hot, but you still lusted for that cold drink.

Joe walked over and sat down in the sand next to me.

"Hey, Gar, wonder where our patrol will go today," he said. It wasn't so much a question, as a greeting.

"Probably the same fuckin area we've been covering for the last three weeks, Hard Core. Getting to know that area pretty good."

Joe laughed. I think he liked the nickname I'd pinned on him.

"I know today is your birthday," Joe smiled. "Happy Birthday. Hope you have many more."

I thanked him.

"Got a present for you," Joe said. "Didn't have much to pick from, but hope you enjoy it."

Joe took his e-tool and started to dig a hole in the sand. I was confused and had no idea what he was doing. He dug a hole about two feet deep and seemed to be searching for something at the bottom.

"Shut your eyes," he said.

I felt a little stupid, but I followed his orders and shut my eyes.

"Hold your hands out."

I felt even stupider, but I held my hands out.

"Happy Birthday."

He had put something cool in each of my hands. I opened my eyes and realized that the two cool objects were cans of Falstaff beer. They were actually cool. I couldn't believe it.

"I buried my two beers from yesterday, so they would cool down in the sand overnight," Joe said. "Got to have cool beer on your birthday. Better drink them fast before they start to warm up."

I opened one of the beers and drained the can in record time. The second beer was different. I drank it slowly, savoring each mouthful of cool, malty liquid. This was undoubtedly the most memorable birthday present I had ever received. It was also the most appreciated. Joe had given me his daily ration of beer as a gift. He had also gone to a lot of trouble to cool the beer.

"Saddle up!" The order came from our fire team leader, Gary Rosser.

It was my birthday and I would be walking point. The bitter aftertaste of the two cool beers was still in my mouth as we started out. The area that we were patrolling was becoming familiar to everyone in the platoon. Our Tactical Area Of Responsibility (TAOR) was about 50 square miles. Most villages within our area of responsibility were not considered friendly and were controlled by officials sympathetic to the Viet Cong. I figured out that I had been in the field a little over three weeks, and twenty-five percent of our platoon had been either killed or wounded. The odds weren't in favor of me spending another twelve months here without becoming a casualty.

The patrol was leaving the village of Binh Minh. We had conducted a comprehensive search of the village without discovering any contraband or suspicious items. As we emerged from the tree line that encircled the ville, we were hit by enemy small arms fire. Although I was walking point, the initial volley of fire had not been directed at me. Usually, the point man gets shot at first, especially if the enemy unit is small. The ambushes are hit and run. A few VC fire at the forward element of a patrol and then quickly vanish into the countryside. They have no desire to engage in sustained battle because they are usually out-manned and outgunned. This time, however, the VC had let me walk halfway across the small dry rice paddy before ambushing our patrol. Instead of firing at me, their shots had been directed at the center of the column.

Since I was almost across the dry field, I continued on toward the tree line. I didn't walk, I ran. Behind me I heard the all too common cry of "Corpsman up!" I wondered who got it. I had my M-14 on full automatic and I was putting rounds into the area where firing came from. The other members of the patrol were also putting out a large volume of fire. I heard the popping of Mac's M-79. Sage and Kranz had made it to my position. We moved along the backside of the tree line in a flanking movement. We were hoping to block the retreat of the VC.

We had moved about 100 meters when we saw two VC run across the trail to our front. They were dressed in khaki shorts and black shirts. Each carried a backpack and a rifle. Three M-14s on full automatic opened up almost simultaneously. A hail of bullets chased the two VC into the jungle. We jumped in a drainage ditch to plan our next move.

"There were only two of them. I don't think an 81 mission is worth it," said Sage.

"Probably not," Kranz responded. "It just pisses me off. We walk around in the jungle as targets for these VC bastards. They set up a two-bit ambush with only two of them, fire about twenty rounds at our patrol, wound or kill one of our men, and then disappear into the jungle. Chickenshit assholes."

It was apparent that the attackers had once again got away safely. We decided to search the area where we had shot at them for signs of blood. Cautiously, we approached the trail intersections where the VC had crossed.

"I found some blood, fucking VC blood," Sage hollered.

"No shit, there it is. At least we put a hurting on one of the motherfuckers," Kranz gloated. "Let's head back to the rest of the patrol. No use to run after these crazy Cong. They're ditty-bopping down some trail, headed for home or whatever."

As we headed back to the patrol I saw a sight that I had seen too many times in the last month, an LZ perimeter being set up. Someone was going out on a medevac. I didn't know who.

I saw the all too familiar sight of Doc Clopton, on one knee, tending to a Marine on the ground. As I approached Doc, I saw who he was working on. It was Joe. I felt the blood drain from my face. I quickly moved to Joe's side.

"How're you doing, Hard Core?" I whispered.

"Doing fine, just fine," Joe replied.

I didn't know if his smile was caused by a shot of morphine or because Doc told him he had the million dollar wound.

"What happened?"

"Took a round in my back," Joe answered. "Doc said it didn't look like it did any serious damage, but it probably will keep me out of combat for the rest of my tour."

"No shit. You lucky bastard."

I was happy for Joe. He had paid his dues. He had spent more time in real combat than most and had been in-country only four months.

I had the routine down pat: the LZ was secured, the medevac chopper landed, bodies were loaded, it departed, and we all carried on. The only difference was that this time the person on the chopper was my friend.

We continued the patrol and returned to the platoon base camp at 1400 hours. After Joe had been hit, the rest of the patrol was uneventful. Mac assigned me to team up with Pat Connors.

Pat was a good tent-mate and my new mentor. Although he didn't say much, he was more talkative than Joe had been. Pat had been in Nam about two months and had been on Operation Hastings. He was very much in love with his wife, reading and rereading her letters. He wanted to survive the war, return home to his wife, and have lots of kids. With his caring manner, he would certainly be a good father.

Chapter 9
Spiders and Lepers

Pat was now my teacher and he was friendly and supportive. We had just returned from a daylong patrol covering seven miles. I was exhausted and thirsty. We had been hit three times but luckily had not taken any casualties. We had killed three VC and found two blood trails, so the patrol could be rated a success. Joe had been gone two days and I missed him.

I had taken off my boots to look at my heel. Every day, I regretted my decision to try to force a size 11 foot into a size 10 jungle boot. The heel on my right foot had been inflamed for almost a month. It was red, swollen and throbbing.

In addition to taking off my boots I unbloused my trousers. We had been told to always keep our trouser legs bloused. By doing so, leeches and nasty tropical insects would be denied access to your lower body. It made sense and I typically complied.

Barefooted and unbloused, I rested on the sand under the shade of a poncho shelter. I was in that dreamlike, not quite sleeping stage, when I felt something crawling up my leg. I abruptly sat up and tried to shake the intruder off my leg. Whatever it was, it was large enough to cause an upward-moving, undulating ripple in the material of my trouser leg. I first thought it was a small rodent, maybe a mouse. Before I could kill it, it bit me.

The pain was immediate and intense. It felt like a combination burn and wasp bite magnified tenfold. I delivered a killing blow and frantically pulled my trousers down. I then saw what had bitten me. It was the largest spider I had ever seen. It was bigger and blacker than a hockey puck.

"Pat, look at what just bit me."

"Holy shit," Pat gasped, "I've never seen a spider that big in my life. Does it hurt?"

"Hurts like hell."

"Maybe you should call Doc."

"Yeah, think I will."

"Shit, look at what's happening to my leg. The son of a bitch is swelling up right in front of my eyes."

I couldn't believe what was happening to my leg. It was swelling so rapidly that I could actually see it increase in size. It reminded me of blowing up a balloon, but this was my leg.

Pat ran to get Doc, while I sat and watched my leg swell to gargantuan size. The veins and muscle tissue were testing the elasticity of my skin. The leg had grown to about twice its normal size and had become immobile. The pain was intense and I was certain I was going to die. How unglamorous, killed by a goddamn spider in Vietnam. I wondered if I would get a posthumous Purple Heart. Jesus Christ, this couldn't be happening. I can't get killed by a fucking spider!

Doc came running to my aid, carrying his medical pack like he did when he tended real casualties.

"The leg looks pretty tough. I think I'll call for a medevac chopper."

"Have you ever seen a spider bite like this?" I asked.

Doc shook his head. "To be honest with you, no. I'll get a bag to put the spider in and send it with you in the chopper," he said as he ran to the command tent.

Doc really couldn't do anything for me. The pain wasn't localized—it was the entire leg. The only non-medical antidote for the swelling and the pain was an ice bath, but we sure as hell didn't have any ice.

Pat and I continued to be mesmerized by my gigantic, swollen leg. Then, as quickly as my leg inflated, it deflated. Like a balloon with a hole in it, my leg started shrinking before our eyes. It took a minute for my leg to return to its normal size. It looked horrible. It was completely black and blue. You could see where some of the smaller capillaries had burst under the unnatural pressure. It still hurt like hell.

I asked Pat to run to the command tent and tell Doc to cancel the medevac. The last thing I wanted to do was to be ferried into the naval hospital with a dead spider and an obscene looking leg. I couldn't handle the humiliation.

At least I wouldn't be killed by a spider. I know dead is dead, but the way you die has to be considered. No death is glamorous, but a Marine getting killed in a combat zone by a spider is too close to high comedy for comfort.

Doc was able to call off the medevac. I would never again lounge around with my trousers unbloused.

The next day we headed for the leper colony. I had not seen a person with leprosy much less a leper colony. This would be another of many firsts I would experience in Southeast Asia. The leper colony occupied a tract of land that was useless for farming, but would have been great for a resort. It was bordered on the east by the South China Sea, the north and west by palm trees and tropical pines. An eight-foot chain-link fence topped with razor wire surrounded the perimeter. I never figured out if it was to keep the lepers in or others out.

Battalion intelligence reported that the colony's hospital was being used by North Vietnamese doctors to treat wounded VC. Our mission was to search the complex.

We rode to visit the lepers on amtracs escorted by three M-60 tanks with 90 mm cannons and turret-mounted .50 caliber machine guns. The trip to the leper colony was typical in that we went through villages instead of around them. This was primarily for safety, not destructive, reasons. Most of the roads around the villages were mined, so the direct route—through the middle of the village—was the safest. I was still somewhat sympathetic to the plight of the ordinary peasant. Consequently, when our tracs or tanks went through a hut instead of around it, I felt sorry for them. In the next few months, this empathy would change.

Our plan to quickly and clandestinely surround an objective was, once again, neither quick nor clandestine.

We entered the colony from three different directions. The chain link fence was cut to allow entry from each side. On the beach, the tanks and amtracs set up blocking positions.

The residents were supposed to be self-sufficient. They grew their own vegetables, raised poultry and pigs and operated a small fishpond. The most prominent feature of the colony was its green water tower that rose high above the rest of the buildings. The colony was laid out in a city-like grid. Buildings with similar functions were grouped together. The support services, such as utilities, hospital, school, and administration building were located in the middle of the complex. The residential sections were on the outer edge. The colony also had an open-air market where vendors sold food, clothes and other commodities.

Children seemed to be everywhere playing like kids do. None of them looked like lepers; they looked youthful and healthy. Several wore t-shirts with logos of American colleges or commemorative t-shirts advertising American festivals, parks and monuments. It was clear that none of them had the vaguest idea what their shirts said or signified.

Our squad was assigned to search the shops and vendors. As we walked down the narrow dirt street lined with tables of merchandise, we got a closer look at some of the older residents.

Our directive was to take into temporary custody any male resident who looked under fifty years of age. All Vietnamese had national identity cards, and we carefully examined the cards of all males who remotely looked underage. Vietnamese seemed to age quickly after their twenties. Women we thought were in their fifties or sixties turned out to be in their thirties or forties.

Many shopkeepers were middle-aged women who were in advanced stages of leprosy. There were discolored, scab-like surfaces where the body parts were missing. Some of the remaining tissue looked like a healed-over amputation, other tissue looked moist and ulcerated.

We found no men under fifty, but we continued the search moving slowly east down vendor alley. The entrance fronted on what had once been a road. On the other side of the road was the sugar sand beach of the South China Sea. After crossing the road, we walked the beach until reaching one of the tanks positioned between the colony and the ocean. A sergeant was standing on the tank looking out to sea with binoculars. His attention was focused on a sampan 300 meters from shore.

"Looks like we got gooks in the boat," he announced.

"How many do you see?" his crewmate asked.

"Can't really tell. Looks like about nine or ten."

"Better call the lieutenant."

"Go ahead. Call Delta One. Advise him of the situation."

The corporal quickly made radio contact with Lt. Sloat. I could see only the corporal's head as he talked on the handset of the radio from his position inside the tank.

Standing next to the tank I could hear the exchange between the tank sergeant and the corporal.

"Lieutenant said he would check with the CO about the gook boats. Said he'd get back to us ASAP."

"Hope they tell us to waste the sons-of-bitches."

In minutes the corporal was back on the phone, then quickly off. Everyone waited.

"Lt. Sloat said he was told to use his discretion and his discretion is 'sink em'."

"Sounds good. Fire a few 50s over the top of the boat to get them to come back to shore," the sergeant ordered.

The corporal quickly followed the order and fired a burst over the canopy of the boat. Instead of turning around, the small craft continued to move farther out to sea.

"Let's blow the bastards out of the water," shouted the sergeant.

The gunner climbed into the tank and adjusted the elevation of the 90mm cannon. The sergeant remained on the turret, his binoculars focused on the target.

"Fire for effect!" He ordered.

A loud blast followed by a three-foot muzzle flame sent the 90mm round toward the fleeing boat. The first round missed its mark—it was high. The second round hit the small craft dead center. The boat flew apart.

The action was almost slow motion. Bodies and pieces of wood from the boat seemed to be floating in the air above the water. Several VC, who had jumped off the boat before the second round had been fired, were trying to swim to shore. They wouldn't make it. The sergeant, manning the .50 caliber gun was picking them off, one by one.

Later, we got an intelligence briefing on the results of our visit to the leper colony. An ARVN patrol boat had picked up pieces of boat and pieces of bodies. They had confirmed that the passengers of the fleeing sampan were members of a VC medical unit that had been using the leper colony's small hospital.

Chapter 10
The Listening Post

I wasn't feeling well. I was nauseated, feverish, and weak. Maybe it was the after-effects of the spider venom. Maybe it was some bug I had picked up from local well water. Whatever it was, I was sick. I didn't want to be branded a whiner, so I didn't go to Doc.

The lowest form of low in the Marine Corps is a malingerer—a person who does everything he can to avoid a duty assignment. Usually it involves faking illness or injury. I didn't want to have that label tied to me, so I decided to tough it out.

Two squads, the platoon commander, and a weapons squad had been directed to establish a temporary patrol base about two miles southwest of our regular platoon patrol base. The first and third squads were selected to move to the new location.

The base was set up in a small hamlet surrounded by rice paddies. The centerpiece of the hamlet was a large combination school and Buddhist temple. The hamlet was abandoned. I had no idea where the previous inhabitants had gone, but the place was empty. The hamlet resembled a small island. It was about five acres surrounded by water, which in this case was shallow rice paddies. The hamlet served as a crossroad for two major trails that connected three smaller villages to the major village of Phong Ho.

I still felt like shit. My fever was raging and I hadn't been able to keep food down for two days. The two-mile hike from the platoon base to our new location seemed like fifty miles. My vision was blurred and I found it difficult to focus my eyes. Several times during the march I almost fainted. I was convinced my illness had some connection to the spider bite.

We quickly established a defensive perimeter around the small hamlet. Pat Connors and I were located about fifty meters from the concrete school that functioned as Lieutenant Sloat's command post. He, along with his radioman, platoon sergeant, and Doc wouldn't have to dig fighting holes. Foot-thick concrete walls would protect them. The inside of the school was also considerably cooler than the 100 degree outside temperature. In the field the advantages of rank were few, but in this case, those four would be slightly cooler and maybe safer.

We usually took turns digging our fighting hole. Pat would dig for ten minutes, and I would dig for ten minutes. Today however, Pat insisted on digging it himself because he knew I was sick. Ideally, a fighting hole is supposed to accommodate two men. In areas where the soil was sandy, this was possible. In other areas, where the soil was hard-packed earth or root-infested muck, a two-man hole was impossible. Our ground was rock hard.

Pat had taken off his helmet and shirt. Dirt-colored sweat streaked down his back and chest collecting at his beltline. As I watched him sweating and hacking at the rock hard ground, I noticed his helmet lying next to his pack and rifle. He had written IRISH across the front. I decided to autograph my helmet even though my vision was still somewhat blurry. I didn't have a nickname, and I didn't know a flattering term for Norwegian, so I would have to come up with a word to make my personal statement. It had to be catchy, but not too cute. I finally decided on ALASKAN KID. I had spent thirteen out of my last eighteen civilian months in Alaska and had filed state taxes there, so I considered myself an Alaskan. I also wanted to be different. Pat lent me his black grease pen and I started writing on the ripped helmet cover.

Suddenly, a barrage of bullets tore through the banana trees surrounding us. Pat, helmet on, but still bare-chested, emptied a twenty round clip into the tree line where the rounds were coming from. Our half-finished fighting hole wasn't large enough to accommodate both of us. Nevertheless, we both dove in.

The firefight stopped as quickly as it had started. It had lasted less than five minutes. Wilson, who was in the position to our right, crawled to our hole and told us that the platoon sergeant got hit.

"I didn't hear the call for Corpsman up," I said.

"That's because Doc was already there. He was standing with Lt. Sloat and the radioman in front of the school when they hit us. The platoon sergeant took a round right between the eyes and it killed him instantly."

Pat looked down and slowly shook his head. After a moment, he looked up at Wilson. "Anybody else get hit?"

"Don't think so," Wilson responded. He moved back to his position.

Sergeant McGougin said that a patrol would be sent to check the area from where the VC had fired. I didn't look forward to going on patrol. I was still feverish and nauseated. What I really wanted was a nice, soft bed and about twelve hours of uninterrupted sleep. We saddled up and joined the other members of the hastily formed patrol.

We moved down the trail leading from our hamlet to a small village on the far side of the paddy. We searched the tree line where the shots had come from without finding anything. No blood, no empty casings, nothing. We continued on through the village to another trail that led to yet another village.

The villages were all starting to look the same. One dirty, little, impoverished group of shacks after another, all with blank-faced peasants warily eyeing you as you walked through their nameless little village. You could see the hatred and resentment in their eyes. We were over here putting our asses on the line so that these ungrateful bastards could experience democracy. At least, that was what we were told.

Mac briefed us on the plan. "Battalion has instructed us to put out a listening post tonight. They want the LP to set up in an old spider hole located about two thirds of the way between here and Phong Ho. Because we're so short of men, this will be a one man listening post. Normally there'd be two, but we're too lean."

A one man listening post almost a mile from base camp! It seemed suicidal. I wondered who he would choose to carry out this mission.

"Tornes, you'll man the LP tonight."

I couldn't believe what I was hearing. I felt like shit, had a temperature of least 101, hadn't eaten for two days and I'm being sent out on an all-night, one person LP a mile from the nearest Marine.

"Sound OK?" Mac asked.

"Sure, no problem," I answered.

The plan was to take the entire patrol down the trail to Phong Ho. We wouldn't enter the village but instead would turn around and return to base camp. The big difference was that I wouldn't be with the patrol when it returned. I would be sitting in an abandoned spider hole 300 meters from Phong Ho. Tomorrow morning, another patrol would be sent out to retrieve me from my hole. I was given an extra canteen of water and a useless PC10 radio. Mac told me to keep the radio off unless it was for emergency communication. I asked him to define emergency communication. He didn't reply.

"Mac, what exactly am I supposed to look or listen for?"

"Any large-scale enemy movements into or out of Phong Ho," he answered. "Intelligence has reported that a battalion-sized VC force is operating in or near Phong Ho. We would like to verify that information with visual confirmation."

The patrol moved down the wide trail toward Phong Ho. We reached the halfway mark where Mac pointed out the spider hole that would be my bedroom tonight. We continued on the trail until it crossed the paddy and was about to meander into the large village. We then abruptly turned around and retraced our steps.

As the patrol once again passed the abandoned spider trap, I quickly jumped out of formation and into it. The hole was about two feet square and about five feet deep with wood reinforced walls. It was dry and cool but musty smelling. Because of its size, I couldn't sit down. As I stood in the bottom of the hole, only my head was out of the ground. I had an excellent view down the trail leading into Phong Ho. Part of the village of Phong Ho was also visible, and I could see people moving between the buildings.

The patrol left and I was alone. Alone and sicker than shit. The listening post idea still seemed stupid. I took a protracted drink of warm water. It would be a long fourteen hours. My PC10 handset radio didn't have a good track record. When it worked, the quality of transmissions was often inaudible. The battery hardly held a charge and most of the time it just didn't work. I decided if I saw a large movement of enemy troops, I wouldn't waste my time with the radio. Instead of calling Delta one, I would run toward it. In military jargon, I would be in a rapid strategic retreat.

Night finally came. I hadn't been looking forward to it. I always felt safer when the sun was up. The darkness of the night was lessened somewhat by a bright full moon. I didn't know if that was good or bad. I really had no desire to see a battalion-sized VC force walking down the trail from Phong Ho.

My fever seemed to be breaking and I was experiencing cold sweats. I didn't know what time it was. I had borrowed Wilson's watch, but it didn't have luminous hands so I couldn't read the time. This was a listening post, so I listened. The only sounds I heard were artillery explosions coming from the direction of Da

Nang and the incessant buzzing from the battalion of mosquitoes around my head. Occasionally, a dog would bark.

I don't know how long I had been asleep, but when I woke up I was shivering uncontrollably. My fever had broken and I was feeling better. But I had fallen asleep. Fallen asleep, standing and leaning against the wood-reinforced walls of my spider hole.

If you are Marine, you do *not* fall asleep on watch. You could be court-martialed for that. Usually, if you fell asleep on watch, you put someone else in danger. At least this time the only person I endangered was myself. I cringed at the thought of what could have happened if the enemy had found me asleep. Never again, during my tour in Vietnam, would I fall asleep on watch. The darkness around me was quiet as I waited for daybreak.

I could hear sporadic crowing coming from all directions. Vietnamese roosters must be genetically programmed to start crowing in the middle of the night instead of right before daybreak. I kept waiting for the morning that never came. The roosters didn't sound like the Leghorns on a Minnesota farm. Their crow wasn't healthy and robust but crackly and sick. But they were roosters and their sound was welcome even if they started too early. Since I couldn't see my watch, it was the first indication that my night was coming to an end. The roosters stopped crowing as the sun rose. I felt much safer during daylight.

I could finally see the hands on the watch—it was 0630, one more hour. For the first time in three days I was hungry. Eating, while manning a listening post was forbidden, so I would have to wait until I got back to camp to dine on C-rat eggs and chopped ham with a fruit cocktail dessert.

At 0710 I spotted the patrol walking down the trail. Wilson was on point, followed by the rest of the squad. As they approached my position Pat said, "You're the biggest gook I ever saw in a spider trap." The rest of the patrol laughed and made a number of comments on what I was probably doing all night.

I had to be helped out of the hole. My muscles and tendons seemed to be frozen in place. I had been on my feet in the small space for more than twelve hours. It took several minutes of warm-up exercise before I could walk.

The hike back to the patrol base seemed shorter. The first thing I did was heat water for coffee and open some C-rats.

Although I legitimately could have refused the LP assignment because of sickness, I was glad that I hadn't. A one-man listening post a mile from camp in the middle of enemy-controlled territory is not choice duty. Because I accepted it without complaining, my status with the other members of the squad was significantly enhanced. I had been with the unit for only a month, but I now felt like one of them.

Chapter 11
Phong Ho

The major differences between Phong Ho and the surrounding villages were size and architecture. Phong Ho was a mid-sized village, not as big as Hoi An or Dien Ban, but larger than most of the villages in our TAOR. Phong Ho was bordered on the west by huge, irrigated and productive rice paddies. These paddies covered more than two grid squares and abutted the Song Vinh Dien river.

Unlike the smaller villages, many of the buildings in Phong Ho were masonry structures. Some had two stories and were architecturally European. The village had a water and sewage system, though they had not functioned for a decade.

It was August 29, 1966, and I was starting my second month of combat duty. It seemed like I had been in-country a whole lot longer. Not having weekends to break up the month contributed to that feeling. Weekends were like any other day, and the workday was twenty-four hours, not eight. Everything was intensely serious and deadly. You couldn't call for a time-out if you ran into an unusual problem or situation. Decisions had to be made quickly and definitively–you couldn't vacillate. Lives depended on what you did or didn't do and how quickly you responded. I still didn't feel combat-hardened, but I was getting there.

We moved back to the platoon patrol base. It wasn't much better, but at least I felt somewhat safe within it's perimeter. I was getting to know Pat Connors. He was a patient teacher with a quiet sense of humor and not into one-up-man-ship. Pat had well-anchored values. He was unusual both in his generosity and in his calm approach to things. Because of his age and time in-country, he was the closest thing to a mentor I had. Mac, of course, had more time in the Corps, but Mac was a sergeant, not a mentor. I followed Mac's orders, but I learned from Pat.

A company-sized search and destroy operation was planned for Phong Ho, a village obviously under the control of the VC. The first squad would have point, and Mac selected me to walk point for the squad. Unlike the listening post assignment, this time I felt honored to be selected. Mac said that I would be attending the pre-operation briefing with him and Lt. Sloat, our platoon commander.

Since the operation was scheduled to depart from the battalion command post, the majority of the platoon had been transported to the battalion area. We had a chance to revisit the Enlisted Men's Club, and for the first time in over a month we had something cold to drink. The beer was cold, cheap, and you could drink as much as you wanted. There was supposed to be a nightly quota that the club could sell, but I don't think anyone took it very seriously.

As I looked around the club, I thought back to when John, Arturo, and I had been here. At that time, none of us knew what to expect. I still didn't know what to expect, but I had a much better idea how to react. I had been in the field for more than a month, and I was still alive. Many in our platoon hadn't been as lucky.

The conversation in the club was less ominous than it had been during our first visit. The talk today was about the USO show that had performed for the battalion a week earlier.

"Did you see the tits on the redhead doing that go-go dance? What a set. It's been months since I've seen a round-eye."

"I liked the blond–the one who looked like Joey Heatherton."

"Yeah, no shit, Man. I could get a hard-on just looking at the tracks in the sand that were made by the six-by that took her skivvies to the laundry."

A hearty round of laughter followed that remark. More beer was ordered and the jovial banter continued.

After quickly downing two cold beers, Mac said we should probably get back to the operation staging area. Reluctantly, we followed his lead and trailed him out of the club.

The operation was to begin at 2000 hours and the briefing started at 1800 sharp. In addition to Captain Kelly and Lieutenant Sloat, several intelligence officers attended the meeting. The briefing started with an overview of reported enemy activity in the Phong Ho area. An intelligence officer crisply delivered his message with Naval Academy authority. Captain Kelly followed, defining the mission.

Our initial task was to move cross-country to the bank of the Song Vinh Dien River, cross the river and set up blocking positions along the river's west bank. Another company from 1/1 was supposed to sweep south through the village of Phong Ho. They weren't scheduled to start their drive until 0600 hours, so we had ten hours to move about eight miles through unfamiliar terrain at night.

Once we reached the river, we were supposed to walk across it. We were assured by intelligence that the deepest spot was only five feet. After crossing the river, we were to set up our blocking positions and kill whatever tried to cross the river—like a deer drive in northern Minnesota except these deer could shoot back. After hopefully killing many VC, we would re-cross the river and move north, through downtown Phong Ho.

If any VC had been stupid enough to hang around town, we expected them to move north and be picked off by another blocking force of ARVN troops. After completing our northward sweep through Phong Ho, we would retrace our steps back through the village. The last act of the operation was a three-mile hike back to battalion. The operation was scheduled to terminate at 1400 hours, August 30. At that time, those who were still alive could go to the EM Club for a cold beer.

Our circuitous route to the river was designed to disguise our intentions and confuse the enemy. Not only was it indirect, but also much longer. At 2000 hours the company-sized formation was ready to leave the battalion perimeter.

I was at point. Wilson was behind with Mac following Wilson. The task ahead was formidable. We had an eight-mile, company-sized patrol to move through enemy-controlled territory. We would be in unfamiliar jungle and crossing many streams and rivers. It seemed impossible that we would ever get to our destination. As was usual in night maneuvers, silence and blackout conditions were in effect.

I spent ten minutes going over our route with Mac. I felt good about having him to consult with during our march. I also had a map in my hand. This was the first time that I had carried the map—a small step up the food chain.

The sky was black as I started leading the unit of ninety Marines in a southwesterly direction. Because the darkness made it difficult to see the man in front you, we moved much slower than during the day.

The first couple of hours were easy. We were on trails and in villages that were familiar to us. At about midnight, however, I went back to Wilson and told him to tell Mac that I had to talk to him. Wilson passed the word back to Mac, and movement was halted while we talked.

"I don't know where we are, Mac," I whispered. "I have to look at the map."

"Can't, we're operating under a no light directive," Mac responded.

I continued to plead my case. "If we can't look at the map we'll never get where we're supposed to."

Mac was a good Marine—he believed in following orders, all orders. I finally suggested that we crawl under a poncho and use a Zippo to read the map. He reluctantly agreed. While under the poncho, we took a compass reading and carefully examined the outdated map. We finally decided on a course of direction, and the long column moved on.

If I could make it to the river, the rest would be easy. We continued moving eastward. I still didn't really know where we were, but the review of the map had given me a vague sense of direction.

It was 0300 and I still had no idea where we were. The only thing I knew for sure was that I was lost in the jungle in the middle of Vietnam. Since I was point, the eighty-nine Marines behind me were also lost. We had crossed several rice paddies, forded three small streams, walked through a number of small villes and crossed what seemed to be a major road. I was concerned. Mac and Lieutenant Sloat had given me a vote of confidence by selecting me for point. Failure was not an option.

I was getting worried that we wouldn't reach our objective in time. We were scheduled to be in position on the west bank of the river before sunrise. Then I smelled it. I smelled water. Not the cool, crisp smell of a northern Minnesota stream, but the musty, earthy, rotting smell of a languid Vietnamese river. I told Wilson to call Mac up.

Mac joined me, and he, too, smelled water. The river probably had the scent of a slowly moving catfish stream in southern Alabama. We continued west for about fifty meters before reaching water.

Our next task was to get the long line of tired Marines safely across the river. Once across, we would move north along the west side of the river and establish blocking positions facing east.

The only time a combat patrol purposely bunches up is when crossing a river of undetermined depth. We would cross hand in hand. Each Marine would grasp the hand of the Marine in front of him and the Marine behind him. Consequently, if you hit a deep hole or dangerous current, you would be in the grasp of two Marines.

Since I was the point, I only had one Marine's hand to hold, Wilson's. I started across the river taking short deliberate steps. The current was slow and I only hit one hole deeper than four feet. It was the dry season, and most Vietnamese rivers were low. It would be suicide to try to cross this river during the fall monsoon season.

The entire company made it across the river. We quickly moved north along the bank and established blocking positions. It was 0530 hours, and the sun had not appeared above the horizon. I had reached our objective on schedule. I felt proud.

The company-sized driving force started sweeping south through Phong Ho at 0600. We heard heavy, prolonged exchanges of gunfire for the first hour. Later, only sporadic bursts of gunfire and an occasional grenade explosion were heard. The retreating enemy had not yet tried to escape by crossing the river. My partner in the blocking position was Sergeant McGougin. I felt special to be teamed up with a sergeant and the squad leader. We watched the river for any sign of fleeing VC. We heard several shots from positions south of us, but our sector was quiet.

As I continued to scan the opposite shore for signs of VC, I spotted three armed enemy troops pushing a small boat into the river. They emerged from one of the many irrigation canals on the opposite shore.

"Mac, do you see what I see?"

"Yeah," he whispered. "Let them get into the river a ways before we take 'em."

The three VC had no idea they were in our sights. They started paddling their small dugout directly toward us. I waited until

Mac gave the order to fire. He zeroed in his M-79, and waited for the right moment to fire. With a barely audible grunt Mac said, "Fire!" I emptied my 20-round magazine in seconds. At the same time, Mac fired the M-79. We both hit our target. The 40mm round from Mac's M-79 blew away the front half of the shallow boat. Boat debris and three dead bodies floated slowly downstream in the sluggish current.

Word from the company commander had been passed up the line. We were ordered to cross back over the river and take the road into the village of Phong Ho. Once we got there, we would sweep north. If there were any VC or NVA still in the village, we would either kill them or drive them into the ARVN blocking force.

Once again I took point and crossed back over the river. Everything was so much easier in the daylight. Crossing the river at night had been frightening; crossing in the daylight was almost refreshing. We would be washing our clothes and taking a bath as we splashed across.

I made it across the river and quickly located the road leading into Phong Ho. During the French occupation, the road had been a major highway, but thirty years of war and neglect had turned it into a pot-holed, washed-out, barely navigable trail. The only vehicles that could use it were tanks and amtracs. Every 100 meters, the road would pass over structurally intact stone culverts. These culverts were part of an elaborate irrigation system for the huge rice paddies bordering Phong Ho. Stone-lined irrigation canals had been built to divert river water into the rice fields. Each canal had a large stone culvert to carry the water under the road.

I was approaching the first fringe of homes surrounding the village when we received the order to hold up. I welcomed the chance to rest a few minutes. I took off my helmet and wiped the sweat from my face and neck. I lit a Viceroy and took a drink of my "Funny Face" flavored water.

Someone in the squad had received a whole case of artificially sweetened, flavored drink packets. The flavors had cute little names like Goofy Grape and Lefty Lemon. The taste was sickly sweet with a bitter aftertaste, but it made the stagnant water drinkable. The irony was that the U.S. Government was about to ban cyclamates, the artificial sweetener used in the drink mixes. Supposedly, it was harmful to your health. We never thought twice about drinking Goofy Grape.

Mac had gone back to the command element of the patrol and returned with one of the intelligence officers who had briefed us the previous night. They had received information that troops from the last driving force had found freshly dug graves on the southern edge of the village. Intelligence felt that the graves contained bodies of dead VC or NVA. The order from battalion intelligence was, "Dig them up."

We continued moving down the road until the S-2 officer stopped us. He was looking at his map and walking at the same time. He motioned us to follow him as he walked off the trail into what appeared to be a vegetable garden.

On the west edge of the garden we could see the dirt mounds of three new graves. The graves were unmarked and seemed out of place in the garden.

The S-2 officer looked at us and said, "Dig them up."

"What?" Pat blurted out.

"Dig them up!"

The order was clear.

We had been selected to dig up the graves because we happened to be at the head of the column and closest to the officer.

It didn't feel right to be digging up graves. Even if the graves held VC, it didn't seem Christian—or even civilized—to be disturbing the dead.

Pat and I grabbed our e-tools and turned into grave robbers. Since the dirt had been recently worked, the digging wasn't too difficult. I had removed the mound and was about two feet into the ground when my e-tool hit something hard.

The S-2 officer, who had been watching my progress, peered over my shoulder as I scraped dirt off the object I hit. It was the coffin. It was made of wood with a red lacquer finish. It didn't resemble any coffin I had ever seen. It was much shorter and narrower with one end wider than the other. I scraped the dirt off the entire length of the colorful casket and waited for the order I knew would come.

"Open it up," said the S-2 Officer. His voice was almost gleeful with anticipation.

"He must be a sick motherfucker," I thought.

I used my e-tool as a crowbar to pry the top off the casket. The top came off easily. I had expected to see a dead VC dressed up in his black pajamas. What I saw was a body wrapped with yards of gauze-like material.

"Get that goddamn gauze off the body, around the head," ordered the morbid one.

The odor wasn't immediate. It took a few seconds to escape from inside the casket, and when it did, the stench was overpowering.

I really did not want to unwrap the gauze with my hands, so I tried to remove the material with my e-tool. My progress was not pleasing the officer.

"Get that stuff off the gook's face, NOW!" He screamed.

I was pissed off. I had just walked point all night and half the day. I was tired, thirsty and hot. And I didn't enjoy digging up graves.

"If you want this shit off the gook's head. I'll get it off real quick."

With my right hand, I brought the e-tool backward so it was positioned behind my head. I then swung the tool downward as hard as I could. My target was the head, not the gauze. The sharp point of the small shovel cut through the gauze skewering the skull. The e-tool was firmly imbedded in the head.

If the S-2 Officer wanted the gauze off, I'd get it off and a hell of a lot more, I silently fumed. The officer covered his face with a green handkerchief as he leaned over the opened casket.

"I still can't see what it is. I have orders to visually confirm the contents of these graves. Pull that away from the face."

My e-tool was stuck in the corpse's head. The last thing I wanted to do was to use my other hand to dislodge the blade from the skull. I started twisting the trapped blade side-to-side, hoping that it would come loose. It worked; it came loose. The problem was that it was the head that came loose, not the e-tool blade.

I couldn't believe it. Here I was in the middle of a garden, straddling a gook casket, holding an e-tool with an old ladies head hanging from the end. I had pulled the whole head off the body. I lifted the head-embedded e-tool out of the casket and pushed it toward the young lieutenant.

"Here. Look for yourself," I said.

The officer, still covering his face with a handkerchief, visually examined the head.

"It's a goddamned old woman," he muttered.

It was obvious he was disappointed. I'm sure he planned to take credit for confirmed enemy kills if the body had been a VC.

"Put the head back in the casket and rebury her."

I pried the head off my e-tool using my foot as a brace. Carefully, I placed the head back into the casket, replaced the lid, and covered the grave with dirt. I tried to be respectful of the old lady. She was someone's mother and grandmother.

Pat's experience with the grave he dug up was similar to mine. His corpse also was an old woman. The difference between his experience and mine was that he didn't pull the head off. The third grave wasn't dug up.

The grave-robbing episode had taken about an hour, and, as a result, our mission was modified. Instead of continuing through the entire village of Phong Ho, we only would go half way. We would stop at the village square, replenish our water supply, and exit the village. We would then move east for about 1000 meters before heading south toward battalion. We expected to be back in time for happy hour at the EM Club.

The well in Phong Ho's village square looked like the well in the movie, *Robin Hood of Sherwood Forest*. It had a diameter of about five feet and a casing made of ancient weathered brick. A discolored wooden bucket was attached to a knotted rope draped over a wooden sawhorse that straddled the top of the well. The end of the rope was tied to an iron hook embedded in the brick outer casing.

We filled our canteens with the well's greenish water and dropped a halazone tablet into each canteen. You were supposed to wait for at least thirty minutes before drinking halazone-treated water. Supposedly, it took that long for any bacteria or other contaminants to be neutralized by the tablets. Often, your thirst was so great that you didn't wait the thirty minutes. We knew what the consequences could be, but we did it anyway.

Mac said he was taking me off point. I was devastated. He assured me that I had done nothing wrong. He said I had done a great job at point, but deserved a break. Although, I had been walking point since yesterday, I still felt like I was being demoted. I tried to persuade him to let me finish the operation as point man, but he was unwavering. He had made his decision. Pat Connors would replace me at point. Like me, Pat enjoyed walking point.

Most guys didn't. I always felt more in control of my fate when I walked point.

With Pat leading the way, the single-file formation headed east out of Phong Ho.

As we departed, I appreciatively gazed at the village's architecture. The trees lining the trail towered above everything. They were the tallest trees I had seen since arriving in Vietnam. They provided a protective canopy from the sun during the dry season and an umbrella during the monsoons.

Ahead, I could see where the path through the village became a trail that turned into a dike connecting Phong Ho to a neighboring hamlet. The distance across the small rice paddy was about 200 meters. I was fifty meters and four men behind Pat, and I watched as he started across the dike.

Wilson was twenty meters behind Pat, followed by Sage. Kranz had just started across the dike when I heard a heavy volume of fire coming from my left front. I couldn't see Pat, Wilson or Sage because the dike trail took a sharp left about twenty meters into the paddy. I could see Kranz behind the dike firing his M-14. Mac had run to the edge of the village and was lofting 40mm M-79 rounds toward the enemy. Then I heard the call, "Corpsman up!"

It had to be either Pat or Wilson since they were the only guys on the dike when the firing started.

Mac motioned for the rest of the squad to advance to where he was kneeling behind one of the towering trees. Doc had already run past us heading to the front of the patrol. He ran with abandon and determination, without regard for his personal safety. I followed Doc, stopping at Mac's position. Doc continued running. As we slid to a stop, I asked Mac who got hit. His response was, "Connors."

Jesus Christ, I couldn't believe it. Pat replaces me at point and gets shot after only ten minutes. I wondered how bad it was. Maybe it was the proverbial million-dollar wound.

"Listen up!" Mac barked.

His eyes, usually squinting, were wide open, almost trance-like. His expression was emotionless as he told us the details of his plan of action.

"We have to secure the tree line on the other side of the field immediately. Tornes, you, Villarreal and Kranz cross the dike. Wilson's with Doc, so pick him up when you go by."

The mission was clear. We were to secure the tree line and search for the enemy.

Without hesitation, we ran toward Kranz. As we ran by, he joined us. We approached Doc, who was frantically trying to do whatever he could for Pat. Wilson stood up and joined the group. Wilson was crying. He and Pat had been assigned to Delta Company about the same time. He probably knew Pat as well or better than anyone in Vietnam.

Pat was conscious when I briefly wished him well. From the placement of the battle dressings, it looked like he had been shot through the lungs. A bloody foam was bubbling from his nose and mouth. Although, I wasn't a corpsman, I thought Pat had the symptoms of a sucking chest wound.

He had a look of disbelief in his eyes. Pat gazed at Wilson and me and said, "I'm going to die, ain't I?" We didn't answer his question. Doc was vigorously trying to help Pat.

As I looked at Pat, I couldn't help but think that it could have been me. I could be lying in this paddy with a bullet in my lungs if Mac hadn't taken me off point. If Mac had listened to my pleading and changed his mind, I would be the one with the sucking chest wound, not Pat.

We continued across the dike, still taking fire.

We moved down the trail toward the ambush site. We found several empty .30 caliber casings and some cigarette butts. The cigarettes were Salems. Some fucking gook had been sitting in this ambush smoking Salems! How in the hell could the gooks get Salems when we have to smoke Chesterfields or Viceroys? Pat's lying out in a rice paddy, dying and the gook that shot him is smoking Salems.

We found a blood trail, so our anger was somewhat appeased, but the gooks were gone. We turned around and walked back to where Doc and Pat were. A medevac chopper had been called and a secure LZ was in place.

I felt strange, stranger than I had ever felt in my life. I wanted to kill something. I really didn't give a shit what. I just wanted to kill something. I wanted to kill something Vietnamese. It really didn't matter if it was a VC or not.

The medevac chopper landed and Pat left. His face had become ashen. He was still alive, but he had the look of death.

The company operation was one man short. We moved south on the trail that led directly to Cau Ha, a village abutting the battalion. As we walked down the familiar trail, I still felt the powerful sensation. I wanted to kill something. We were walking through a small hamlet about a mile from battalion, when I spotted it. It was large, ugly and Vietnamese.

I surreptitiously removed an M-26 fragmentation grenade from the pocket of my flack jacket. I pulled the pin, and tossed it underhanded at my target. Several seconds later, I heard the explosion and watched 300 pounds of pork instantly turned into sausage. I had killed something Vietnamese. I felt foolish, but I still felt good.

The explosion caused the column to halt. Mac came back to where I was and asked me what happened. I told him I had blown up a spider hole. He left without asking any details. I was sure some of the guys behind me had seen what I had done, but nobody said a word. Their feelings were probably the same.

Two days later, we heard that Pat died in the chopper on the way to NSA. The bullet that hit him severed his pulmonary artery. There was no way he could have made it.

Weeks later, the company received a letter from Pat's wife. She said he looked good lying in the casket in his dress blues, but his wedding ring was not on his finger. Someone had taken it after he was medevaced out. Every man in the squad could have put a bullet in the head of the son-of-a-bitch that had stolen Pat's ring.

The end of August continued to be bloody. On August 31, an amtrac carrying a unit from Charlie Company hit a large anti-tank mine. One Marine was killed instantly, and eleven others were seriously injured. All were medevaced to the Naval Hospital in Da Nang.

The battalion CP was mortared on August 31st. Since our platoon patrol base was several miles from battalion, we missed that event. We heard that a Combined Action Corps (CAC) unit operating in our area had been overrun while battalion was getting mortared. The battalion intelligence officer said the mortar attack was a diversionary action. The CAC unit had been the VC's primary objective.

Chapter 12
Battalion Bait or Security?

It was September 2, 1966, my sister Debra's birthday. She would be twelve years old today. I knew Mom would bake her a cake and have a neighborhood birthday party. Since I didn't have a birthday card, I decided to write to her. The letter was pretty generic. I wrote about the weather, the geography of Vietnam and the people. I asked her questions about what she did during summer vacation and if she was looking forward to school. After several sanitized paragraphs, I couldn't think of anything else to write. We had been required to convert all American dollars to military payment currency (MPC), so I didn't have a five-dollar bill to send to her as a gift. Instead, I sent her a five-dollar MPC note. She wouldn't be able to spend it, but she would probably be the only twelve-year old girl in International Falls with a five-dollar MPC certificate.

On September 8, we packed up and moved from the patrol base that had been home for the last month. Wilson and I dismantled our poncho lean-to and gathered up our few personal belongings. We walked to what would be our new home. Our platoon had been selected to provide security for the abandoned battalion command post. We couldn't figure out what we were going to provide security for since the entire battalion was moving. They were headed for the newly constructed battalion command post eight miles south, near the town of Hoi An. We were down to twenty-six men, certainly not enough to provide adequate security for such a large perimeter. Many of us thought we would be nothing more than bait—an attractive and vulnerable target for our foe.

Compared to our previous living accommodations, the old battalion CP seemed palatial. We had real tents with wooden floors and mosquito netting under the canvas wall flaps. We would also have the use of a real shitter, a four-holer. No more squatting over cat holes. Our major disappointment was that the battalion had taken the mess hall and EM club with them. We would still be eating C-rats and drinking warm beer. Nevertheless, it seemed like a fair trade-off.

Fortified, sandbagged bunkers guarded the perimeter of the base. The bunkers were about twelve feet square with timber reinforced walls and roofs. Each bunker had an entrance on the side facing the center of the base, and a narrow elongated opening facing outward. In front of the bunkers, various patterns of tanglefoot, razor, and concertina wire encircled the entire base. It was a formidable defensive structure when adequately manned. Because we were understaffed, only a third of the bunkers would be manned. This resulted in huge gaps in perimeter security. We continued to think of ourselves as bait.

Lieutenant Sloat came up with an ingenious plan that he hoped would provide our platoon with additional security. We all knew that the residents of the villages abutting the base were Viet Cong and Viet Cong sympathizers. They used children and women to monitor every move we made during the day. The lieutenant said the Viet Cong excelled in planning, but if something unexpected developed before the plan could be executed, they floundered. They were inflexible and unable to quickly modify a preconceived plan of action. He decided to play to that weakness.

Two squads spent several days planting mines in designated areas between the concertina and tanglefoot wire. This was done at midday so the VC informants would be sure to see what we were doing. The mines were unusual in that they were not mines at all. They were either empty or unused C-rat cans. We used our e-tools to dig the holes into which we placed our fake-mines. He even had us put up warning signs in both English and Vietnamese by the pseudo mine fields. Although a company of VC could have easily overrun the base, they never tried.

Providing security for the base was only one of our responsibilities. We continued our routine of patrols during the day and ambushes at night. Two new guys had joined our squad so we were up to seven men.

The two replacements were quite different from each other. One was a corporal with more than three years in the Corps. The other new guy, Langley, was a boot with fewer than four months in the Corps. Langley was assigned to me. With two months of combat experience, I was now the mentor.

In early September, the remaining artillery group was conducting Forward Observer (FO) training sessions for a group of Marines from three different battalions. The school used a hands-on, learn-by-doing teaching method. Classes were conducted in a large open area near the northwest corner of the perimeter. The classes lasted two days and were attended by thirty Marines.

We were returning from a daytime patrol and approaching the main entrance to the base. Gary Rosser, my fire team leader, had Langley walk point. It was his first time and he did well.

Langley was a farm boy from east Texas. He was more comfortable walking through woods and fields than on streets and sidewalks. He had hunted as a teen, and possessed a hunter's sense of location, alertness and attention to detail—ideal qualities for walking point. I was point on the majority of squad patrols, so I appreciated a capable back up.

As we entered the perimeter, two huge explosions erupted from the area where the Artillery Forward Observer School was being conducted. Smoke and sand billowed skyward. From our location near the main gate, we were unable to see exactly what happened, but we instinctively knew it wasn't good. Quickly, we headed in the direction of the explosion.

The training area was a disaster. Wounded Marines were everywhere. Chunks of metal, wood, and clothing had been scattered over the entire compound. Uninjured Marines were confused and dazed. Two corpsmen were already working with the wounded. The Artillery Liaison Officer for 1/1 had been severely wounded along with eight other Marines.

A Marine FO officer took charge. He directed our squad to move outside the perimeter and establish defensive positions between the training area and the nearby hamlet of Cau Ha. Apparently, the officer thought there could be a VC attack from that direction.

As we moved northward toward Cau Ha, I overheard a Marine saying the explosions had been electrically detonated mortar rounds. Apparently, the VC had been able to infiltrate the Forward Observer training area and plant the explosives. Since they had been electrically detonated, whoever triggered the explosions would have to be nearby. The closest Vietnamese village was Cau Ha, our destination.

We entered the small village and began searching for any evidence of VC. As usual, the residents of the village all looked outwardly innocent. Our questioning consisted of, "Where VC?" The answer was usually a sing-songy, "Cam biec" (I don't know or understand) followed by animated pointing to anywhere away from the village. In our hearts we knew they were all lying. They knew who the VC were and where they were hiding.

We searched the huts without success. We found no VC or anything related to electrical detonation. In fact, the youngest male in the village was about seventy-five years old. In the middle of the village, I spotted a local entrepreneur hawking her wares. A grandmasan standing behind a display table covered with mostly useless junk. The table was made out of a U.S. Navy shipping crate.

As I approached the old lady, I looked at the variety of goods she was selling. In addition to fresh vegetables, she offered Zippo lighters, toothpaste, Fanta orange soda, beer and condoms.

The old lady had about five tar-colored teeth in her mouth. She waved a Zippo lighter in front of my face and shouted, "You buy! Good Zippo. Only five bucks. Numba-one Zippo. You buy!"

Since I didn't need another Zippo or anything else she was selling, I decided to rejoin the rest of the squad. As I turned to leave, I spotted something behind her that stopped me in my tracks. Stacked neatly on the ground, partially covered by a piece of canvas, were about twenty cartons of Salems and Marlboros.

This old gook grandma has twenty cartons of quality American cigarettes, and I'm ruining my throat smoking Chesterfields! I could feel my anger building. She was no longer some innocent, old woman trying to make a few bucks selling vegetables and junk. She had Salems, and I didn't.

I felt like kicking the table over, knocking her down, and taking the cigarettes, but I didn't. I knew that nothing would happen if I did what I felt like doing, but I couldn't do it. Instead, I angrily asked her how much for a carton of Salems. She answered, "Ten bucks." Ten bucks! It was fucking robbery. If you had access to a PX, a carton of Salems cost $1.50. This old gook bitch is trying to rip me off while I'm supposedly fighting for her freedom. Something was wrong, big time. I decided to leave before I did something stupid, like kill the old broad.

We left Cau Ha without finding anything worthwhile, other than the cartons of Salems. Whoever detonated the booby-trapped mortar rounds won today's battle. The war was still up for grabs.

Chapter 13
The Rat

It was rumored that we were to remain on security detail until October 26th. Then the rumor was that the battalion would be sent to Okinawa to regroup and rebuild. After several months in Okinawa, we would be assigned to a float phase as a battalion landing team. This would mean that we would float around in the South China Sea waiting for the call to make a landing or to replace a battalion that was being pulled out.

This rumor, like most, was false. Nothing ever materialized, but at least it gave everyone something to look forward to. We spent hours fantasizing about the debauchery of an Okinawan liberty.

The residents of our tent at the old battalion command post were Mac, Kranz, Sage, Rosser, Wilson, Langley, Hicks, Rice, and me. Rice was attached to the weapons squad, but lived in our tent. He was a tall, skinny, black PFC with pockmarked skin. His eyes were unusual. They were very small with a slight oriental slant. Rice was a fearless machine gunner.

I doubt whether he had known many white guys before being drafted into the Marine Corps. He had been born and raised in Harlem. His first trip outside New York City had been to boot camp at Paris Island. Rice didn't trust Whites. You could see the resentment in his eyes.

Packsacks and personal gear were stored under our cots. Personal gear consisted of razors, letters from home, stationery, any treats we may have stashed and cigarettes.

Platoons periodically received sundry packages or gifts from the government that included such necessities as cigarettes, Red Man chewing tobacco and plug tobacco. Almost all Marines smoked, but only a few good ol' boys chewed. I did both. I preferred snuff, but a wad of plug tobacco would do in a pinch.

There was an established pecking order to receive a carton of cigarettes from a sundry pack. The package would first go to the platoon commander and his staff. They, of course, would select the most popular brands: Marlboro, Winston and Salem. Then the second tier would move in—sergeants, corporals and squad leaders. They would select L&M's, Kools, Viceroys and Pall Malls. The leftovers would be passed down the line to the lance corporals, PFCs and privates. During my first month in the field, I smoked unfiltered Chesterfields, unfiltered Camels and Lucky Strikes. One of the greatest perks of being promoted (other than money and status) was an upward move on the sundry pack smoke chain.

The inside of our tent was hot and dark. The side flaps had been down all morning and the air was sticky. I had returned to the tent to get a pack of cigarettes. Luck had been with me during the last sundry pack distribution and Viceroys were still available when the cigarettes dropped to my level.

As I entered the dark, sauna-like interior of the tent, I saw someone sitting on my cot busily digging through my packsack. It was Rice. He turned his head abruptly toward me and his eyes fell to the floor. He had a pack of Viceroys in one hand and my opened packsack in the other. He said nothing as he continued to guiltily gaze at the floor. I didn't know what to say.

Finally I blurted out, "What the hell are you doing in my pack?"

Rice didn't respond. He had dropped both the pack of cigarettes and the packsack. Several uncomfortable seconds passed before I decided to give him a chance to save face and exit the embarrassing situation.

"If you were out of smokes, you should have asked me, I would have given you a couple of packs," I said. "Just ask me next time. I'll be happy to share my cigarettes with you."

Rice grunted and headed for the door. I reached into my pack, got two packs of Viceroys. "Here," I said tossing them toward Rice. "Take these with you."

He caught the packs of cigarettes, muttered an almost inaudible "Thanks," and left.

I didn't know much about Rice's life in Harlem, but I assumed that it was much different from life in northern Minnesota. For some reason, he had been reluctant to ask me for cigarettes. He had probably never asked a "chuck dude" for anything. The incident was forgotten, and Rice continued to live in our tent. His intrepid M-60 support of our operations continued.

Our daily schedule was changed slightly by the additional responsibility of guarding the perimeter. We would be on perimeter guard during the night and run patrols during the day, or the schedule could be reversed with perimeter guard during the day and ambush at night.

Two Marines were assigned to a bunker and each would stand a two-hour watch. After your shift, you would wake your bunkermate so he could relieve you. This continued until daybreak when the security of the perimeter was decreased and only the corner bunkers and the main gate were manned. The Marines who had been on night security guard would then return to their tents and prepare for a daylong patrol. This demanding schedule took its toll on everyone. We were perpetually exhausted. Our schedule would not be reduced in the months ahead.

Wilson was my partner and we were in one of the larger bunkers on the north side of the perimeter. The sun had set, and he would take the first shift. I was still awake, so we talked about what young Marines usually talked about—women (girlfriends, wives and mothers), what you wanted to do when you got out of the Corps, and where you were going on R&R. I don't remember ever having a conversation about communism, winning the war or the domino theory. Our main concern was to stay alive and intact until our tour was over. For us, our war would end when we boarded a plane heading for Travis Air Force Base in California. Alive or dead, you would go home by plane.

Tonight, the topic was women. The first platoon had been adopted by a sorority from Georgia Southern University. The college, located in Statesboro, Georgia, was obviously pro-military. The school had initiated a program where individual sororities received the names of Marines in a specific field combat unit. The names were then assigned to girls in the sorority, and they would write letters to the adopted Marines.

Both Wilson and I received letters. The idea was great since all Marines enjoyed getting mail. It was especially rewarding for me since I didn't have a wife or girlfriend writing to me.

The first letter was generic. The girls each wrote a brief personal biography, told us what they were studying, and described the school and their sorority. They encouraged us to write, promising a quick reply. Wilson and I spent a few minutes comparing our letters and the bios of our Southern belles before I decided to go to sleep.

I was in the middle of a dream, when something caused me to wake up. There was a weight on my chest and I couldn't determine whether it was part of my dream or real. I was in the twilight zone between sleep and lucidity, lying on my back in the corner of the bunker. My head was propped at an uncomfortable angle against the bottom tier of the reinforced wall.

As I opened my eyes, I saw *its* eyes. They were small and red, and about five inches from my face. The biggest rat I had ever seen was on my chest looking into my eyes. I could feel his tail twitching against my bare chest. Instinctively, I brought my right fist across my chest, delivering a solid blow to the startled rodent. The rat shrieked as it was propelled off my chest into the log wall.

Wilson had been unaware of the rat. His attention had been properly focused on the tree line two hundred meters away. Startled by the squealing rat hitting the wall, Wilson lurched up, then fell backward against the bulkhead. The rat hit the wall and dropped to the floor. This rat was not about to be intimidated. It quickly regained its composure and assumed an aggressive stance.

I rolled to my right and grabbed my M-14. The rifle was at the ready position: I was prepared for combat. The rat's path of egress was blocked because I was between it and the door. The rat made a run for it. I was quicker. As I lunged for it, I brought the heel of the stock downward. The stock hit the rat's head squarely. There was a crunching sound as the butt of the rifle drove its head into the earthen floor. The rat quivered, then died. It looked like a dead muskrat. I felt good. I had killed the enemy.

Chapter 14
The Pit

We continued to operate out of the old battalion area during the month of September, enjoying simple luxuries while we could. Many still felt the platoon was being used as bait to encourage a large-scale attack. We were still seriously understaffed with occasional replacements arriving to take the place of those rotating back to CONUS (continental United States). Casualties from small arms fire and booby traps continued to deplete our ranks. Temperatures ranged from 100 degrees during the day to a low of 80 at night. Humidity varied from 80 to 95 percent. We were still in the dry season, however the wet season, the monsoons, would be starting in October. This was the status of the first platoon in mid-September 1966.

Gary Rosser was still my fire-team leader. He was enthusiastic about his responsibilities and genuinely concerned about the safety of his team. He had joined the Corps earlier than me, so his tour would end in January of 1967. Rosser said that his brother had received the Congressional Medal of Honor in the Korean War. Most of us didn't really believe him. I had never known anyone related to a Congressional Medal of Honor recipient. I didn't think Rosser was purposely lying about his brother. He was probably just confused about what medal his brother had been awarded.

Rosser was from Southern Ohio, an area as hillbilly as any place in the country. His spare time had been spent hunting the hills and creek beds near his home. As a result, he had an excellent sense of direction and a hunter's sense of stalking and ambush.

I continued to walk point every other day, and we often collaborated on location, direction, and tactical decisions. Rosser had a knack for remembering obscure landmarks that frequently helped us determine exactly where we were. Knowing where you were could be a life or death issue.

Today's patrol would be shorter than usual. We would be out for only three hours instead of seven or eight. Two tethered water buffalo were working the field that we crossed. Their handler, a pre-teen boy, ignored us as I led the squad along the top of a nearby dike.

Our first checkpoint was about 500 meters from the perimeter. The patrol had been without enemy contact. After calling in our position, we continued west toward the second checkpoint. The temperature was cooler than normal and the patrol was almost fun.

In many ways, Vietnam was beautiful. There were places that rivaled Bali and Hawaii in natural beauty. Today, I felt like I should have been carrying a Nikon instead of an M-14.

We made it to the second checkpoint without incident. I had been unusually careful in selecting what paths and trails we used as we moved from checkpoint to checkpoint. The area was heavily booby-trapped and I didn't want to be added to the long list of casualties it had produced.

The second checkpoint was the village of Quang Ha. Rosser stopped the patrol and called in our location. Everyone took a short break, and most of us had a cigarette. After I had smoked my Viceroy, I took a large bite of plug tobacco. The chunk of "Days Work" was sweet and produced a thick syrupy juice that could be spit great distances.

We had lost the only other person who chewed tobacco, the squad leader from second squad. He had been killed the week before when he stepped in a punji pit that was booby-trapped with an 81mm mortar round.

Chewing tobacco satisfied my nicotine addiction, and it also helped conserve my cigarettes. Another benefit was increased saliva production. Although the presence of tobacco juice in your mouth didn't quench your thirst, it did keep your mouth moist and eliminated the "cotton mouth" that accompanied dehydration. On the negative side, it was a messy, low-life habit.

I continued leading the patrol through the small village to Phong Ho (1), our third checkpoint. This wasn't the same Phong Ho where Pat Connors had been killed a month earlier. Phong Ho (1) was the northern suburb of that Phong Ho.

For safety reasons, I had taken an indirect route to Phong Ho (1), avoiding trails that looked unused as well as those that looked even remotely suspicious. Often, it was a gut feeling that made me avoid certain trails or roads. I was proud of my ability to effectively lead patrols. The years I spent hunting deer, rabbits and grouse were yielding dividends.

We approached Phong Ho (1) from the north. Rather than take one of the many trails leading to the center of the village, I took what looked like a safe corridor between two rows of tall trees. The branches from the opposing rows of trees were intermingled overhead creating a thick green canopy.

As I led the patrol down the slight incline of the trail, I noticed that the ground was covered with fallen leaves. They looked like the yellow, autumn-colored aspen leaves of northern Minnesota. For a brief moment, I was back home stalking grouse, my .410 at the ready and a loyal dog at my side.

About half way down the wide path I noticed a suspicious pile of the yellow leaves. I picked up a long piece of bamboo and carefully approached the unusual mound of foliage, probing the ground in as I walked. Suddenly, I felt the ground beneath me give away. Half my body was falling; the other half was safely anchored. Instinctively, I threw myself away from the collapsing groundcover. I had fallen on my left side and part of my right leg was invisible. It was in the pit. I had almost fallen into a large man-trap. I pulled my right leg out of the hole and rolled to my left.

Rosser had seen me fall and he quickly moved to my side. Together, we peered over the edge of the man-trap. The hole was about four feet square and five and a half feet deep. Five sharpened bamboo stakes, between four and five feet long, were imbedded in the bottom of the pit. They rose menacingly from the base of the hole. Anyone unfortunate enough to fall into the pit would be impaled.

It was the largest man-trap that anyone in the patrol had seen. I was lucky. If my left foot had been six inches closer to my right foot, I would be sitting on the bamboo stakes. We called Delta One to report what we had found. We were instructed to destroy the pit. We happily complied by depositing two M-26 grenades in the bottom of the hole.

Shaken, but alive, I continued down the pathway toward the center of the village. I had walked only five meters when the ground collapsed. This time it happened all at once, not gradually. In a matter of seconds, I was standing at the bottom of a man-trap identical to the one we had just destroyed.

My rifle was jarred from my hands as I fell and my helmet flew off. I could feel the pressure of the sharpened bamboo stakes on my back and both legs, but I felt no pain. Maybe the body's natural pain-killing analgesics had kicked in. I was afraid to move. I didn't want to look downward and see the damage.

"Tornes, you okay?" It was Rosser.

"Don't know. Don't feel any pain or anything," I yelled.

"Don't move. The bottom of the pit may be booby-trapped with a pressure-release explosive. I'll call Delta One and ask them what we should do."

I was alone in my pit. Many punji pits, whether foot traps or man traps, were booby-trapped with explosives—usually variations of pressure-release mines. The mechanics of pressure-release is a simple and effective two-step process. The first step involves depressing an activating mechanism, and this happens when you step on the triggering device. The second step, the actual activation of the explosive, happens when you remove the weight of your body or foot.

The secondary goal of pressure release explosives was to maximize enemy casualties by injuring the rescuers as well as the trapped. Consequently, Rosser and the other members of the patrol would not be coming to my aid. If I died, I would die alone.

I decided to survey my body and see what damage the bamboo stakes had done. Slowly, I dropped my chin to my chest and let my eyes wander over my lower body. There were five sharpened stakes. One had gone through my trousers above my boot and had exited my trousers near my crotch. Another stake was pressed against the crack of my ass with the tip touching my back just below the shoulder blade. A third stake had sliced through my jungle utility shirt on the inside of my elbow and was menacingly close to my neck. The forth piece of sharpened bamboo was pressed against my left knee and extended upward toward my left armpit. The last stake was about six inches in front of my body, the sharpened tip chest high. I still could feel no pain or see any blood.

Was it possible that all five of the bamboo stakes had failed to find a target? The configuration of the stakes and the small size of the pit made that scenario highly improbable.

Rosser had contacted Delta One to inform them of our situation. His orders were, "Extricate him in the safest possible manner without endangering additional Marines."

In other words, they didn't have a plan that would guarantee success. We had to do what we had to do.

Rosser, positioned a safe distance behind me, checked on my condition, " You still okay, Tornes?"

"Yeah," I answered. "Don't think any of the stakes hit me."

"Are you sure none hit you?"

"If they did, it ain't bleeding. Still can't feel pain anywhere."

"The lieutenant said you should try to carefully climb out of the pit. We're to stay clear while you climb out."

"Fuckin hole's probably booby-trapped," I shouted.

"I know, but what you gonna do?"

I knew I didn't have any choice but to climb out of the pit. I also knew that the odds were high that the pit was booby-trapped. If that were the case, the pressure-release triggering device would activate the explosive charge the second I lifted my foot. I tried not to think about the damage even a small grenade would do to a body in such a confined space.

"Bring me a knife so I can cut some of my clothes away from these stakes."

Rosser responded to my request and brought me his K-bar. I cut away clothing that had been skewered by the stakes. By doing so, I hoped to eliminate anything that would restrict my jump out of the hole. The top of the pit was eye level, and if the pit wasn't booby-trapped, I didn't want anything catching on one of the stakes that would cause me to fall back into the hole. I knew I couldn't cheat death three times in one day.

After I cut away all potentially restrictive clothing, I threw the K-bar toward Rosser.

My life didn't flash before my eyes as I mentally prepared to jump out of the pit. If it was booby-trapped, I would be dead in minutes. If it wasn't, I'd be alive. Not too complicated. To be killed in a combat zone by a booby-trap was still preferable to being killed by a fucking spider. I jumped.

I was still alive. Instead of heading for the Pearly Gates, I'd be heading for the platoon base and a warm beer. The gooks had lost this one. They probably didn't want to waste an explosive device booby-trapping a man-trap that they thought would be certain death.

After climbing from the hole, we blew it up as we had the first pit. Rosser said he would take me off point. I declined. I felt lucky. I continued down the path to Phong Ho (1). About ten meters from the mantrap I'd just jumped out of, I spotted the third hole. Leaves that had camouflaged the cover of the trap had been blown off, probably by the concussion blast when we destroyed the second trap. We destroyed this pit, too.

As we neared the entrance to the camp, we took a few sniper rounds. A lone sniper shot at us nearly every time we departed or entered. We assumed he was the same guy because he always shot from the same hill. The hill was about 400 meters too far for his underpowered rifle and he was a terrible shot. We nicknamed him Luke-the-Gook. I'm sure there were many enemy snipers nicknamed Luke-the-Gook in Vietnam, but this was our Luke-the-Gook. We would usually give him the finger and holler in unison, "Ho Chi Minh sucks Marine cock!" We didn't even return fire. Luke-the-Gook was our mascot, even though he supported the other team.

Chapter 15
A Case of Beer

Someone in the squad received a bottle of Tabasco sauce from home. It was amazing how a few drops of the hot red pepper sauce could improve our C-rats. A couple of drops sprinkled into a can of ham and MFs would produce Creole ham and beans.

We got very creative at modifying C-rats. Peaches and fruit cocktail continued to be the C-rats of choice. A can of peaches could be traded for just about anything. Peach shortcake dessert was our favorite. We would make it by opening a can of pound cake, poking holes in the top of the cake with a bayonet, then pouring the fruit and juice from a can of peaches over the top.

Lieutenant Colonel Van D. Bell, the battalion's commanding officer, designed an incentive plan to increase the productivity of field forces. Productivity was defined as dead VC. He placed a bounty of a case of beer on any confirmed VC KIA. The killer would receive one case of beer for every dead gook. Like most incentive plans, it didn't make us try harder; it just cost the government more when we did what we would do anyway.

We had been directed to provide a blocking force for Charlie 1/1 whose TAOR was north and slightly east of ours. We were ordered to move three miles northwest and set up blocking positions for their sweep. The area they were driving was under VC control and supposedly a recently captured NVA officer had confirmed that a combined VC and NVA Regiment was based in the area.

Our blocking force was small: two reinforced squads—about twenty-five men. We had moved into position on both sides of a road that led to a bridge crossing the Song Vinh Dien River. It was the only intact bridge for miles in either direction. If any VC or NVA wanted to leave the area, they would have two choices: boat across or take the bridge. If they decided to take the bridge, we would be positioned to ambush them.

If, in fact, there was a regiment operating in the area, there could be a large number of enemy wanting to use the bridge. Although we wanted to kill as many enemy as possible, our blocking force was limited, and we would be greatly outnumbered if the intelligence report was accurate. None of us felt the intelligence was credible. We didn't have any special information, just a long history of useless intelligence information.

Langley was my fighting hole companion and I continued to be his mentor. We worked well as a team and quickly dug a deep and spacious two-man fighting hole. Digging was easy in the moist sand of the riverbank.

It was 1700 hours and we settled in for the night. The main driving force was supposed to start sometime in the middle of the night or early morning. Once again, we really didn't have much information on what was supposed to happen. Our assignment was simple: kill anything that tried to cross the bridge. We decided on one-hour watches for the night. Earlier in my tour, a two-hour watch was easy. I could stay awake and alert for two hours. As my tour continued, my body slowly wore down. A two-hour watch was now too long and I would probably fall asleep. Some of the Marines, who had been in Nam longer than I, couldn't make it an hour.

I was awakened by Langley pulling on my arm.

"Think I see something crawling toward us," he whispered.

Quietly, I rolled off my sleeping ledge, and looked in the direction Langley was pointing. I couldn't see anything. The night was dark and moonless. I couldn't even see the embankment of the road leading to the bridge.

"I don't see anything."

"Look over there, to the left front 'bout twenty meters out. Doesn't that look like someone lying on the ground?"

"Could be, but I'm not sure," I answered, trying to keep my voice as quiet as possible.

"Look, it's moving toward us," Langley excitedly whispered.

I looked toward the prone profile. It was moving slowly in our direction.

"What should we do? Should we shoot it?"

"Let's blast it," I said.

We both zeroed our M-14's in on the prostrate target.

"Fire!" I whispered.

I fired a short burst and Langley fired three deliberate shots. There was no reaction from the target.

Everything looked like it had before we shot. Whatever it was, it wasn't moving. Maybe it had never moved and we had killed a mound of dirt.

"What the hell is going on over there?"

Mac had heard the shots from his position on our left and wanted a report.

"Thought we saw something crawling toward our position," I answered.

"You shouldn't shoot unless you are sure," he admonished. "It gives away your position."

The rest of the night was quiet. Shortly before daybreak, Mac walked up to our position with information about the operation we were supposed to be participating in.

"We're going to pull out at first light and go back to the platoon area," he announced.

Apparently, someone up the chain of command had decided during the night to cancel the operation. It was rumored that intelligence had identified the wrong village as being a VC stronghold. Nobody, including Mac, really knew what was going on or why the operation was canceled. The only thing we knew for sure was that we were going back to our platoon area.

The sun broke the horizon and we could see once again. In front of our position, about twenty meters away, was a body. Scrambling out of our fighting hole, we ran to look. Our rifles were at the ready as we approached the contorted figure.

It was a young Vietnamese male, dressed in Khaki shorts and a light green shirt. He was wearing a small backpack and a cartridge belt. A Chicom grenade lay in the sand near his clenched fist. His eyes and mouth were open and most of his face and neck was covered with dried blood. We had got him before he got us.

Mac inspected the body and took the backpack, cartridge belt and unexploded Chicom. The body, riddled with M-14 rounds, was left where it was. Relatives would eventually retrieve it and give it a proper Buddhist burial. We decided Langley would be credited with the kill. It was his first confirmed kill and he would get his case of beer from Col. Bell. Since Langley didn't drink, the rest of the squad would party.

The celebration with Langley's beer was short. We had got into the habit of eating and drinking any extra or unexpected food or beverages as soon as we received them. You didn't save anything for tomorrow. You might get killed today and never have the chance to enjoy it.

We divided up the case of beer and had five beers each. In an hour, it was gone. The warm beer with C-rat crackers and cheese had tasted great.

Chapter 16
Watermelon and Snakes

The area that we were going into was outside our normal tactical area of responsibility. Intelligence reported that the area had been infiltrated by a regiment of VC with NVA advisors. Our mission was to locate and engage the regiment. I felt honored when Mac told me that I would lead the patrol.

The trek to the unfamiliar area took about four hours. Today was unusually hot and humid, a precursor to the monsoons that would arrive in October bringing cooler temperatures and welcome rain. Fresh water would be available and your clothes would be washed as you wore them. None of the members of our squad had experienced a monsoon. We naively looked forward to its arrival.

We moved south, parallel to a major road, which in Vietnam was any road that could accommodate a wheeled vehicle without breaking an axle. Although the road was drivable, it was empty. Occasionally, we would meet a peasant woman, dog-trotting down the road carrying large baskets of vegetables suspended from the ends of a bamboo shoulder pole. It was remarkable how much weight these slight women could carry.

We were on the eastern edge of the Que Son Valley, an area covered with large rice paddies and irrigation canals. Networks of dikes connected many small villages. Some of the rice paddies were irrigated but others were bone dry.

The entire area had been designated a "free fire zone." The official definition of free-fire zone was ambiguous, but what it really meant was that you could shoot first and ask questions later. All residents were considered unfriendly to Americans and sympathetic to the Viet Cong and North Vietnam.

I led the patrol into a large village bordering a dry paddy that was separated from an irrigated field by a four-foot high earthen dike. Although the village was in a free fire zone, women and children continued to live there. They had no other option–this was home.

The lieutenant ordered the patrol to halt and called the squad leaders together to review the route of the patrol. Since I was walking point, I was included in the meeting. Although I was only a PFC, I felt like an important member of the patrol's leadership. Peer pressure in the Marine Corps probably creates more heroes than either genes or training. We finalized our plan of action and moved forward.

We were thirty meters apart and moving faster than normal. Dry rice paddies weren't typically booby-trapped and I felt comfortable with the accelerated pace.

About half way across the field I spotted what looked like a mutant cucumber. The strange looking vegetable was the only fruit on a single shriveled vine. I was tired, thirsty and generally pissed-off so I gave the weird cucumber a kick. The foreign fruit exploded when hit, covering the ground with seeds and chunks of ripened flesh. Then I smelled it. I had destroyed a vine-ripened Vietnamese watermelon. I would have killed for a piece of watermelon, but instead I had just killed the watermelon.

I looked at the scene of destruction. The largest surviving piece, about the size of my hand, was lying flesh down in the dirt. I picked it up, brushed it off, and devoured the juicy morsel. The flesh wasn't red like a real watermelon; it was green like honeydew. The taste was unfamiliar, but definitely melon. Unfortunately, the remaining pieces were too small to salvage. Momentarily refreshed, but angry at myself for damaging most of the melon, I continued across the dry paddy.

I approached the dike separating the dry field from the irrigated one. Thick jungle bordered the southern edges of both fields. The area looked ripe for an ambush.

Thigh deep water met me as I climbed over the dike and started splashing through the irrigated paddy. My destination was a road-sized dike on the eastern edge of the flooded field. The large dike functioned as both a trail and a water retention wall.

The muck sucked at my boots as I plodded ahead. My eyes were focused on the large dike in front of me, waiting for the ambush that I thought was imminent. Suddenly a uniformed, armed figure ran from the middle of the dike toward the southern tree line. Without hesitation, I fired a short M-14 burst at the fleeing figure. Several shots found their mark causing the figure to do a partial cartwheel before hitting the ground. Seconds later the patrol column came under intense fire from the southern tree line. I was the only person who had made it into the flooded paddy, and I was trapped in the middle without any place to hide.

Mini geysers erupted around me as the singing bullets entered the water. Since there was no cover, I decided to do the next best thing—minimize the target. I quickly submerged my entire body in the water with only my head and rifle exposed. In my underwater kneeling position, I offered the VC a lot less to shoot at.

The volume of fire had not lessened, but I was no longer the main target. Although I was a closer target, the firing was directed toward the main body of the patrol behind me. They were caught in the middle of the dry field but with some available cover. It seemed possible that the ambush had been triggered prematurely when I shot the fleeing VC. They probably planned to have the main body of the patrol trapped in the flooded paddy before firing. Some VC had fucked up and fired too soon.

My fear suddenly switched from the VC to a snake with a girth bigger than my arm. It was the largest snake I had seen since the San Diego Zoo. It was about 10 feet long, and it wasn't caged. It was gracefully gliding through the water about a foot in front of my face.

I quickly forgot about the bullets kicking up water around my head and redirected my fear. I had no idea what to do, so I did nothing. I froze. To my dismay, the snake didn't seem to be in a hurry to get to any destination. Its tail was in front of my face and it seemed to be treading water instead of moving away. My trance-like state was interrupted.

"Tornes, you okay?" The call was from Mac. Because of the height of the dike, he couldn't see whether I had been hit or not.

I was reluctant to answer. I didn't want to do anything that might irritate or startle the large reptile.

"Tornes, you okay?" Mac called again, concern in his voice.

I decided to answer, snake or no snake.

"Yeah, I'm okay." My voice could barely be heard above the noise of the firefight.

"Can you see where most of the firing is coming from?" Mac hollered.

"Yeah, most is coming from the middle of the tree line about a hundred meters to my right," I answered.

"We've called for an arty mission. Be prepared."

Mac's warning was barely out of his mouth when I heard the blast of the 105's leaving the battalion four miles away. In a matter of seconds, I heard the whistling of the large projectiles as they headed for their target. They had fired for effect on the first volley. Four rounds hit at the same time.

They tore into the tree line one hundred meters to my right. I felt the concussion from the blast and saw tree trunks and large hunks of soil erupt from the targeted coordinates. Another volley followed the first. We stopped taking fire.

The concussion from the artillery explosions created a ripple on the surface of the water. The ripple didn't quite reach my submerged position, but the concussion was enough to spook the snake. I was as relieved by the snake's departure as I was by the cessation of fire.

All firing had stopped and I hadn't heard the call for "Corpsman up."

I moved to the dike on the edge of the paddy. Maybe we had won the battle today. Maybe I would find the dead body of the enemy soldier. Once on the dike, I walked south where I thought I had dropped the VC. I didn't find a dead VC, but I found blood—lots of blood and a trail leading to the thick foliage of the tree line. I didn't have a body for proof. I wouldn't get a case of beer.

As Buddhists, the VC believed that to have an afterlife, the dead must have a proper burial. As a result, the VC were very conscientious about removing their dead from the battlefield. By doing so, they were able to salvage a small strategic victory from what was often an operational defeat. We had no proof that we had killed anyone. Psychologically, it devastated us. We knew we had killed the enemy, but we didn't have a body.

It is similar to deer-hunting. You see a buck and shoot it. It's hit. The wounded buck runs deep into a cedar swamp. You find blood but no deer. You know you hit it and it will die, but you have no proof. You can never celebrate success. You have no trophy.

Chapter 17
Saddle Up

At almost any time in a grunt's tour, a left nut would be sacrificed for a job in the rear-with-the-beer. Although we felt superior to those in the rear, we would join them if the opportunity presented itself. For most of us, the chance for such a skating assignment was about as probable as getting hit in the head with a meteor from Pluto.

We were grouped around the platoon sergeant for mail call. Once he finished distributing it, he asked, "Would anyone like a job in Da Nang with a non-combative status? Those interested, raise your hands." Every hand in the platoon went up, including mine. This was great, a chance for assured survival and future life.

"What's the job?" one of the volunteers asked.

The platoon sergeant hesitated, then said, "It's in Graves Registration."

Every hand dropped except Corporal Washington, the new right guide who had been with us only a few weeks. He had four kids and sixteen years in the Corps. He wanted to see his family again and retire in four years. Although we understood why he took the job, an incentive didn't exist that would entice us to work in Graves Registration. The personnel there did the cleaning and embalming of all combat fatalities before shipping the bodies home.

We wished Washington well, but each of us would rather stay where we were.

Gary Rosser, the fire-team leader of the first squad, had been in the field for almost five months and had proved himself many times. Early in his tour, he volunteered for "tunnel rat" assignments. He had the ideal build and personality for crawling through tunnels and caves. Rosser was small, strong, and fearless. Although still a PFC, he was going to be promoted to L/CPL on October 1st. If anyone deserved to be promoted, Rosser did.

The order from Rosser was, "Saddle up!" Although we weren't cowboys in a Saturday afternoon matinee, the command was clear. "Saddle up!" was the order to get ready to go out on patrol or ambush.

Rosser's Southern Ohio accent made "saddle up" sound like "saddoe up." I used to joke with him about his accent and his habit of omitting l's. He took the kidding without getting upset. Usually he didn't respond, but gave a sardonic smile. I suspect he thought my flat Midwestern accent sounded strange, too.

It was September 19th. I had been in Vietnam about six weeks. I had lost a lot of weight, but since I didn't have access to a scale, I didn't know exactly how much. Nevertheless, I was happy to be alive and contributing to the platoon's efforts.

We had been on a patrol for several hours. I was hot, sweaty and thirsty, so everything was normal. I would have committed almost any atrocity for a glass of clean, cold water. In the field, the quality of water was terrible. I wouldn't have let my dog drink the water we drank. Whenever we started to piss and moan about the quality of water, Doc Clopton would tell us about an incident on Operation Hastings. After hearing the story, our bitching usually stopped.

Doc had been one of the corpsmen with Delta 1/1 during Operation Hastings, the first major battle between Marines and NVA regular forces.

Doc's story went something like this:

"We had been fighting for control of this hill for about four days. The fuckin gooks were everywhere. Finally we made it to the top of the hill, but we paid a price for it. Lots of good Marines and a number of corpsmen didn't live to see the view from the top of that hill. After we got to the top, do you know what we did? We walked back down to the bottom. We hadn't been re-supplied with water for two days; didn't get anything—no C-rats, no ammo, no nothing.

We went back down to the bottom of the hill a different way than we went up. We're all thirsty as hell—dehydrated is what we were. Well, you know what we saw at the bottom of that hill? I'll tell you what we saw. We saw a little ol' stream just bubbling down from the mountain. We all rushed over and started filling our canteens and swigging down the water. The water was the worst tasting shit we had ever had, but we were thirsty enough to drink it anyway. We almost puked. Finally, another squad comes down the hill walking along the edge of the stream. They tell us we should walk upstream a bit before we fill any more canteens.

So I take this Marine, and we start following the stream up the hill. We hadn't gone but twenty meters upstream when we come across two dead, bloated NVA soldiers lying in the water. They didn't even look human. They looked like some kind of inflatable toy. They had bloated up so much that their clothes were skintight. They smelled worse than a garbage can full of rotten fish guts. The Marine I was with started puking. But since he hadn't had much to drink or eat, he only dry-heaved.

We each grabbed an arm of one of the gooks to pull him out of the water. We each got an arm and gave a pull. And we still each got an arm, only the arms don't have a body. We pulled those rotten gook arms right off the bastard. End of story. This water may taste like shit, but it will never be as bad as the water we drank from that stream with the dead gooks in it."

After hearing Doc tell his story, we usually drank our water and shut up. He told the story every time a new guy complained about the water. I heard it many times.

The patrol we were on was a two-day roving patrol. The route of the patrol had been established, and the only thing I had to do as point was find all the checkpoints and stay alive.

Our patrol was made up of two squads with an M-60 and a weapons team. The weapons "team" consisted of Arturo carrying a 3.5 rocket launcher. Tanks would accompany us today; tonight they would be placed in defensive positions on our perimeter.

Most patrols were not as long as the one that had been planned for us. Initially, we would travel east from our patrol base to the village of Viem Dong, a distance of two miles. From Viem Dong we would move south to the hamlet of Cam Sa (2). The trail south from Cam Sa (2) followed the western edge of a huge irrigated rice paddy to the edge of the horseshoe.

The horseshoe was a notorious VC stronghold. It got its name from the horseshoe looking curve made by the Song Ha Xau River. Many dwellings inside the horseshoe resembled old French villas. Someone said the area used to be a resort community for the French during their occupation.

We would follow the western bank of the horseshoe for about one mile before heading south through the village of Dong Thoi to a large hill where we would set in for the night. The next morning we would move west through the village of Cuo Lu and continue until we hit the major road that ran from Da Nang to Hoi An.

Although the road was drivable, most traffic, both military and civilian, used Highway One. We would follow the east edge of the road in a northerly direction for almost six miles, walking in the jungle, seventy-five feet from the road because of mines and booby-traps.

The first leg of the patrol was unremarkable. We reached Viem Dong without taking fire or triggering any booby-traps. Hicks, our radioman, called in our positions. We continued south along the edge of a large, flooded rice paddy. This area was known for booby-traps, and I was being exceptionally cautious as I led the group of Marines.

We were on the trail bordering the paddy when I saw something that many grunts only dream about: a group of VCs caught in the middle of a rice paddy, without cover. Wilson and Rosser were directly behind me. Both saw the VCs right after I did.

The enemy was about two hundred meters away, sitting in a circle eating when we surprised them. They jumped up, one at a time, like little, gook jack-in-the-boxes. We had them and they knew it.

Since the rice plants in the paddy were three feet high, we could only see the heads and shoulders of the trapped prey. They seemed confused and uncertain about what to do. Several started running in one direction, then turned and ran back. It was almost humorous to see them jumping around, not knowing what to do. The only thing they knew for certain was that they would meet their Buddha real soon.

Rosser and Wilson quickly joined me at the front of the column. Without saying a word, we brought our M-14's to our shoulders and emptied our magazines at the pop-up targets. I called for Arturo to bring up the 3.5 rocket launcher. I loaded the tube with a rocket; he aimed and fired. The rocket landed almost on top of the jumping figures. Water, rice stalks, mud and body parts flew through the air. It was the classic turkey shoot.

We all felt good. Usually, the roles were reversed and we were caught, exposed and without cover.

Before we could move to the center of the field to claim our trophies, we got word to keep moving. The rear element of the patrol would verify the kills. Several days later, we heard that five VC and three VCS had been confirmed killed.

"Tornes, what the fuck is hanging out of your boot?" Arturo's voice sounded an octave higher than normal.

"Look at your right foot, Man! You ain't gonna believe what's coming out of the top of your boot. Looks like some sort of snake."

I hadn't felt any pain in my right foot, so Arturo's warning came as a surprise. I looked at my foot and saw what had to be the world's largest leech. In Vietnam, leeches were almost as common as flies or mosquitoes. Usually they would drop off when touched with a lighted cigarette. They were small—fishing bait in Minnesota. This leech was different. About five inches of the leech hung over the top of my boot. It was apparently attached to my ankle. I quickly removed my boot and instinctively grabbed and pulled its slippery twisting body from its blood-sucking position. Not only was it huge, it was also aggressive. It wanted to continue feeding on my right hand where it hungrily tried to reestablish suction. I grabbed it with my left hand and managed to throw it to the trail where I stomped on it with my left boot. The eight-inch leech exploded like a ruptured artery. Blood flew in all directions—my blood. Oh, what I wouldn't give to be fishing walleyes on Rainy Lake with a dozen of these gargantuan leeches.

We moved south toward the horseshoe, following the western bank of the river for 2000 meters. Eventually we found the trail that would take us into Dong Thoi. As we moved single file through the village, it was obvious that the village did not support the Government of South Vietnam. Instead of the usual blank-faced peasants, the expressions on the faces of the residents of Dong Thoi were hostile and defiant. Although the chance of being ambushed in the center of a VC controlled village was remote, we remained cautious and vigilant while moving through the hamlet.

A sand hill, our destination for the night, was about 500 meters southwest of Dong Thoi. I assumed the location had been selected because of the elevation. The topography of the coastal plain was flat, barely above sea level. A night position on the sand hill would provide us with an elevated view of the surrounding area. Although the local relief of the hill couldn't have been more than one hundred feet, it was still one hundred feet higher than everything else.

The patrol moved toward the low hill with tanks leading the way. One tank positioned itself on the western edge of the hill, overlooking a large trail. The other tank remained on the opposite side of the hill facing the village of Dong Thoi. Between the tank positions, fighting holes would be dug at twenty-five meter intervals. I was teamed up with Wilson. Since the hill was a big sand pile, we expected easy digging.

I had just started digging when I heard an explosion. The sound was muffled, not loud and thundering like the booby-trapped pagoda. Two positions to our right, we saw a small cloud of smoke and sand billowing above a prone body. Immediately, I started running toward the fallen Marine. As I ran, I once again heard the scream of "Corpsman up!" Doc Clopton beat us there.

The wounded Marine was PFC Larry Glover. I didn't know him well, but I knew his name.

Doc asked if we had extra battlefield dressings. We gave him what we had. Glover's wound was ghastly. Whatever had exploded had shredded his legs and lower body. Bone and muscle tissue were everywhere. He was still conscious and was trying to lift his upper body up to see his wounds. Doc knew that Glover would probably go into shock if he saw what was left of his legs. He was both comforting and restraining him.

Unfortunately, Glover managed to rise up on one elbow and see the damage that had been done.

"Doc, my balls, everything is gone," he screamed.

"You'll be okay, you'll be okay," Doc consoled.

Glover's upper torso fell back into the sand. He had seen his frayed body, and it was too much for his system to handle. He became less agitated and his screams ceased. He was going into shock. Doc had done everything he could with what he had to work with. Glover's fate would now be in the hands of the doctors at the Naval Hospital and God.

A medevac arrived and Glover was loaded. As it departed for NSA, most of us knew in our hearts that he wouldn't make it. Our foreboding was confirmed: two days later we heard that he had died.

We never knew exactly what type of explosive device killed Glover. The best guess was that it was a booby-trapped 60mm mortar round. Apparently, he walked to the top of the hill, took his backpack off and dropped it on the ground. The backpack triggered the detonating device when it hit the ground and the mine. We were lucky that there weren't multiple casualties.

We continued to set up our perimeter for the night. Talk was subdued, with the usual bullshit and horse-play noticeably absent. Wilson had known Glover well. They were both black and had grown up in similar environments.

Wilson was as tough as any Marine, but he was one of the few who would outwardly show emotion. I had seen him cry several times. He had been devastated when Pat Connors was killed. He cried then, and I could see tears in his eyes now. That Wilson cried openly didn't diminish his stature as a Marine. Many of us wanted to, but couldn't.

I wanted to get Wilson thinking about something other than Glover, so I asked him about the co-ed from Georgia Southern University who had adopted him.

"Heard from your Southern belle lately?"

"Yeah, just got a letter at the last mail call."

"What'd she say?"

"I don't know, Gary, she's getting all mushy and stuff when she writes. She says she loves me, and that she is going to break up with her boyfriend. Says she is waiting for me. I can't figure out why she's saying all that stuff. I haven't written any love type stuff to her."

"Andrea's not like that," I said. "She writes nice letters, about school and all that. She doesn't even sign her letters 'Love, Andrea'."

"This girl is a white girl, you know," Wilson added.

"Yeah, I know. Bet there's not a black chick in the school. Haven't told her you're black, have you?"

"No, but I think I should. What you think?"

"I wouldn't tell her yet. Wait a while."

The talk about our Southern belle pen pals seemed to take Wilson's mind off Glover's death. We continued to dig our fighting hole in silence. When we finished, we ate a meal of cold C-rats. We were both too tired to take the time to heat the food. I volunteered to take the first watch. Other than the sound of distant artillery fire, the night was quiet.

Later, I had the last watch of the night and the opportunity to see the sunrise. I have always been a morning person. I enjoyed all mornings, even in Vietnam. I always felt less vulnerable in the daylight. I remember as a kid, when watching WWII movies, I almost stopped breathing during the scenes that took place at night. When the sun came up, I relaxed and breathed normally.

Shortly after sunrise, Rosser came by our position and ordered us to "saddoe up." Wilson and I buried our trash, and moved to the head of the patrol. Wilson would be on point today. I would be behind him.

The weather was like yesterday, and the day before, and the day before that—sunny and hot. The monsoons were coming and a few wispy clouds drifted across the blue sky. It felt more humid than usual.

Our patrol followed the road with no name north toward Da Nang. We passed through many nondescript villages on the seven-mile trek. Most of the villages were familiar to us: Co Luu, Binh Minh, Quang Ha, and Phong Ho. All had negative events associated with the names. When I heard the name Phong Ho, I immediately thought of Pat Connors.

We had five hours to go ten thousand meters, or about six and a half miles. Since we would not be walking on the road, our patrol time was tripled. After picking two Marines to walk the flanks, Rosser gave the order, "Move out!"

The villages we would pass through today were all considered sympathetic to the National Liberation Front. We entered the village of Co Luu, the first checkpoint. Like Dong Thoi, the villagers seemed hostile and resentful.

The next checkpoint, Binh Minh, came and went without incident. Between Quang Ha and Phong Ho, our left flank took a few sniper rounds, but the shots fell short. We didn't bother to return fire.

As we passed along the eastern edge of Phong Ho, I thought about Pat Connors' death less than a month ago. Mac always wanted to be fair to the men in his squad. He felt that I had fulfilled my obligation for that day, so he assigned Pat to point. Mac's sense of equity and fairness was the only reason I was alive and Pat was dead.

The midday sun was cooking as we entered the ville of Ngan Cau (2), not far from the old battalion command post. Suddenly, we received word to hold up. Wilson stopped the formation and we dropped to one knee. I wondered why we had stopped. It was usually the point element of a patrol that would decide to stop movement, but this order came from Sgt. McGougin who probably got the order from Lieutenant Sloat. A few minutes later, Mac came to the front of the formation. He had his head down and was moving it from side to side as he approached us.

"I know you guys are tired, we all are. But we've been told to keep going to provide security for a mine sweep team that is coming south from Da Nang. Yesterday, an Ontos detonated a large anti-tank mine on this road. One crewman was killed and the other two are in tough shape. We're supposed to provide flank security for the mine sweep until it gets to Ngan Cau (2). From there, we will escort them back to our base. They'll stay there overnight before going back to Da Nang."

After Mac finished giving us the word, he moved back to the main element of the patrol, and we headed north. Everyone was bitching about having the patrol extended, and, as usual, we were all thirsty, hot, and tired.

The mine sweep team we were to meet had a security escort of Marines from 2/1. Their battalion CP was located between our old battalion area and Da Nang. They would provide security for the mine sweep until they reached the village of Xaun Tra. At that point, we would relieve them until we made it to our patrol base.

After about forty-five minutes of bitching and shuffling, we spotted the mine sweep team moving slowly southward on the road. As we approached, we noticed three trucks following the sweep element. The security detail from 2/1 apparently would ride back to their battalion area. We would walk. There was some good-natured banter between our patrol and the security detail. We called them pussies for having trucks to haul them back to their base. They told us to have fun and stay low.

Our patrol did an about face and started back in the direction we had come from. To provide appropriate security, we switched from a single-file patrol to a formation with two flanking elements. One squad would be on the left side of the mine sweep, the other on the right. Several Marines would be assigned "tail-end Charlie" duties for each squad.

Rosser gave our fire-team the order to move to the end position of the squad on the left flank. He edged through the thick jungle with the rest of us close behind. When we got into position, he gave the command, "Move out!"

The going was tough. The hedgerows consisted of briar patch vines entwined with brushy bamboo.

I couldn't figure out what the land surrounded by the hedgerows was used for. The hedgerows were in a checkerboard configuration. Some had small openings allowing us to move easily from field to field. Most didn't, and we would hack, cut and curse our way through. Movement was slow and our already tattered utilities were shredded some more. The sharp briars were like fishhooks snagging whatever disturbed them.

Rosser was about twenty meters to my left, Wilson the same distance on my right. Rosser and I were battling the same hedgerow. Wilson was in the next grid, hidden by dense undergrowth.

"This stuff is a bitch," Rosser muttered. "Can't move fast enough to stay even with the minesweeper."

"Where's the minesweeper, Tornes?"

"Can't see shit," I answered. There was a hedgerow on my right and I couldn't see Wilson or the mine sweep.

We were in the kill zone of a claymore anti-personnel mine. The explosion was loud and brassy. I could hear the deadly buckshot-sized pellets tear through the hedgerow. It was over in seconds. Somehow, I had not been hit. Rosser wasn't as lucky.

He was lying on his back, one arm flailing. I could hear him moaning. Maybe, it wasn't too bad. Maybe he took a pellet in the arm. As I ran to his fallen body, I started screaming, "CORPSMAN UP!! CORPSMAN UP!!"

Rosser's helmet was off and his M-14 was partially under his body. I slid to a stop on both knees. I grabbed his waving arm and said something to him. I can't remember what, but I said something. As I bent helplessly over his body, I continued to scream "Corpsman up! Corpsman up!" I knew he was dying. The arm movement was involuntary, and the sounds coming from his mouth were unconscious throat gurgles.

I could see only one wound on his body, but it looked fatal. A single claymore pellet had hit him in the left eye. There was no exit wound; it was still in his head. His other eye had rolled back into his head. Maybe I couldn't do anything for him, but Doc probably could. He was still alive. Doc would know what to do.

"CORPSMAN UP!! CORPSMAN UP!!"

Doc was having a tough time getting through the thick growth. I could hear him swearing at the vines and razor sharp briars as he struggled through the last hedgerow. As he ran toward us, I took one last look at Rosser before moving away to provide security.

Several minutes later, Mac arrived with the rest of the squad. He ordered us to move to the outside edges of the hedgerows surrounding Rosser and Doc to secure an LZ for the medevac. The chopper arrived faster than usual. It took only seconds to load Rosser into the chopper. I watched as the chopper gained altitude before leveling-off and accelerating toward the Naval Hospital.

He was a good friend and good Marine. The longer I survived in the field, the more personal the casualties became. I didn't cry. I just felt empty and angry. Wilson cried and that gave me some relief. He cried for the whole squad.

The claymore had been remotely detonated, so we knew whoever triggered the mine had to be in the area. A Marine, who had been walking tail-end-Charlie for the sweep, said he saw a VC run into a small grouping of huts between the road and a small stream. Mac called the squad together.

"Listen up! We're going in those huts, and we're gonna get the son-of-a-bitch that got Rosser! Sage, take Wilson and start with the last hooch and work this way. Tornes, you, Langley and Kranz start with the hooch on this end and work toward the middle. I've positioned two guys on the creek bank, behind the hooches. I'll be in the front. Let's get the gook bastard!"

Langley went around the back of the first hut. Kranz and I went through the front entrance. The first house was empty. We noticed a timber-reinforced entrance to an underground shelter next to the hut.

"Lai Dai, Motherfucker!" Kranz screamed into the tunnel leading to the main chamber of the shelter.

"Hear anything in there?"

"Don't hear anything. Maybe we should throw a couple grenades in there to make sure."

"Shoot a few rounds in first," I said.

Kranz cut loose with a ten round burst into the walls of the tunnel. Suddenly the wailing began. The sound that came from inside the underground shelter was an unintelligible mix of crying babies and sing-song Vietnamese chanting. A few minutes later, they began emerging from the hole. The first person out was an old gray-headed, toothless gramasan. A younger woman carrying a small baby followed her. The baby was crying as were the two toddlers crawling behind their mother.

"Where VC?" I yelled.

"Cam biec, cam biec".

Always the same response, "I can't understand; I don't know."

We knew she knew. And she knew we knew it. Fucking lying bitch.

"Cam, biec, cam biec, cam biec."

Author far left, John Williams, middle.
Santa Monica Beach, June 1966

Author far right, Arturo second from left.

photo - Harry Brown

Grace Tornes, Gary and Harold Tornes before leaving for Vietnam.

photo - Harry Brown

Unidentified marines on "Operation Hastings."

photo - Gary Tornes

PFC Gary Tornes at Platoon Patrol Base near Quang Ha.

Sage far left, Wilson second from right.

Marble Mountain

photo - Harry Brown

Typical two man fighting hole.

photo - Harry Brown

Riding across the sand dunes on tanks.

Sgt. James "Mac" McGougin

photo - Harry Brown

photo - Steve Mollica

Lt. Sloat and "Mac" checking outside of old 1/1 battalion CP.

photo - Harry Brown

Cpl. Brown on Operation Hastings.

Mollica far left, Sanchez middle front, Arturo far right.

Captured VC

Jim Kranz on the right outside of BAS.

Villagers fleeing Phong Ho prior to fire fight.

Vietnamese during monsoon floods.

Patrol supported by an Ontos (left) and tanks.

photo - Jim "Doc" Clopton

Doc Clopton with Vietnamese baby.

Gary Rosser

Medevac with security perimeter.

Dead VC from County Fair I-21. Lt. Sloat far right.

Remote platoon patrol base.

Full issue field gear 1967, M-16 not M-14 rifle.

Gary Tornes, November 15, 1966 – minus 60 pounds

photo - Gary Tornes

Author with Casual Company, Camp Hansen in background.

Lieutenant (Tim) Sloat and Gary Tornes 02/04

I felt like hitting the woman with a horizontal butt stroke to the head with my M-14. I felt like crushing the head of this lying gook, but I did nothing. We decided not to crawl into the shelter but just in case a VC papa-san was still in the hole, we tossed in two grenades. The explosion partially collapsed the earthen roof of the underground chamber.

Immediately, the two women started wailing and crying. They were on their knees, throwing the upper part of their bodies from side to side on the ground, like a deer shot in the spine. Apparently, a VC or papa-san had been in the hole. We moved to the next house.

I approached the second hooch from the rear. The house was more than a hut. It had a pink stucco-like exterior, a tiled roof and a private well. Cautiously, I crawled to a position under a large window on the backside of the building. I raised myself up and looked through the uncovered window. I was hoping to see a uniformed VC that I could blow away, but I didn't.

I saw a family similar to the one in the first house. Their backs were toward me, unaware of my presence. The bottom of the windowsill was about chest high. Although the window didn't have any glass panes, it had sturdy wooden cross-members. I suppose I could have walked around the side of the house and entered from the front but I wanted to make a dramatic entrance. With the butt of my rifle, I smashed the wooden grid system, and climbed into the house through the window. I felt like John Wayne.

If the roles had been reversed, I'm sure my mother and sisters would have reacted the same way. The horrified Vietnamese family cowered in front of me. I was almost three times as big as the mother. I was uniformed, unshaven, and armed. I am sure they knew what had happened and probably knew who we were looking for. They could see in my eyes I was seeking revenge. The intensity of their crying and wailing increased, but not loud enough to mask the sound of shots coming from the next house. I heard a burst from an M-14 and what sounded like .30 cal. carbine shots. Then I heard Wilson hollering.

My first fear was that Wilson had been shot. I charged out of the hooch, leaving the terrified family cowering on the floor. They probably thought that some Buddhist god had intervened to save their asses.

Wilson was already on the road in front of the adjacent hooch. He was obviously anxious and was talking so fast that I could hardly understand him.

"The gook was behind this screen by the altar. He just jumps out, sees me and opens fire. I shot back, and I think we both missed. Shit, he was only ten feet away. Jesus, I should of got him. He was probably the one that killed Rosser."

Wilson felt guilty. He felt like he had let us down. He had a chance to get the gook that may have killed Rosser, but he failed. None of the squad blamed him. We had all blown opportunities for kills.

Mac ordered us to surround the hut. Langley and I went around the back of the hooch, Kranz and Sage covered the sides, and Wilson and Mac were at the front. I heard Sage screaming, "I think I saw him, over by the north side of the hooch. Looked like he was crawling along the wall."

I was standing in the creek behind the hut. The water was shallow and the sloping bank provided protection from potential friendly fire. I was close enough to reach the end of the hut with a grenade. I pulled the pin, yelled, "Fire in the hole," and threw the son-of-a-bitch as far as I could. I ducked behind the creek bank, and seconds later heard the grenade explode.

"Throw another one!" The command came from Mac.

The second grenade flew a little right of the target and the back half of an adjoining wooden building collapsed. The silence immediately after the blast was broken by a high-pitched squealing sound emanating from the rubble. The sound was almost human, but not quite.

Langley, an old farm boy, said, "You nailed the pig-pen."

Mac yelled, "Move toward the hooch."

Langley and I climbed up the muddy creek bank and moved slowly toward the back of the building. We didn't know what to expect, other than a dead hog. With our backs against the masonry wall, we cautiously moved to the end of the house. The only noise was an occasional muffled pig squeal.

"Mac, you and Wilson on the other side of the hooch?"

"Yeah, we're here. Don't see anything."

"Where's Sage?"

"He's on the other end. Let's move to the end and see what's there, okay?"

I moved around the corner of the house. Langley was about ten meters behind me and to my right. The entire squad converged on the area where Sage thought he had seen someone crawling. Much to our dismay, the only thing we found was a dying pig and a partially collapsed entrance to an underground shelter.

"I wonder if anybody is in the hole?" Sage's question wasn't directed at anyone in particular.

"Let's blow the hole," Mac said.

Before anyone could pull the pin on a grenade, Kranz emptied his rifle into the tunnel entrance. Without exchanging a word, the whole squad followed Kranz's example and 120 additional bullets entered the tunnel. Three of us pulled the pins from our grenades and tossed them as far as we could down the shelter entrance. Maybe one of them would be lucky enough to reach the main chamber. If it did, and anybody was there, they were dead meat.

Two of the grenades exploded at almost the same time; the third a few seconds later. The explosions were muted by the sand overburden. The elevated dome of the shelter seemed to jump a few inches before it sank below the level of the ground. One or more of the grenades had made it to the interior of the manmade cave.

"I should have had him. I should have had him! I can't see how I missed him." Wilson was still anguishing over his failure to hit the VC.

"He was right there in front of me. How could I miss him?"

Mac put his arm around Wilson.

The mine sweep team had stopped in front of the row of huts we had just searched. The squad that had been on the west side of the road had quickly set up a security perimeter around the mine sweep equipment and personnel. Rather than continue with "on line" flanking elements for the duration of the journey, one squad would be in patrol formation on each side of the road. We covered the last two miles in about 45 minutes and arrived at our base at 1700 hours.

As I entered our tent, I noticed Rosser's sea bag and extra backpack on his cot. Apparently, someone in the company had been notified of his injury. We still hadn't heard if he made it or not.

Mac entered the tent. He looked at the five of us sitting on our cots and said, "Rosser didn't make it. He died on the chopper. Someone should take his sea bag and other stuff to the company tent." Mac turned and left the tent without saying anything else.

Kranz volunteered to take Rosser's stuff to the Gunny. Sage sat quietly on his cot, his head in his hands. Wilson was blowing his nose. The three of them had been assigned to the platoon about the same time as Rosser. The four had been through a lot together.

Rosser would have been twenty years old in two days. He shared his birthday with my mother, September 22nd.

Mom would be forty-three years old. She was almost twenty years older than Captain Kelly, and Captain Kelly was old. I didn't have a birthday card to send her so I decided to write her a birthday letter. I dug out a pad of Marine Corps stationery and borrowed a working pen. I sat on the edge of my cot, paper and pen in hand. I couldn't think of anything to write.

The image that kept reappearing was Rosser on the ground, arm waving, gurgling and dying.

Someone had entered the tent, but I didn't bother to look up. I continued to think about Rosser lying in the cooler at Graves Registration.

"Hey, Gar, what's happening?"

I recognized the voice. Joe Cullens had just re-entered my life.

"What the hell you doing, Joe? Thought you got the million-dollar wound."

"They just patched me up and sent me back. Got to stay longer than I should have. Pretty good duty: nice bed, good food, and cold beer. Doesn't get much better."

I was overjoyed to see Joe back. I had been closer to him than anyone in the squad. I had lost one friend, but had been reunited with another. Although Joe's arrival did wonders for my morale, I'm sure he would have rather been somewhere else. Without asking, Joe took Rosser's cot. He knew Rosser was dead, but didn't mention it. We were silent for several minutes before I started asking him about his stay at NSA. It was good to have Hard Core back.

Chapter 18
A Real Live Cong

Fishing for walleyes in Minnesota had never been like this. The two grenades resulted in an erupting plume of thick water and a muted explosion. Seconds later, hundreds of fish floated to the surface of the slow-moving river. Most were unidentifiable species of Asian carp although others looked like bass. Before they floated downstream, we grabbed several for dinner. Someone in the squad suggested that we cook fish tonight instead of dining on C-rats. Nobody knew much about cooking, but a menu change sounded enticing.

The remainder of the dead or stunned fish floated slowly away. Downriver, a Vietnamese fisherman was methodically casting and retrieving a room-sized fishing net. As the dazed and dead fish started floating by his boat, he became a blur of motion netting the unexpected bonus. After several minutes, he started waving his arm at us in a friendly manner. We could barely hear him as he waved and chanted, "Marines numba one." Although I would hear this statement many times during my tour, it was the only time that I believed it was genuinely meant.

Our platoon established a night perimeter around the hamlet of Tu Cau (4). The small village was located on a hill overlooking the Song Vien Dien river, the source of our eagerly anticipated evening meal. I had filleted and boned many walleyes in my short life, but these weren't walleyes. My attempts to skin and bone the fish failed. The K-bar was too large and the internal bone structure of the fish unfamiliar. Finally, I decided to simply scale, gut and gill the fish. We would grill them like trout.

Hopefully, the fish would taste better than the meal we cooked last week when the squad decided that our menu needed some variety. The entrée of choice was chicken and our mission was simple: procure one.

We decided to shoot a chicken during the landing of a re-supply chopper. We felt that the noise and flying sand during the descent would create enough distraction to complete our mission undetected. Our recon team selected the target before the arrival of the chopper. The chosen chicken was a rooster that lived near the LZ, a safe distance from his Vietnamese owner. One squad member was the designated sniper. When the noise of the chopper's landing peaked, the sniper would shoot. Once the chopper left, we would retrieve the rooster and cook it.

Everything went as planned except for the cooking part. Since we didn't have any oil or shortening, we boiled the chicken in an appropriated Vietnamese cooking pot. After boiling the bird for an hour, we cut the chicken in pieces and started eating. The chicken was undercooked and rubbery with a strange metallic flavor. We gave it to two dogs tethered to a nearby tree. They eagerly devoured our discarded entrée. The dogs themselves would be the entrée on the next Vietnamese holiday.

Cooking the fish presented a major challenge. The only utensils suitable for cooking were the metal covers of our field mess kits. Once again we had no cooking oil or spices, so we decided to poach the fish. With several hunks of C-4 as our heating source and thick water from the Song Vien Dien river as our poaching liquid, we started our meal. It was a disaster. Scales from the fish floated to the top of the liquid and one fish split in half exposing sharp y-bones. A gray scum with specks that looked like fly shit danced on the surface of our poaching liquid. We weren't brave enough to even taste it. We dined on C-rats.

After Rosser was killed, I became fire team leader. The promotion was due to my major accomplishment—staying alive. Others more experienced and accomplished were not there to compete.

My fire team consisted of Joe, Wilson, and a new guy, Corporal Dakron who had more than three years in the Corps. He had been with regiment for the last seven months. I didn't know the story surrounding his transfer to the field. Initially, it was uncomfortable to lead someone who was two grades higher and older than me.

The hamlet selected for our night position was neither VC controlled nor government supportive. Like many villages and hamlets, it was on the cusp. Loyalties could and would change quickly. If the government forces seemed to be winning, the villages would support the South Vietnamese. On the other hand, if the VC seemed to be stronger, the soft support would tilt toward them.

The position assigned to my fire team was terrible. Although it was on the edge of the hamlet, it was also the highest point in the village. Because of the thick vegetation on the hillside, we couldn't see much of anything. It was impossible to establish realistic fields of fire, but worst of all, we were skylined. Our hooch was perched atop the highest piece of real estate in town. I wasn't an accomplished military strategist, but common sense told me that this was not good. A trench line dug in the 1950's by the French was at the bottom of our hill, encircling the entire village.

For the first time, I was carrying an M-79 grenade launcher instead of a rifle. Although I also had a .45 pistol on my belt, I still felt vulnerable. My confidence in the M-14 was unquestioned. It was an amazing weapon that you could use, abuse, and always depend on. I felt naked without it.

The hut we commandeered was a typical Vietnamese peasant home, about 300 square feet, bamboo walls and a thatched roof. A cooking pit dominated one corner. Two bamboo beds, several wicker baskets and a small religious shrine made up the rest of the interior. The floors were petrified dirt and, as in many Vietnamese peasant homes, there were no chairs.

Each of us would have a two-hour watch during the night. Three Marines would sleep in the hut while the fourth would stand watch. By offering to take the first shift, I had a chance of getting six hours of uninterrupted sleep.

I positioned myself about ten meters down the hill, between the hut and the jungle. I had no protective cover and felt ridiculously exposed. My shift was about half over when I happened to turn and look at the hut where the fire team was sleeping. A single figure was crawling along the wall of the hut toward the door. Whoever it was, had not spotted me. Since the intruder was next to the hut, I didn't want to chance hitting the sleeping Marines with rifle fire. Instead of shooting, I would take a prisoner – a real live Cong.

Time was limited to plan my attack, so it wasn't complex. With my .45 in hand, I charged the enemy. I covered twenty-five feet in seconds hurling my body on top of the surprised insurgent. The young VC suspect offered no resistance. Maybe the .45 under his chin influenced his passive reaction or maybe he just wanted to surrender. His body was shaking violently as he whispered, "Me no VC. Me no VC." His response wasn't a surprise. That's what they all said. I knew this skinny little prick was a Cong.

The commotion of the capture had awakened my sleeping fire team. They charged out of the hut not knowing what to expect. Joe was the first to emerge.

"What the hell's going on? Who the fuck is that?"

"Captured me a little VC. Doesn't have any weapons or grenades, but he's got some papers and other shit on him."

"Here, blindfold him with this towel." Corporal Dakron said, as he handed me his sweat encrusted neck towel.

"Why the fuck do we have to blindfold him? It's pitch dark and you can't see shit anyway," I answered.

"Cause that's what they always do. You always see captured enemy with blindfolds on."

Rather than argue the merits of blindfolding the VC, I tied the towel around his head covering his eyes. The young Vietnamese man couldn't stop shaking. He looked like a drunk with the DT's.

"Better take him to the lieutenant," Dakron said.

"No shit, where do you think I'm going to take him?"

Dakron was starting to irritate me with his know-it-all attitude. He was a corporal and senior to me in rank, but I was still the fire team leader. I wondered again, why he ended up with a line company when he had been in the rear-with-the-beer for the last seven months.

I had a trophy, of sorts. Although the VC was not armed, he had to be the enemy. The more I looked at the blindfolded, 120-pound trembling teen, the less he looked like a trophy, but it was better than a blood trail leading nowhere.

The fire team remained near the hut while I stumbled down the backside of our hill toward the lieutenant's position.

Lieutenant Sloat, along with several others, had established a temporary command post in one of the larger houses near the middle of the village. The house had thick concrete walls and was not sky lined. With one hand grasping the back of his black cotton shirt and the other pointing a .45 at his head, I pushed my prisoner to the ground in front of the lieutenant's hooch.

The prisoner's welcoming committee included Lieutenant Sloat, the platoon sergeant, and an ARVN soldier who functioned as our scout/interpreter. The prisoner's head snapped backward as I jerked him from the ground to a standing position in front of the lieutenant. "Me no VC! Me no VC!" The prisoner continued to stutter as he stood blindfolded and shaking in front of his captors.

Lieutenant Sloat was the first to confront him. He ripped off the towel blindfold, and with an intense but controlled voice said, "You VC. You VC!"

The answer of course was, "Me no VC; me no VC."

The lieutenant's pre-interrogation had begun. Since neither the interrogator nor the interrogated was bilingual, the exchange of information was minimal. The lieutenant's first move was not what the prisoner had expected.

Instead of putting a razor-sharp K-bar to the throat of the quivering teen or crushing his skull with a rifle butt, the lieutenant hit the suspect across the face with a pair of leather gloves. Six years later, when I saw George C. Scott hit an army malingerer with his gloves I thought of Lieutenant Sloat and his Pattonesque move.

The lieutenant was a class act. Everyone in the platoon liked and respected him. Most of all, we trusted his judgment. He was from California and had graduated from the University of California, Berkley. He wasn't an academy officer like Captain Kelly, but in our opinion, he was more effective.

After the lieutenant completed his brief interrogation, the Vietnamese interpreter took over. I never trusted the ARVN interpreters assigned to field units. It was a gut feeling. They all looked too slick and smart. They wore new-looking jungle utilities and well-fitting jungle boots. They probably smoked Winston's and Salems too. They were better educated and more politically connected than the average ARVN soldier. Consequently, they ended up with less demanding and safer assignments.

Vietnamese interpreters wouldn't stay with any individual unit too long. Supposedly, they rotated back to the ARVN interrogation units in Da Nang and Hoi An after brief field assignments. Most of the real hard-core interrogation took place there instead of in the field. In addition to being better educated and politically connected, the interpreters probably came from families with money. The combination of these three elements could be enormously influential in determining not only what your military assignment would be, but whether you even had to serve or not. It really wasn't much different from back home. The slick ARVN interpreter took the prisoner inside the hooch. I returned to my fire team.

Joe was on watch and it was my turn to sleep. Hopefully, the night would be quiet, and I could get five hours of uninterrupted sleep. Wilson and Dakron were sleeping on the larger of the two bamboo beds. The remaining bed was much smaller and looked like a child's bed, a Vietnamese crib. It was about four feet long and the surface was made of woven strips of bamboo. To fit on the bed I had to assume a fetal position. My pillow was a small block of wood with a head cradling indentation. I was ready for five hours of sleep.

I was abruptly awakened from a deep sleep by straw and pieces of wood falling on my face. The roof had been partially blown away by an enemy RPG round and I could see tracer rounds sizzling across the dark sky through the opening. I rolled from the small bed to the floor, landing on Wilson and Dakron.

"Get some cover," I screamed, as the three of us crawled for the door. The silhouette of our hut against the sky offered an inviting target to anyone below the hill or outside the perimeter.

I had to locate Joe. It was his watch and I wondered where he was.

"Joe, you okay.?" I yelled.

"Yeah, I'm okay! Lot of shit coming at us."

"Where's it coming from?"

"It's coming from all ways. I think the whole perimeter is getting hit."

I heard the throaty rattle of one of our M-60's on the far side of the village. Someone had fired an illumination flare and I could hear the thump of 60mm mortars. A steady stream of incoming rounds continued overhead. A rifle grenade exploded 30 meters away.

"Let's try to get down the hill to the trench line," I shouted, as another rifle grenade exploded nearby. Firing as we ran, the four of us stumbled down the hill toward the trench line that surrounded the village. Since I was carrying an M-79, I was the only one in the fire team not firing. I couldn't fire. An M-79 round is centrifugally activated after rotating a certain number of times. The projectile will not explode until the specified number of rotations has been completed. This feature allows you to launch the small grenade through a tree canopy without having it explode in your face.

The formerly terraced hillside was covered with thick underbrush and clumps of bamboo. Other than tracer rounds whizzing by our heads and the occasional mortar illumination round, we were running into the black.

We took turns falling before reaching the bottom. The hill was small, and it took only seconds in "real time" to descend. But in "movie time," it took forever. We knew we had made it to the bottom when we stopped falling. I had lost visual contact with the others, but could hear them crashing and cursing to my left. I found the old trench line by tumbling into it.

I landed on my stomach. My helmet had fallen off and my face was an inch from the musty trench floor. It smelled like the old potatoes in my grandfather's root cellar. It was dark coming down the hill, but the bottom of the trench had less light than the middle of a tar pit.

I heard a noise on my right. It was close, real close. I knew that the rest of the team was on my left, so who was on my right? An illumination round exploded overhead and the landscape momentarily was as bright as a high school football field on an October night.

He was about my age. He had a soft, drooping, green hat. I was helmetless. He looked scared. I was scared. He had a rifle. I had an M-79. Reacting on instinct, I fired my M-79 from the hip before he could fire his rifle. Because of the short distance, the round did not explode when it hit him. But it hit him. I heard the thud and a grunt as the 40mm payload punched his torso. Then it was quiet. I didn't know whether he was dead or unconscious. He may have been only momentarily dazed. He could have gone somewhere into the blackness. I didn't go look.

After the illumination flare burnt out, it returned to a sightless dark. It was quiet in my little personal battlefield, but a heavy volume of both incoming and outgoing fire continued elsewhere on the perimeter.

I had retreated around the corner to another segment of the trench line. I had my .45, but I still felt defenseless without a rifle. Tomorrow I would assign the M-79 to someone else.

Like many night attacks, the fighting stopped as quickly as it had started. We regrouped to assess the effects of the battle.

Mac told us to stay in the trench line for the rest of the night. My plan for five continuous hours of sleep was put on hold. Mac said that the platoon had made it through the attack without a fatality, but seven Marines had been wounded. Fortunately, none of the wounds required a medevac. Most were superficial and Doc had been able to do his thing.

The wounded would be transported out in the morning. Mac said that Corporal Dakron had been hit by a small piece of shrapnel. I wondered when that had happened.

At daybreak, an amtrac loaded with wounded Marines including Dakron departed for the battalion aid station. The rest of us were ordered to join an ARVN force on County Fair I-21. The County

Fair was about five miles southeast, in the village of Lai Nghe. As usual, we would walk, not ride.

During the night, Corporal Brown, the second squad leader, had an experience with his M-79 similar to mine. He, too, had confronted an enemy soldier in the trench. He, too, had hit the VC with an M-79 round that didn't explode because of distance. Brown continued to carry his M-79 but I gave mine away.

With Corporal Dakron gone, my fire team was down to three. In my mind, I continued to question the authenticity of his wound. I never saw him again.

Chapter 19
County Fair I-21

The trail to Lai Ngne(2) was almost a road. Since we didn't have to struggle through jungle and hedgerows, we covered the five miles in less than two hours. About 1000 meters from Lai Ngne (2), the road intersected with a heavily used east-west trail. We turned east, toward a predetermined coordinate where we were to link up with an ARVN unit. We were about 500 meters south of the sand hill where Glover had been killed. Wilson also knew where we were and his eyes were tearing up.

A cordon had been established around Lai Ngne(2) and most civilians had been herded out of the village to the county fair head-quarters. This county fair would be somewhat special. Not only would the standard food and medical care be provided, there also would be entertainment. A temporary stage had been built to accommodate the troop of Vietnamese actors that were performing before a passive audience.

As we passed the Vietnamese vaudeville act, the theme of the play was obvious. Although my knowledge of Vietnamese was limited to a few basic phrases and curse words, this was clearly a black hat—white hat presentation. The good guys were portrayed as government officials helping the struggling peasants. The bad guys were the VC who raped the farmer's daughter while demanding protection money. Although the script was animated and noisy, the actors looked bored.

Intelligence reports had confirmed that the village of Lai Ngne(2) harbored a company of Viet Cong with North Vietnamese advisors. We rarely believed the so-called intelligence reports that trickled down to our level. I questioned both the sources and the motives of those sources. Nevertheless, we were uneasy as we linked up with the ARVN soldiers and started our sweep through the village.

Immediately, a major firefight erupted on our right and several grenades exploded to our left. It was the beginning of what would be a four-hour battle. Our integrated unit swept on-line through the village. We were the guests, and we followed their lead.

It was my first combat experience with our allies. Marines were aggressive, but the ARVN troops seemed to be maliciously combative. They had little respect for personal property and would laugh and joke as they trashed the interiors of peasant huts. They also seemed to enjoy killing penned pigs and fowl. Although they appeared undisciplined and rancorous, they managed to find caves and tunnels that we probably would have missed.

An ARVN officer informed us that the remaining VC had retreated to underground tunnels and caves. Our mission was to find and destroy the subterranean foe.

The only available size of jungle utilities was small. My choice was either to wear my heavier regular-issue utilities (that were too hot) or wear the lighter cargo-pocketed jungle trousers (that were too small). Once again, my judgment was flawed. My first jump across a small ravine ripped the new utilities. The rip went from ankle to groin exposing my entire right leg and then some. If I were back in Minnesota instead of Vietnam, I would have been arrested for indecent exposure.

The ARVN soldier on my left was laughing as he taunted a young mother and her children. He said something in Vietnamese as he pointed his rifle at one child's head. The mother fell to her knees in a praying position before this little prick. Tears streamed down her face as she looked up at him. You didn't have to understand the language to know what she was saying. Finally, the little bastard got bored with his game and left. The woman continued to tremble and cry.

An ARVN soldier discovered the entrance to what appeared to be a large VC cave and tunnel complex. Quickly, we fanned out to search for air vents and additional openings. As we plodded and poked our way through the sparsely vegetated sandy soil, I heard an M-60 machine gun rip-off about 100 rounds. An ARVN cowboy wannabe was firing wildly into the tunnel's entrance. He wore a green, brimmed hat with one side of the brim bent upward secured to the hat with some sort of Vietnamese medal or pin. A red, silk scarf encircled his arm-sized neck. He looked like a real dip-shit.

"Hey, Gar, look what I got!" Joe sounded like he had opened a Christmas present. "Think I found an air hole or something."

Hidden in a clump of stunted bamboo brush was a wood-cased air vent hole. The opening was about 12 inches square, with four inches of casing above ground.

"Let's blow the bitch up," I said.

We each pulled the pin of an M-26, and almost delicately, dropped them down the vent. Although the distance from the vent opening to the point where the grenades exploded was difficult to determine, the almost inaudible blast suggested that they had traveled far into the tunnel.

Sand and some unidentifiable debris erupted from the vent tunnel as a large section of sandy soil slowly sank below its previous level. We found other vents and openings and repeated the process. The sounds of grenades and C-4 explosions could be heard throughout the village. We had the VC trapped in what would be their underground tombs.

The combined action sweep element continued blasting and blowing its way through the village of Lai Ngne(2). By the time we reached the southern edge of the cordon, the hamlet was a mass of collapsed tunnels, blown caves and burning hooches. ARVN troops had torched several huts on our march south. None of the Marines in our squad had participated in their pyromania, nor had we purposely terrorized any of the few remaining civilians.

Near the outer edge of the village, the density of the hedgerows increased. Sparse bamboo thickets became impenetrable walls. It reminded me of the tree lines that surround midwestern farms. When first planted, the spacing seems fine. But as they grow, the tree's branches and runners begin to intertwine, weaving an almost impregnable barrier. In the Midwest, they functioned as windbreaks and provided cover for pheasants. In Vietnam, they brought your movement to a halt.

"Fucking goddamn bamboo shit," I muttered, to nobody in particular, as I tried to force myself through a solid wall of vines and vegetation. I twisted to my right and attempted to penetrate the barrier sideways. As I turned, I heard a "pop" and saw the smoke. A bamboo tentacle had ripped the pin from a green smoke grenade attached to my cartridge belt.

The pin had been pulled and the grenade was activated; spewing smoke and a fountain of phosphorous sparks. I dropped my rifle, threw off my backpack, and with one hand, tried to unhook my cartridge belt. My exposed right leg offered an easy target for the sputtering smoke bomb and the pain confirmed a hit. As I stumbled backward, the pain in my right leg brought tears to my eyes. The inside of my right thigh had been burned in two places and was still burning.

I hadn't realized that smoke grenades contained phosphorous and would continue to burn until the flame was deprived of oxygen. Phosphorous residue had stuck to my leg in two places, feeding inch long orange flames. The smaller of the two fires quickly went out, the larger continued to burn. I had nothing but my hand to smother the flame, but instinct prevented that.

The only non-body object that was available to extinguish the burning circle was my helmet. I ripped it off my head and pressed it firmly against the flaming phosphorous. I held the helmet to my leg for several seconds. When I lifted it, the fire rekindled. I repeated the process, only this time I kept the helmet smothering the flame for thirty seconds. It worked, the fire went out and stayed out.

"What the fuck is that smoke for?" The question came from someone on my left.

"Don't worry, it was an accidental detonation," I answered, and in the same breath called for Doc.

Since my wound wasn't life threatening and had been self-inflicted, I didn't yell "Corpsman up!" I simply called for Doc.

Skin and surface flesh had melted away from the two perfectly round leg burns. One was about three inches across, the other less than an inch. Doc had seen the green smoke cloud before he heard my call. As always, his response was immediate. He didn't know what he was running toward, he just ran. As he approached, he realized what had happened and started laughing.

"What the hell happened to you?"

Doc's laughter, with a note of relief, continued. The battle scene that he had been called to was more humorous than horrific. He would enjoy helping me—I was fixable.

"You're goddamn lucky you didn't fry your dick," he chuckled, as he dropped to one knee to examine the burns.

"Was pretty close, you know—another three inches higher and your little Yankee prick would look like a French fry." His laughter continued as he examined the two wounds.

Sergeant McGougin joined us. He, like everyone else, had seen the green smoke. He wasn't laughing. He was pissed.

"What in the name of Jesus happened here?"

Mac was a good Baptist and didn't swear as much as the rest of us. When he did, you knew he was mad.

"I was trying to get through a hedgerow, and the pin on a smoke grenade on my belt got pulled out."

"Jesus Christ, you got to attach them right. If that had been a frag you would be a dead son-of-a–bitch. And if we were on a recon mission, our location would be compromised." He completed his ass chewing before asking about my burn.

"Can you walk okay or do you need a ride back to Battalion Aid Station?"

"I'm okay. Doc's taking me back to the medcap tent to patch me up."

The smoke grenade casing was still hot as I removed it from my cartridge belt. I dug a small hole and buried what was left. Viet Cong ingenuity was legendary. They could find a use for almost any kind of junked military material. The spent smoke grenade canister could easily end up as a crude booby trap. Limping slightly, but alive, I followed Doc as he headed toward the temporary medical tent that had been erected near the holding area.

The medical tent was full of mothers and children receiving treatment and medication for a variety of conditions. I was the only Caucasian patient. Doc quickly applied a salve and field dressings to both burns. He put extra tape over the dressing on the larger burn.

"We better get back in case the guys run into some shit." Doc said.

We had just left the medical tent and were walking back toward our unit when I heard snarling sounds coming from a nearby straw hooch.

"What the hell's that noise, Doc? Sounds like two dogs fighting."

"That's where the ARVN are interrogating some VC. They use a dog to put the fear of Buddha into the VC. The Cong are scared shitless of dogs. These aren't the cute little motherfuckers that the gooks eat on holidays; these are big mean-ass German Shepherds. Lets check it out; you can see for yourself."

It was a typical straw hooch with a dirt floor and no openings on three sides so it was semi-dark—even in daylight. There were six or seven ARVN and one was holding a German Shepherd on a leather leash. The VC was stripped down to just a pair of black cotton skivvies, his arms tied tightly behind him at the elbows. Two ARVN held the VC in a standing position and the others shouted questions, one after another. The ARVN with the German Shepherd commanded the dog to attack and let it close enough to jump and bite at the VC's stomach, crotch, and thighs—hard enough to tear skin. The handler pulled the dog back and the interrogators fired more rapid questions. They apparently didn't hear what they wanted to and the handler let the dog forward to bite again.

When this technique didn't get the answers they wanted, the ARVN had another truth-producing tactic. The VC was laid on the dirt floor, arms still bound, face up with one ARVN holding his legs and another his shoulders. They took a dirty white hand towel, soaked it in water, and rubbed a bar of common white hand soap over it. They placed this completely over the VC's face so he was almost, but not quite suffocating. What little air he could get was mostly soapy water that caused immediate coughing and retching. One ARVN would place his boot on the VC's stomach and violently press down, causing more retching and loss of air. More water was then poured on the cloth while it covered the face. The cloth would be removed, re-soaped and re-applied until they got whatever answers they wanted. They explained that the advantage of their soap method was that it left no obvious evidence of torture. We all wondered who would care about any evidence.

As we were leaving, Lt. Sloat approached.

"Are our ARVN allies getting any results with their soap torture routine?" he asked, somewhat cynically. He had seen the act before.

"Doubt it, Sir," Doc answered.

I was still favoring my right leg as we walked to rejoin the squad.

The plan was to sweep the ville and set up a night encampment on the edge of the village with our ARVN allies. Sporadic explosions could still be heard behind us. The ARVN Lieutenant conferred with Lieutenant Sloat and Mac before a location was chosen for the night. We had taken over the vacated village and commandeered the hooches. The villagers would be spending the night in the county fair complex watching propaganda plays while we slept in their homes.

Joe, Wilson and I were bunking together. Our hut was a typical peasant home. The ubiquitous Buddhist altar had an offering of small green bananas. They were sweet and meaty.

One of the ARVN soldiers was barbequing a pig over a cooking pit; today's trophy would be the meal. The soldier acted like he knew what he was doing. Somebody said that larger ARVN units took a cook along on extended field operations. The spit-roasted pig smelled good, but it looked ghoulish. It was being cooked whole, head and all. I couldn't take my eyes off its protruding tongue. The tongue was bent backward toward the jowl and the goddamn pig looked like it was smiling at me. It was having its last laugh as the chef basted it with a red sauce. Several side dishes simmered near the edge of the pit's glowing coals.

While waiting for dinner to be served, we sat around shooting the shit and smoking. Since we didn't speak Vietnamese and the ARVN didn't speak English, there was little allied interaction. I was irritated because they all seemed to be smoking Winstons and Salems when I was lucky to have Pall Malls.

I remembered the Salem butts we found at the ambush site where Pat was killed. I flashed back to the Salems that were being sold for ten dollars a carton by the old gook woman. Once again, it didn't make sense, and I was pissed off. As I continued to eyeball our friends, I noticed that they all had new jungle boots that actually fit. Needless to say, there was little camaraderie as we waited to eat.

The meal was served buffet style with the chef dishing up portions on dented metal plates. Each serving consisted of meat, boiled rice, and pieces of Vietnamese squash slathered with a pungent red sauce. The large slice of pork roast had been cooked medium rare. I momentarily thought about trichinosis before devouring the food.

Everything was delicious, even the rare pork. The sauce that had been ladled over the rice and squash was hotter than Tabasco, but tolerable. I learned later that it was Nuoc Mam, a Vietnamese condiment made from fermented fish.

The three of us had our best night's sleep in weeks. We slept undisturbed until awakened by a rooster who had somehow escaped the previous day's slaughter. The hut's hard bamboo beds were unquestionably more comfortable than the ground, and being excused from night watch was a luxury.

I couldn't remember the last time I slept uninterrupted for more than three hours. We assumed that ARVN troops had stood perimeter guard during the night. Whether they had or not was now immaterial. The night was over and we were alive.

Breakfast wasn't as exotic as dinner had been. I smoked a cigarette, warmed water for coffee and downed a can of C-rat crackers and cheese. The burns on my leg throbbed as we saddled up and moved toward the county fair headquarters.

Mac said they had retrieved many of the dead VC. A working party of Popular Forces had dug out the bodies from the blown caves and collapsed tunnels.

The thespians were through and the show was over. ARVN troops were busy dismantling the stage as we made our way into the county fair headquarters area. Villagers who had been entertained and fed for the last two days were drifting back to their homes.

What they left was not what they would find when they returned. Many homes had either been burned to the ground or trashed by ARVN soldiers. Dead pigs, chickens and dogs littered the landscape. If the ARVN troops on this operation were indicative of all ARVN forces, I could easily understand why the hearts of the peasants were not with the government.

A jubilant crowd of ARVN troops had congregated near the headquarters tent. Being curious Marines, we decided to investigate.

"Holy shit, look at all those gooks!" Joe's reaction was a combination of surprise and glee.

It was another ARVN theatrical production with actors even less enthusiastic than yesterday—they were all dead. The PF forces had done a good job salvaging the enemy from their underground burial vaults.

The dead VC, all between fifteen and forty years of age, were lying side-by-side on the sand. Some were missing body parts, others looked asleep. The only thing they had in common besides being dead was their exposed genitals. Their trousers had been pulled down to their knees exposing little shriveled dead dicks: twenty-six dead gooks with their lifeless family jewels on exhibit.

The cheering ARVN soldiers seem to be enjoying the spectacle a little too much. Was there an Oriental obsession with genitals that prompted this behavior? Whatever it was, this genital fixation was demonstrated by both ally and foe. I remembered two months ago, when the VC emasculated one of our Marines and after severing his penis, stuffed it into his mouth. The Marines I knew would eagerly kill a Viet Cong, but wouldn't lop off a lifeless dick. They may be the enemy, but to mutilate them in death would be obscene.

As I looked at the Viet Cong corpses, I wondered if one of my grenades had killed any of them.

War and killing becomes enormously personal when you see the person you've killed. Artillery, mortars and air support probably account for larger numbers of enemy dead, but the victims remain anonymous and invisible. The killer never sees the killed.

We rode back to the platoon base on tanks. Tanks aren't made to carry troops, but we always managed to get a squad aboard. Holding on to each other and whatever piece of the tank we could grab, we would fly across the sand at 25 MPH. Although riding was less exhausting than walking, it had a downside. The noise of the tank's engine made it impossible to hear enemy small arms fire. They would shoot at you and you couldn't hear where the shots were coming from. Often, the first sign that you were under attack was when a Marine next to you slumped over with a bullet in his chest. Nevertheless, we never refused a ticket to ride.

Back at base camp, Doc checked my wounds. The original dressing on the smaller burn was gone, washed off crossing a river. Dirt and sand covered the wound. The larger dressing was still attached, held in place by the additional piece of tape Doc had applied. He gave me a tetanus shot, cleaned my burns and applied new dressings.

As I watched Doc clean my wounds, I was amazed at how gentle his touch was, almost mother-like. He was obviously trying to make the process as painless as possible.

On the way back to the tent, I ran into a couple of guys who were romping around like two kids on Halloween.

"We're going on R&R! We're going on R&R! Gonna get some cold beer and hot pussy. We're all going, the whole platoon."

Then I ran into an excited Joe, who yelled, "Did you hear we get a three day R&R in Da Nang?"

"Da Nang? Why do we want to go there?"

"Cause that's where China Beach is."

"No shit, what's there?"

"It's this real nice navy rec area . . . has a restaurant, bar, pool hall, swimming beach and all the rest. It's down the road from NSA where I went when I got shot. Drove by the entrance when I came back to the field."

"Why do we get to go?" I asked.

"Don't know really," Joe responded. "Mac said he heard it was because the First Platoon killed the most gooks this month."

Chapter 20
China Beach

We rode in style to our China Beach vacation, thirty thrill-seeking Marines crammed into two six-bys. We were Roman gladiators riding into Carthage. We felt like gladiators, but we certainly didn't look the part. Our faces were unshaven, our body odor tolerable only to each other, and we carried M-14's instead of swords.

To get to China Beach we had to cross the often-repaired Cao Do Bridge, pass by the large U.S. airbase, and drive through downtown Da Nang. In October of 1966, the City of Da Nang was still open for business and not yet off-limits to American military personnel. We stared in disbelief at what we saw.

Had we taken a wrong turn or were we all dreaming the same dream? We had to be on another planet—this couldn't be Vietnam.

The streets of Da Nang were teeming with unarmed, clean-looking Americans. Some looked like tourists in their Bermuda shorts and sport shirts. Others wore starched utilities and spit-shined jungle boots.

Who the hell were these guys? This was a war zone. What were they doing strolling the streets listening to radios balanced on their shoulders? The sidewalk cafes were filled with cigarette-smoking, beer-drinking, bar-girl-groping guys. They had to be military personnel—there weren't *that* many reporters.

We started to feel like real gladiators. We were fighting a war while these guys were fighting boredom with booze and broads. As we looked down at the spring-break-boys, we experienced an over-whelming sense of superiority. We were warriors. They weren't.

Our convoy stopped at a security post guarding the entrance to China Beach. The sharply-dressed MP who manned the gate directed the trucks to a large metal building near the center of the complex. The trucks emptied in seconds and we filed into the visitor orientation center where a navy officer met us.

"Listen up, Marines." His voice sounded patronizing. "You are scheduled to be here for three days. During that time, you will be billeted in one of our Quonset huts. You will each be assigned a bunk and provided with sheets and pillows. You will be required to make your own bunks and police your assigned area. You can leave the China Beach compound, but we advise against it. We are a considerable distance from Da Nang, and most of the local shops and skivvie houses will rob you blind or give you the clap. One last thing, you have to check your weapons."

"What do you mean? Check your weapons?" The question came from Corporal Brown, one of the squad leaders.

"For those of you who may not understand the term, 'check your weapons' means I take them away from you until you leave China Beach. Does everyone understand that now?"

The inflection of the naval officer's voice reminded me of a kindergarten teacher admonishing her class.

"What if we don't want to give 'em up?" This question came from the back of the room.

"If anyone refuses to turn in his weapon, he will immediately be returned to his unit and a situational report will be sent to his commanding officer."

Although none of us were happy about turning over our weapons, we all wanted the three day R&R. Reluctantly, we lined up and signed them over to one of the assistant beach managers.

Our quarters were palatial. The bunks had soft four-inch mattresses, the sheets were clean and crisp, and the shower was just down the hall. I hadn't slept in a real bed or taken a shower for three months. This was living. Everyone made their bunks and rushed to the showers. As the warm water washed off months of dirt, crud and grime, I shut my eyes and returned home.

There was much more to China Beach than a real bed and a warm shower: there was a real restaurant serving real food. I ordered a cheeseburger and fries with a strawberry shake. I couldn't believe how good it tasted. It is one of four meals that I will remember until the day I die. I remember not only how it tasted, but also how it looked. I remember every bite and swallow. We all ordered a second round.

Cold beer was everywhere. It was in large tubs of ice. I hadn't seen ice for months. Not only was the beer cold, it was real beer: it wasn't Crown Beer, San Miguel or Black Label. It was Schlitz, Bud and Stroh's. There was music, a real jukebox with the Beatles, Stones and Animals. For country fans Buck Owens, Patsy Cline and Marty Robbins wailed on about a tough life, tough times and tough luck.

White sugar sand, tropical pines, and wooden lounge chairs adorned the beach. It looked like Acapulco. A group of Marines played a true sand lot game of football. Most of the beach crowd sat in Vietnamese-made lounge chairs, sipping beer and looking out to sea.

They looked east to their past and hopefully their future. As I sat in one of the soft bamboo chairs, my mind was ten thousand miles away. What were my parents doing at this very instant? It wasn't even the same day in Minnesota. I couldn't remember if they were a day ahead or a day behind, but it really didn't matter. Dad was probably going to work at the paper mill and Mom was getting my sisters off to school.

Too much food, too much beer and a soft bed highlighted the first day at China Beach. By 1900 hours we were asleep in our bunks, drunk, full of cheeseburgers, and dreaming about the other side of the ocean.

I have no idea how many hours I slept, but when I awoke I heard the roar of pulsating showers. The sound of the running water was like the voice of sirens beckoning. I took another lengthy shower, the warm water massaging my body, a metaphysical marriage of body and soul.

I had teamed up with three Marines from other squads, Graystone, Martinez and Taylor. We all had another cheeseburger and fries before we left the complex. The whole scenario seemed unreal. We were in a war zone, but we couldn't carry a weapon.

The MP at the main gate made us sign out and list the unit we were attached to. We were supposed to specify our destination, so we all listed NSA. We told the MP that we were going to visit a couple of wounded Marines from the platoon. They didn't ask any more questions, and we walked out of the gate, rifleless and vulnerable. It was the first time in three months that I had been anywhere without a weapon.

We headed south toward NSA, but with no intention of going there. Our destination was the skivvie houses south of China Beach. The four of us left the secure confines of China Beach, unarmed and ready for action from any young Vietnamese "boom-boom girl" willing to spend three minutes with a horny Marine.

Our leader was Graystone, a squad leader. We followed him and obeyed orders as if we were on patrol. A cottage industry dealing in sex and black market goods had established a foothold on the road from China Beach to NSA.

Both sides of the dusty road were lined with small shacks constructed of discarded wooden packing containers, irregular pieces of sheet metal and the ubiquitous bamboo poles. There was a wide variety of products for sale and almost anything imaginable could be bought from the enterprising, middle-aged, female vendors.

"Hey, Marine, numba-one boom-boom girl. Good time. You come here. Good boom-boom girl. Five bucks MPC." A middle-aged female shill was calling us in. She was puffing her wares as she waved her hand for us to visit her stall. The Vietnamese hand signal for "come here" is the same as the American good-bye wave. She continued to wave and advertise her goods.

"Girl good boom-boom. For you Marines numba-one. For you only five bucks, good time."

We lingered briefly in front of her business, but not briefly enough. The mamasan had detected interest. The hook had been set. Now she went for the sale.

"You, Marine, you come here." Her comments were directed at Graystone, our leader. "Come and see beautiful boom-boom girl."

"I'll handle this," Corporal Graystone said, as he walked toward the woman. "You guys stay put while I get us a deal."

His negotiations were fast and furious. He returned with a smile on his face. "Got a hell of a deal. We get four for the price of three. Fifteen bucks and we all get our ashes hauled."

The prize that we had purchased stood in the doorway to the back room of the shack. She was the quintessential Oriental beauty: long silken black hair, smooth unblemished olive skin, and mysterious almond eyes. She was less than five feet tall and about ninety pounds. She looked like an innocent child but had probably taken more inches of Marine dick than a bar full of Tijuana whores. In Minnesota she would be jail bait.

There wasn't a question about who would go first or last. The genius of the Marine Corps' organizational structure was once again affirmed. The most senior Marine would go first and the least senior would go last. Ties would be determined by time in grade. Corporal Graystone was first. I was last.

Our leader wore a shit-eating grin as he entered the back room of the ramshackle bordello. He emerged from the love nest before we had time to smoke half a cigarette. He smiled sheepishly and said, "Rusty load."

Martinez was second. He played the role of the macho Chicano better than anyone I knew.

"Man, what do you call that, Graystone? You got to know how to satisfy your women, you know, like me, Man. Got to have that Latino lust, you know, Man?"

Martinez entered the back room without bothering to pull the sheet hanging over the door. Mamasan jumped up from her haunches and quickly slid the curtain shut. It was the first action relating to modesty that I had seen in Vietnam, and it probably had nothing to do with discretion. We had almost finished another cigarette when Martinez stumbled out of the back room rambling on with his macho bullshit.

"That boom-boom girl ain't ever going to be the same, man. She finally had a real man and she knows what she's been missing. Who's the unlucky bastard that follows me?"

Number three in our foursome was Taylor, a black PFC from Los Angeles. Although he had been a PFC three months longer than me, he had only recently joined our platoon. Taylor had told us some unbelievable stories about the Watts riots. We were familiar with some of the scenes he described, but they had happened in a war zone, not in the United States.

Taylor didn't last much longer than his predecessors. He later confided to me that it had been the first time he had sex with a woman who wasn't black.

I was next. My father had never preached to me on how to live my life, but one of the few bits of advice he had given me when I left home for Alaska was, "Always wear a rubber if you sleep with a woman before marriage." Of course, his concern was fathering a child out of wedlock, not catching the clap.

I entered the back room of the combination store/brothel. The teenage prostitute had a wet rag and was busily cleaning her genital area when I entered. Although I felt embarrassed to be watching such a personal activity, the young girl seemed nonplused and continued washing her crotch. Once she finished her task, she looked up at me and smiled.

She couldn't understand English and I didn't speak Vietnamese, so there was no verbal foreplay. As she fell backward onto the hard bamboo bed and spread her legs, it was obvious that neither would there be physical foreplay. The thunder of F-4 Phantoms flying overhead, trucks grinding gears on the road outside, and sing-song Vietnamese voices on the other side of the shared wall didn't exactly create a romantic atmosphere.

But I wasn't after atmosphere, and I didn't want romance. A twenty-year old Marine doesn't need much to get aroused, and I was ready. I dropped my ripped utility trousers to my ankles and prepared to mount my purchase.

Suddenly, the middle-aged madam entered the room. She went to the back of the room and opened a metal box. Carefully, she counted a wad of MPC bills and stashed them in the box. As far as she was concerned, I didn't exist. I didn't even rate a fleeting glance. Her visit had no effect on my lust, and hormones overpowered embarrassment. My need was satisfied in two minutes.

I had followed my father's advice and used a condom. The others hadn't. A week later, they were all getting penicillin shots for the clap.

Physically satiated, we continued south toward NSA. We soon tired of our shopping trip that meandered from one vendor of cigarettes and junk to another.

"Why don't we just go back to the beach, drink some beer and relax? This stuff doesn't interest me," Taylor said.

"Let's go back then," Graystone responded, as he did an abrupt about-face and headed back in the direction we had come from.

I agreed with the change in plans. I was actually sick of looking at Vietnamese people in general. At least at China Beach, you wouldn't have to worry about some gook taking a shot at you.

Back at the beach, I bought a couple of cold Bud's, found a peaceful piece of sand, and just kicked back. The sand was hot and felt good on my bare back and legs. A breeze off the ocean kept the flies at a tolerable level. If it hadn't been for an occasional Phantom screaming overhead and the wumping of medevac choppers heading for NSA, I could have been at a first class beach resort.

As I slowly sipped my beer, I thought about how unbelievably lucky I had been during the last three months. The downside was that it didn't seem possible that I could continue riding lady luck for nine more months. After an hour or so of trying to look across the ocean, I returned to the Quonset where the first squad was billeted.

Mac and Kranz were sleeping. Several guys were singing in the shower and Wilson was sitting on his bunk writing a letter.

"Still writing to that Southern belle, Wilson?"

"Yeah, she's really getting all crazy and stuff. Said she broke up with her fiancé and wants to see me when I get back. Keeps on saying she loves me and all that. I'm writing to tell her I'm black. Maybe she will continue to write me, don't know. Nice to get her letters but I know the real world. Ain't gonna be too many white girls from Georgia writing some black dude from Brooklyn."

"Yeah, you're probably right. It'll be interesting to see if she answers your letter," I said. I doubted whether she would write again. This broad sounded like she was living somewhere up in the clouds.

On the way to the shower I decided to weigh myself on the scale that sat outside the exercise room. I was seeing bones in my body that I had never seen before.

The scale looked like the one that used to be in the sick room at Holler Elementary School. It weighed you as well as measured your height. We were measured and weighed twice a year, in the fall and spring. The teacher wrote your personal statistics on your report card so you could track how much you grew during the year.

I always wanted to be taller and lighter. When the teacher measured my height, I tried to stretch my neck and sneak in an undetected tiptoe. On the other hand, when I was weighed, I tried to step lightly on the scale. Sometimes almost all my weight would be on one foot. By doing so, I thought I could shave a pound or two off my real weight.

I stepped on the scale and pushed the larger of the two counterweights to the two hundred pound setting while leaving the smaller one at zero. The balance assembly didn't move. I pushed the larger counterweight to the one hundred fifty setting and the smaller one to thirty pounds: still no movement. I continued to push the smaller counterweight to the left. The balance assembly started rising as I neared fifteen pounds. It was perfectly balanced at eleven pounds. One hundred and fifty plus eleven was one hundred and sixty-one pounds.

This couldn't be right. I was two hundred and thirty pounds when I graduated from High School. After boot camp I was two hundred and twenty. On the USS *Gordon*, I was at two hundred and twenty-three pounds.

I had lost sixty-two pounds in three months.

I had always thought of myself as a big guy, but not anymore. I was now one of the little guys. I was a defensive back instead of a tackle. I wished I hadn't got on the scale. I felt better when I still thought I was big.

The entire platoon drank too much beer and ate too many cheeseburgers again that night. Bedtime came early, and most of us slept ten hours. We were up early and after showering, headed for the mess hall. Breakfast consisted of greasy fried eggs, bacon, grits and the always tasty shit-on-a–shingle. A large metal coffee machine provided real coffee, not the instant C-rat stuff. The food was fabulous. We were well-fed, rested, and nobody was trying to kill us.

It was a shock when the trucks arrived a day early to bring us back. Apparently, after most of us had gone to bed last night, a group of Marines from the platoon broke into the armory to retrieve their weapons. Then they took several MPs hostage in their effort to take over the complex. As a result of this escapade, our R&R was terminated and we were kicked off China Beach. Lieutenant Sloat got his ass chewed out and court-martials were threatened.

We tried to drink as many cold beers as we could before climbing into the back of the six-bys. It was probably the last cold thing we would drink for weeks, months, or maybe our lives. It was 1100 hours, and most of us had a slight beer buzz as the convoy headed out.

We had to drive north through the city before heading south toward the war. As we drove by the huge airbase with its shower-equipped barracks and air-conditioned clubs, we all regretted not joining the air force or the navy. But then with our luck, we probably would have ended up as navy corpsmen.

The old battalion command post, now our platoon patrol base, was about ten miles south of Da Nang. We were about five hundred meters from our destination when we caught up with three tracs going in the same direction. Clouds of sand and diesel smoke trailed the tracs creating an acrid, particle-laden barrier that blocked our view of the road. Since our driver couldn't see the amtrac in front of us, he had slowed to a crawl.

Our weapons had been returned to us before we left China Beach. The butt of my M-14 rested on the floor of the box, muzzle pointing skyward. My left hand gripped the barrel as my right hand shielded my partially closed eyes from the swirling sand.

The sudden explosion was loud enough to be heard above the noisy amtrac engines and grinding six-bys. The initial blast was immediately followed by several smaller, secondary concussions. Our truck came to an abrupt halt, throwing us forward. Both convoys stopped and we literally waited for the dust to settle before we could see anything. Meanwhile, smaller popping sounds could be heard coming from the direction of the first loud blast.

We jumped off and automatically established a temporary perimeter around the six-bys.

Once the sand and smoke finally settled, we saw what had happened. The lead amtrac had hit an anti-tank mine and was engulfed in a rage of flames, fed by fuel from its diesel tanks. The popping sounds were heat-ignited rounds of small arms ammunition exploding inside the trac.

In utter helplessness, the first platoon and the men from the other tracs looked on as the twisted trac carcass burned. The black and gray acrid smoke irritated our nasal passages and activated a gagging reflex. We knew we were smelling burning human flesh amid the stench of flaming diesel fuel and rubber.

Everyone in the squad silently stared at the soaring flames of the deadly pyre. We were hypnotized and helpless. The exact cargo of the amtrac was unknown, which meant that additional secondary explosions were possible. Everyone kept his distance.

After a while, Mac called the squad together. We walked the remaining distance to camp.

We later learned that three Marines had burned to death and three more were badly injured.

Chapter 21
Friendly Fire

October was coming to an end and the monsoon rains started. At first, the rains resembled midwestern thundershowers. The clouds blew in, the rain fell, and the clouds blew out. Between the showers, the sun came out and the wet earth steamed. Although the temperature was lower than during the dry season, the humidity was stifling.

It was during this early monsoon period that I experienced my first and only episode of heat exhaustion. My vision was blurred and I became disoriented. Everything I looked at was distorted and out of proportion like a carnival's house of mirrors. Luckily, Doc recognized the symptoms and treated me immediately. His quick action stopped the episode before it became severe and potentially lethal.

Our platoon set up a night defensive perimeter around a small village that straddled the intersection of two major dikes. Like always, we established two-man positions at regular intervals on the outer fringe of the jungle surrounding the hamlet. Quickly, darkness engulfed us. A steady rain added to our discomfort as we sat looking outward for any sign of the enemy.

I was teamed with Hicks, our squad's radioman. It was about 0200 and I was trying every trick I knew to stay awake. All of a sudden the silence of the night was shattered by a short blast from the M-60 positioned about fifty meters to our right. One short burst, then silence. Several minutes later, someone popped an illumination flare. The light from the flare quickly went out and was followed by sounds of obvious confusion and concern.

"What the fuck happened over there?" A voice in the darkness demanded.

"Saw movement in front of my position and there was no answer when I challenged it," came the reply. "So I gave it a burst from the gun. Think I hit whatever was out there."

Another voice said, "Where's the new guy?"

"What new guy?"

"The guy in second squad, don't know his name, just got here a couple days ago."

"Was he with you?"

"Yeah he was, but he ain't no more. He disappeared."

"Maybe that's who was out there in front of the perimeter."

"Fuckin' guy couldn't be that stupid."

"Let's check it out."

The banter had stopped, and the only thing you could hear was the sound of two Marines splashing through knee-deep water. The sound of the splashing stopped.

"Holy fuck, it's the new guy."

"Who?"

"The fucking new guy! Jesus Christ. Corpsman Up! Corpsman up!"

Hicks and I stayed in our position as we heard Doc splashing through the water toward the fallen Marine. It was silent while Doc tried to perform another miracle. After several minutes, I heard the Marines and Doc laboring as they returned to the perimeter. They didn't seem to be in any hurry and this was definitely a bad sign. The new guy was probably dead.

The corporal who had shot the new guy was devastated. He had been in Nam seven months and was a "recruitment poster"

Marine. He was fearless in combat and had performed enough heroic deeds on the battlefield to warrant a chest full of medals.

The corporal said the new guy had not responded when he was challenged to "advance and be recognized," so the corporal fired. There were many theories on what had caused the new guy to get that far out in front of our perimeter. One was that he fell asleep on watch and when he woke up forgot where he was. Another was that he had been sleepwalking. A third was that he had gone to take a shit and had become directionally disoriented. The only thing we knew for sure was that the FNG with no name was dead. Nobody blamed the corporal because all of us would have done the same thing.

The body of the new guy was tied to one of our two tanks and transported back to the platoon base the next morning. We all agreed that if you were going to get killed in Vietnam, it was better earlier than later. It would be much worse to live through eleven or twelve months of shit, and then get killed. Think of all the misery you would have to endure and the end result would be the same—dead.

We still had the remainder of the patrol to complete, so after the tank carrying the dead Marine left, the first squad mounted the remaining tank and headed north. A mini sweep toward a squad-sized blocking force was the plan.

The first squad would ride for about 1000 meters, bypassing the village of Cuo Lu. The remainder of the patrol would set up blocking positions in the underbrush growing along the edges of a major east-west dike just south of the village. The plan was simple—we would move south through the village, and the VC would run away from us directly into our strategically placed blocking force.

After circling the village, the tank came to a sliding halt two hundred meters north of Cuo Lu. We jumped off, ready for the drive. The problem was that my military issue glasses preceded me to the ground and I heard a crunch as I landed on them. The frames were broken in several places rendering them useless. I didn't even pick up the pieces. I couldn't think of any way that a VC would be able to use the smashed glasses for sinister purposes.

I started moving toward the village. Once we reached there, we were supposed to spread out and sweep south. Without my glasses, when I looked at the trees lining the trail, I saw a solid green watercolor wash.

I had only walked about thirty meters when Joe called for me to stop. Joe was third in the patrol, behind Wilson and ahead of Hicks.

"Gar, you can't walk point. You can't see shit without your glasses. I'll walk point for you, it's safer for all of us."

Joe's offer made sense. I really couldn't see much without my glasses. If I remembered correctly, my eyes were 20/400. "Okay, okay, take over. You know this area as well as I do."

Joe and I switched places, I thanked him, and the patrol moved on. The trail snaked its way through a grouping of hooches before it turned into a dike that crossed a small paddy. I was about thirty meters behind Joe, and I really couldn't see shit. I couldn't tell whether Wilson, who was in front of me, was black or white.

I couldn't see, but I could hear. And what I heard was a staccato of rifle fire and a hail of bullets tearing through our sparse cover. I hit the ground immediately and tried to locate the direction of the fire. In front of me I saw Wilson behind the stump of a tree that at some time had been severed by artillery fire. I couldn't see Joe, but I heard his call for help.

"Gar, I'm hit--doesn't look too bad, but I took one."

Jesus Christ, poor Joe—offers to take point for me and gets hit again. I felt terrible. I was praying that it wouldn't be too bad. Joe was not a complainer; he was a master of understatement.

I moved forward to where Joe was lying behind a minimally protective mud dike. He was in over two feet of water and holding his arm. As I crawled the last ten meters through the knee-deep water, I was afraid of what I'd find. He could have a shattered arm with major artery damage. If we were unable to get him out in time, he could easily bleed to death. He could go into shock and die without knowing he was dying.

When I reached Joe, I was relieved to see that the wound was not life threatening. I applied a field dressing, took his M-14, and told him to follow me back to the rest of the squad.

With Joe injured, I decided we weren't going to fuck around and complete our hastily conceived mini-sweep. I told Hicks to call Delta One and advise them that we were returning to the blocking force with a WIA. Then I called for an 81-mortar barrage on the coordinates of the ambush.

We found the tank escort and rode south toward the rest of the platoon. We rejoined the rest of the patrol and were told to return to base. I rode with Joe and the rest of the squad on one tank. The other tank had joined us after delivering the dead FNG to base camp.

Riding back to camp, we once again drove through, rather than around the huts. I couldn't help but think what might have happened if I had been on point instead of Joe. I would have been a different target than Joe. I was bigger and without my glasses would have been walking at a slower pace. Maybe the bullet that had hit him in the arm would have hit me in the chest.

When I walked point I always placed the metal breach and action of my rifle directly in front of my heart. Although most of my chest was still exposed, my heart was protected by six square inches of forged steel. It probably didn't protect me at all, but psychologically, it did wonders. I was still riding lady luck.

When we returned, Doc took Joe to the aid station, re-bandaged his wound and gave him a tetanus shot. Doc said he wouldn't have to go on patrol for a week. Joe would be awarded his second Purple Heart.

Chapter 22
Temporary Assignment

We were moving our patrol base to a location near the town of Dien Bahn, about eleven miles south of our present location and five miles from the new battalion command post. Once again we would be reunited with the second platoon and Delta Six.

Instead of going directly to our new patrol base, which didn't yet exist, we were scheduled to spend a few days at the new battalion command post that at present housed H&S Company and several platoons from various line companies.

Our two-day stay at the battalion base turned into two weeks. During those two weeks, I got a new pair of glasses. I also experienced a number of firsts.

The Bullet In The Sock

The second day at battalion I was asked to lead a daytime patrol and ambush to the horseshoe area of the Song Ha Xau River. It was a small patrol with only six Marines and a new corpsman. Doc Clopton was nearing the end of his six-month field assignment, and the new corpsman was scheduled to be his replacement.

Our mission wasn't complex: move in patrol formation to the edge of the horseshoe and set up a three-position ambush on the eastern edge of the curving river. Near the middle of the curve, the width and depth of the river decreased providing a safe and short place to cross. We would establish our ambush positions opposite the shallow crossing area where we could observe anyone trying to move out of the horseshoe. To complete our mission we would simply kill any VC or VCS trying to move across the narrow passage.

The 5000-meter hike to the ambush site was without incident. The rain had stopped and the sun was in full force trying to evaporate the rain. It was unbearably humid, but at least the sun would dry us out.

After selecting our ambush sites, we crawled into the thick vegetation along the riverbank and waited for someone stupid enough to try to cross the river. I was with Hicks; Wilson was with Joe. Langley was teamed with the new corpsman. Ideally, I should have teamed with the corpsman, but then Hicks and his radio would have been with someone other than me.

The sun was cooking and steam was rising. We had been in position for an hour and nobody had tried to cross the river. I was dying for a smoke, but the smell of American cigarettes would have been a dead give-away. Several swans were swimming in the water of the horseshoe. It was a picture that could have adorned an oriental vase. My daydreaming was interrupted by a single muffled shot followed by a shout from Langley.

"Tornes! Tornes! Get over here!"

I responded immediately to the call. Telling Hicks to hold tight, I ran toward Langley's position.

The new corpsman had taken his boot off and was grimacing in pain. Langley was standing at his side with a blank look on his face.

"What the hell happened?"

Neither Langley nor the corpsman responded. Finally Langley said, "He shot himself in the foot with his .45."

"What do you mean, shot himself in the foot?"

"He shot himself in the foot." Langley continued to look dumbfounded.

The new corpsman was silent. His boot was off, and there was surprisingly little blood. I dropped to one knee to examine the wound. The .45 slug had entered the top of his foot and exited the bottom. The weird part was that the slug had not made it through the sole of the sock. The round had been trapped between the foot and the sock. When I held the foot in a horizontal position, the bullet pulled the bottom of the black military issue sock down like a little hanging testicle.

The corpsman's silence continued. Langley finally realized what had really happened and said, "He just took his .45, held his foot up, and pulled the trigger. It wasn't no accident."

The new corpsman was furtively rummaging through his medical pack. I thought he was looking for a field dressing but what he retrieved was one of the morphine doses that he carried. This was too much. This son-of–a-bitch would not shoot himself in the foot and then get high on a morphine shot. I ripped the dose out of his hand and called for Hicks.

Hicks responded to my call wearing his ever-present grin.

"Hicks, call Delta One and tell them we have a WIA and are terminating our mission."

"What the hell happened?" Hicks asked, as he attempted to retune the PRC25 to contact Delta One.

"Fucking new corpsman shot himself in the foot, then tries to shoot himself up with morphine," I answered.

"No shit. Fucking disgrace to the navy."

"This is the first time I ever saw this," I said, shaking my head.

"That's advised," Hicks said.

Hicks had the tendency to use "affirmative" and "advised" interchangeably. By now, everyone was familiar with this aberration so we knew what he meant.

The new corpsman finally said something that none of the rest of the patrol even considered, "Call a medevac to fly me out of here."

I couldn't believe what I was hearing.

"You shoot yourself in the foot to avoid combat and you expect us to call a chopper to fly you out? Fuck you, you chicken-ass motherfucker! We're not risking a chopper pilot's life to get you out of here. You're *walking* back to base. Langley, go find some kind of a stick this asshole can use for a crutch to walk back to the CP."

Langley returned with a sturdy piece of wood that had washed up on the riverbank, a very adequate crutch. We headed back to base with the new corpsman limping along on his makeshift crutch. The trip back took twice as long as the trip out.

When we arrived, I briefed Mac and he told Lieutenant Sloat. I don't know what happened to the corpsman. I suppose he could have been court-martialed, but I never heard. The one thing I knew for sure was that Doc Clopton's field assignment would not come to an end. He would continue to serve beyond the normal six-month stint until another replacement was found.

Wet Feet

We were always wet. The monsoons were in full swing and it rained every afternoon and night. Sheets of rain would fall for hours at a time. Our schedule of patrols and ambushes continued uninterrupted. The difference was that instead of just sleeping on the jungle floor, we slept in water on the jungle floor. Although the temperature never got below sixty-five degrees, we still shivered at night. For warmth, we wore utility jackets retrieved from our sea bags.

Socks were in short supply. I can never remember having more than two pairs of socks at the same time. Usually, we made do with only one pair. This of course was not good for your feet. They were always wet. Although our jungle boots dried quickly, the socks remained wet. There was never enough time between patrols or ambushes to dry your socks. If you were lucky enough to have a second pair, it too, was usually wet. My feet started hurting shortly after the monsoons began. Initially, I thought the burning sensation was a rash or irritation caused by wearing the undersized boots. Days passed without me taking my boots off, and my feet continued to ferment inside their leather and canvas containers.

Every step I took became a test of my pain threshold. Peer pressure and pride kept me going. I didn't want to look weak and whiny, so I didn't go to Doc. Instead, I continued to hope the problem would fix itself. It didn't. Not only did it hurt when I walked, now it hurt all the time. I broke down and went to Doc.

Since we were still temporarily based out of the battalion CP, Doc bunked in the corpsman tent. I picked a time when I knew he was on duty. It was late afternoon and he was alone. I tried to be as discreet as possible entering the medical tent.

"Hey Tornes, how're the burns on your leg healing?" Doc laughed as he greeted me. He continued to think that the whole smoke-grenade burn incident was hilarious. It didn't bother me. Anything that made this corpsman laugh made me feel good.

"They're okay. They're healing up."

"What can I do for you?"

"I got a little problem, Doc. Maybe you can help. My feet are killing me. Don't know what the problem is. Hurt all the time."

"Let's look at them. Take your boots off."

Gingerly, I unlaced the boots and pulled my feet out. I couldn't remember the last time I had taken them off.

"Jesus Christ, what do we have here!" Doc's reaction to my feet was unexpected.

As I looked at my feet for the first time in days, I understood Doc's reaction. About half the black cotton sock fibers were gone. I don't know where. The other half seemed to be part of my feet. In some places the fibers were covered with flesh. In other areas, the fibers were above the skin. Strands of thread were interwoven with pieces of skin.

"I got to get the doc to look at this," he said.

"But you *are* the doc."

"No, the medical doctor, Lieutenant Foley. I've never seen anything like this."

Doc left, and returned in several minutes with the doctor.

Lieutenant Foley, the battalion surgeon, bent down to examine my feet. After a cursory examination, he said, "We want to get some pictures of these. This is a textbook case of Immersion Foot at its worst." He left and returned shortly with a camera. After taking pictures from every conceivable angle, he put the camera down and started treatment.

The first phase of treatment was to soak both feet in a large container of warm water containing an Epsom salt-like ingredient. My feet were underwater for at least an hour. The next step was to try to remove the ingrown sock fibers from the skin of my feet. This step was quite uncomfortable. The pieces of ingrown material had to be pulled from under the overgrown skin. Doc rubbed an analgesic salve on my feet to dull some of the expected pain. Then the pulling and tearing began. Fortunately, the pain caused by the fibers ripping through the overgrown skin was not much more than I had experienced walking.

The process was over in about half an hour. I was given an antibiotic salve to rub over my feet and a two-day reprieve from patrolling. The doctor told me to take my boots and socks off every night to air them out. All this advice made medical sense, but in reality, it couldn't be done.

Fortunately, it was my only episode with Immersion Foot. I wondered if the pictures taken of my feet would ever appear in a medical textbook.

A Taste Of Our Own Power

Our mission was a patrol into the village of Ngan Cau, a small hamlet in the northern part of our TAOR. We were scheduled to move into the ville, search for and destroy anything of military value, set up a night perimeter, then return to battalion the next morning.

We knew the area, so I had Shively, the newest member of the squad, walk point. We weren't going far and we didn't expect trouble. It would be a good experience for him. We made it to Ngan Cau with no problem. The village was considered government sympathetic so our anxiety level was low. We quickly established a perimeter around a piece of real estate north of the village and casually dug fighting holes.

We were re-supplied with C-rats, ammunition and mail. No one was concerned about a night attack.

The sun had set, and most Marines were busy cooking C-rat dinners when a machine gun opened up on our position. The fire was coming from a northeast direction. Our M-60 immediately responded. Automatic fire was exchanged at an unbelievable volume. Several grenades landed close to our positions. They sounded like M-79 rounds, but could have been Chicom rifle grenades.

The level of fire was much greater than previous enemy encounters. The tracer rounds flying over our heads were red not green. After an intense ten-minute firefight, an order to cease-fire was given. We stopped firing and the enemy did the same.

It was only then that we figured out that the enemy wasn't the enemy. We had been fighting a platoon from Second Battalion,

First Marines. We didn't know where they were, and they didn't know where we were.

It didn't say much for the accuracy of our fire, but no one from either unit was killed or wounded. It was a mistake that happened more than once during the war, but at least our firefight had been without casualties.

Where's My Life?

Patrols continued unabated during our extended stay at battalion. Several days before we were scheduled to move to our new company patrol base south of Dien Bahn, we went on a routine night ambush in the ville of Tan My (1). Because we were still undermanned, the patrol consisted of only four Marines: Hicks, Wilson, Joe and me. Joe's few days of skating duty were over. He was back with the squad without light duty restrictions.

It was still daylight when we left for Tan My (1). We crossed a heavily flooded rice paddy on an elevated, slippery dike. About half way across the paddy, we started taking heavy fire from the western tree line. I jumped into the water on the left side of the dike.

The water looked like a continuation of the paddy water, but it wasn't. It was an eight-foot deep canal paralleling the dike. My heavy backpack, rifle and other gear quickly took me to the bottom of the trough. Frantically, I struggled to rise to the surface. My helmet had fallen off during my plunge, and when I made it to the surface, it was floating nearby. My cigarettes were also floating. I kept them inside my helmet liner since that was the only dry place on my body.

I retrieved my helmet with one hand, while the other hand was frantically trying to find a secure grip on the slick dike. I never liked swimming, and the plunge to the bottom of the deep trough had scared me.

As I tried to climb onto the dike, I heard "Whomp!" as a .50 caliber round removed a clod of mud about a foot from my head. It was apparent that the VC had zeroed in on me.

"Ca whomp!" Another slug disintegrated a basketball-sized piece of dirt. I looked around and saw I was definitely the duck in this duck-shoot. I felt helpless as I struggled to keep my head above the waterline.

Hicks and Joe were behind me, protected by a large earthen bridge. I was confident that they would call in an 81 mission to go after the attackers. Another .50 caliber round produced one more "Whomp!" while yet another piece of dike flew. Then I heard the thump of the mortars. They had called them in and were firing for effect. The .50 caliber gun that had me targeted, stopped. The sun was setting as quiet returned.

After successfully climbing onto the slick dike, I ran toward the tree line. I sought the cover that a jungle provides. I also thought that there was a chance of finding an enemy casualty from the mortar barrage. I assumed Hicks, Wilson and Joe would follow.

As I entered the tree line moving fast, two VC nearly ran into me. They were running north on the trail bordering the paddy. Even though it was dark, I could see the .50 caliber gun that had been trying to put me away. The first member of the team had the gun over his shoulder; the other carried the pod and ammo. I opened up with a quick burst and they disappeared. I didn't think I hit them, but I wanted to check.

The trail they had run down veered left into a small hamlet. The path led to an abandoned hut, almost encircled by a large fishpond. I quickly searched the interior of the squalid, partially destroyed hut before moving to the backside of the structure. I was behind the hut when I heard several intense volleys of fire–but the firing was at least 300 meters away.

It was then that I realized I was alone.

I had made a huge mistake: I had lost both visual and voice contact with my team while on a night mission. For whatever reason, the rest of the patrol had not followed me into the tree line.

I recognized the sounds of M-14's hammering away as well as the quieter popping of VC .30 caliber carbines. I knew I was in deep shit.

The firing finally stopped, replaced with something much more frightening—the sound of a large body of enemy troops moving and talking on the trail I had just left. How could I have been so damned stupid to get separated from the rest of the patrol? It had to be the dumbest thing I'd ever done and could very well be the last dumb thing I would ever do.

It was difficult to determine how large the enemy force was, but I heard many different voices sing-songing away in Vietnamese. The bulk of the force was about twenty meters away. They were on the main trail near the secondary path, which led to the hut I was hiding behind. The VC troops seemed in no hurry. If they decided to move into the village, I would either be dead or a captive in a matter of minutes. The layout of the carp pond that nearly surrounded the hut limited my exit options. It would have been impossible to move quietly through the water to the relative safety of the dark jungle.

The enemy force continued to congregate at the juncture of the two trails. They talked and smoked rancid-smelling gook cigarettes. At least they didn't have Salems. Other than language and cigarettes, they could have been a platoon of Marines. I knew I was dead meat. The first person to walk down the trail to the water-encircled hut would almost certainly see me, since there was no place to hide. I started preparing for the showdown that I felt was imminent. I didn't have any grenades with me. Recently, they had been in short supply and we had rationed them among the squad members. It was me and my M-14.

I had two tactical options: start firing before they got to the hut or wait until they looked behind the building before firing. I chose the latter. My other decision was whether I should be standing or prone when they encountered me. This was more difficult. I didn't like either option. I decided to open fire from a prone position. Maybe they wouldn't expect fire coming up at them from such close range. If they were surprised, I could kill more of them before they killed me. I dropped to a prone position, placed my extra magazine next to my rifle, and waited.

The conversation among the enemy combatants became more animated. Clearly, the force was not in agreement on some issue. First, it seemed like they were moving toward my position. Then they stopped and moved back.

The rain and wind had stopped and it was cold, yet every inch of my body was covered with sweat. It wasn't your typical perspiration; it was the sweat of a soon-to-be-executed prisoner.

I didn't think about my life, my parents or friends. All I debated while sweating profusely was if I should be in a prone or standing position when I opened up with my initial blast.

The VC platoon made their move. They decided to go north. I heard the clank and clatter of their equipment, as they clamored down the trail. I waited until I could no longer hear their noise before rising from my prone position.

I now had a different problem: how was I going to find the rest of the patrol?

I had left my map with Hicks, so the basis for my direction would be knowledge of the area and landmarks. I walked back to the trail where the VC had been talking. They had gone north, I would go south.

I stepped as quietly and as quickly as I could in the general direction of where I thought the rest of the patrol would be. Not only did I have to worry about being shot by the enemy, but I also had a concern about being shot by someone from the patrol. They had no idea where I was or for that matter if I was even alive. I knew they wouldn't leave without me, but the dangers of re-establishing contact were obvious.

I followed the trail south for about 300 meters before heading west on what seemed to be a major trail. I still didn't know exactly where I was, but I was at least headed in the direction of the battalion CP. Tall grass hugged the sides of the trail. I didn't know what it was, but I knew it wasn't rice. It was probably one of the many species of bamboo, which could grow over a foot in a day.

I was making more noise than I would on a normal night mission, but this time the noise was planned. I was hoping that a member of the patrol would hear me and challenge me with the "Who goes there, advance to be recognized" routine. My wish was granted.

"Who goes there?" It was Wilson's voice.

"It's me, Gordon," I answered. I could hear the relief in my own voice.

"God, Man, we were afraid you were dead or captured," Wilson said as he put a welcoming arm around my shoulder.

"That's advised," Hicks said, his grin even more pronounced than usual. "We thought you were dead meat."

Joe approached and slapped my back. I barely heard him whisper, "Gar, you dumb Fuck."

Without another word, the four of us headed back to battalion.

Chapter 23
Dien Ban

Our long-awaited and much-delayed move to the new company patrol base finally was underway. We packed up what little personal gear we had, climbed atop amtracs, and headed to our new home.

The new base camp was 7000 meters southwest of the battalion CP near the village of Dien Ban. A labyrinth of rivers, streams and canals surrounded the village. We commandeered a suburb of Dien Ban and started our urban renewal project.

Our defensive perimeter was about 500 meters across. In the center of our appropriated living area was a large masonry schoolhouse. Next to the schoolhouse was another smaller concrete building. The schoolhouse and adjoining building would function as the company command center. Captain Kelly and his entourage would live in the big house. His platoon commanders and senior NCOs would occupy the little house. The rest of us were looking for temporary shelter.

Permanent defensive positions had not yet been established since it was our first night. An Ontos detachment had strategically placed three six-gun mini-tanks on the main roadways leading into the complex. The M-60's had also established temporary positions for the night.

Several squads from the second platoon had moved into a number of houses on the eastern edge of the perimeter. The majority of the 1st Platoon was without housing.

The obvious choice was a red brick, cylindrical structure on the southern edge of the perimeter. We decided to explore.

The tall brick building looked like a cross between a power plant smokestack and a farm silo. As we walked through the larger-than-usual arched entrance, we were met with air that smelled like it hadn't moved for decades. The stagnant air had a sweet-smoky odor. The only natural light beamed through a large hole in the top of the cylindrical column. We were inside some type of smokestack.

The light from the overhead hole allowed us to explore the internal architecture of this strange fortress.

"What are those?" Hicks pointed to the bed-sized brick benches that were built into the base.

"Looks like made-to-order sleeping compartments," someone answered.

A worldly and educated Marine in our group told us what we were in. "This is a crematorium, and those bed-like structures are where they put the bodies before they torched them."

"No shit. We're inside a crematorium! Fucking unbelievable." Hicks looked around in amazement.

Without hesitation, we climbed onto the benches that probably never held a live body. Everyone felt safe that night. It was by far the most secure and invulnerable defensive position we had ever slept in.

The next day we were assigned two houses on the western edge of the perimeter. Mac, Wilson, Hicks, Joe, and I would live in one; Heatley, Shively, Langley and Sage would live in the other one.

The house was better than average by Vietnamese standards. It had concrete walls and floor, four window openings, a heavily thatched roof, and, of course, a religious shrine. It was definitely better than some of the other houses on the perimeter. After selecting our personal floor space area, we started working on perimeter defense.

Our first task was to string hundreds of yards of concertina and razor wire around the perimeter. The wire was strung seventy-five to one hundred meters from each security bunker. The bunker for our group was about ten meters from the house and had a sand-bagged and wood-reinforced roof with two outward-facing windows. Fields of fire were determined for each position, and in short order we had ourselves a formidable-looking perimeter. Anyone trying to breach the defenses in front of our bunker would have to slog through one hundred meters of barren rice paddy before reaching us. This, of course, would be only after they had successfully penetrated our concertina and razor wire defenses.

Water and More Water

The rain continued. Day after day, night after night, it fell. Everything was wet all the time.

My personal space in our appropriated house was comfortable and usually dry. I was in the southwestern corner of the house. I had a window opening directly above my head on the west corner and another on the south edge of the house.

Although the windows were open and uncovered, rain could not reach me unless driven by a strong wind. The concrete floor was hard and cold, but dry. Often, before falling asleep, I would watch a family of small green snakes crawling through the thatch of the roof. I didn't know what kind of snakes they were, but assumed they were venomous. Someone said they were small pit vipers. I had stopped worrying about snakes months ago. Snakes didn't like the monsoons either, and like us, migrated to the high and dry ground. The snakes in the thatch were comfortable and content. They wouldn't mess with us if we didn't mess with them.

Our new company TAOR was virgin territory. None of us had patrolled the area before and we didn't know what to expect. The only thing we had heard was that battalion-sized units of the enemy were supposedly working the area south of the Song Dien Bihn River. Intelligence had identified the primary unit as the 307th VC/NVA Battalion.

I was scheduled to lead my first patrol into the new area the next day. The first squad had been replenished, so we had nine Marines available for patrol. At 0545 hours, Mac and I went to the command center for a briefing with the lieutenant. The briefing was cursory, Mac gave me his map, and I left. Our course was predetermined and we would call in at designated checkpoints.

We walked south toward the Song Dien Binh River. The monsoons had swollen the rivers and streams. What had been a trickling stream two months earlier was now a raging river. I had no idea how deep the river was. The only thing I knew was that we had to cross it. Today we were without a corpsman. There simply weren't enough corpsmen to go around. Doc Clopton had just come off an all night ambush so he was sleeping. Doc's replacement had yet to be assigned, so Doc continued to serve beyond the normal six-month field assignment. I put Langley on point. He was good and getting better. I followed Langley with Hicks and the radio behind me.

The river looked like a white-water rafter's dream. Clods of dirt and pieces of wood were moving at fifteen miles per hour toward the South China Sea. We put our cigarettes in our helmets, held our weapons above the water, joined hands and started across. The river was about seventy-five meters across, and we were in no hurry.

Each step was careful and deliberate. The water was already to our chests and we hadn't made the halfway point. Langley's grip on my right wrist tightened, his steps were careful and deliberate. Luckily, the water didn't get higher, and the patrol successfully made it to the opposite shore. The major downside to our company location was that any patrol going south had to cross the river. You were soaking wet before starting your patrol.

The patrol was fairly short as far as distance, but the many surging streams slowed us down. We walked south for about an hour on a well-used trail. We called two checkpoints in to Delta One, the last of which was Dong Ban Dong. At this small ville, we changed direction and headed northwest. We were supposed to continue north to the river hamlet of Cam Lau Trung (1) before re-crossing the river and returning to the CP.

Langley struggled to get up the greasy bank of a ravine on the edge of a large rice paddy. I was ten feet behind, slipping and sliding as I tried to climb the same incline. When Langley finally made it to the top, he came under intense small arms fire from the tree line on the western edge of the rice paddy. He dove for cover as I ran to the top of the bank to determine where the fire was coming from.

The source of fire was in the thick foliage on the western edge of the paddy. As I surveyed our personal battlefield, I saw a figure wearing a typical VC black pajama uniform running on the dike that crossed the paddy. The figure was about 300 meters away, and it was carrying what appeared to be a weapon.

The VC was less than halfway across the paddy and I would have several unobstructed shots at the fleeing foe. This was great. Usually I was the target in the middle of a field. I brought my M-14 to my shoulder, centered the running target in my sights, and fired.

The figure kept running. Once again, I zeroed in on the target and squeezed off a round. Once again, I missed. My third shot was successful. It had found its mark. The fleeing figure dropped. Even from my distant vantage point, I knew I had a kill.

The firing from the tree line stopped as abruptly as it had started. Rather than use the interconnected dikes to reach my trophy, we followed the eastern tree line until we arrived at the dike that my prize had tried to cross. A small village was on my right. Apparently the village had been my target's destination.

"Langley, Let's go see what the gook looks like."

I felt good. I had bagged one of the bad guys. We walked the short distance to where the body was floating in the water. I didn't notice a weapon, but a weapon wouldn't float. It was probably under the water in the paddy muck. The body was floating face down so Langley kicked it over with his foot.

"It's a little girl, not a VC," he stammered.

"Shit." My response was frustration, not regret.

I felt no remorse. It was an accident. Things like this happened. I had thought the figure running across the dike was a VC combatant. Her shoulder pole looked like a weapon from 300 meters. That's war. Innocent people get killed. It shouldn't happen but it does.

"Leave her there. Her relatives will find her and give her a proper burial."

I couldn't agonize over the premature death of this girl. I had my squad and myself to worry about. If I let myself agonize over this, where would it stop?

We entered the ville that had been the young girl's destination. After a brief search, we found a VC flag in one of the huts. I took the flag. At least it was something tangible. Although the village was vacant, it was obviously VC controlled. After a short smoke break, we headed north, re-crossed the river and returned to base. The dead girl was called in as a VC confirmed KIA.

Chapter 24
The Six Week Day

My six weeks in Dien Ban were the most miserable and fearful of my life. It seemed like one long continuous day and night. Patrols were indistinguishable from each other. Ambushes were identical. We were continually wet and cold. Everything was in short supply except water—which was everywhere. Our TAOR was basically one big free fire zone occupied by large numbers of NVA and VC. In addition to daily patrols and ambushes, our company participated in two operations during my month and a half at Dien Ban—Operation Arcadia and Operation Trinidad.

The Boots

One of the company's first casualties at Dien Ban left an indelible image on my memory. The guy was part of an Ontos team assigned to Delta Company. I didn't know him, but I will never forget part of him.

This particular incident involved an Ontos that was in a defensive position straddling the road on the southeast edge of the perimeter. It just sat there with its six 106 recoilless cannons pointing outward, looking more ferocious than it was. I always thought it was a useless offensive weapon. Its mobility was limited, it was lightly armored, and you had to climb out of the minimally protective cabin to load the cannons. Nevertheless, the Marine Corps—having bought them—was trying to use them. For permanent defensive positions, they were probably acceptable.

The driver of the Ontos guarding the southeastern road, for some unknown reason, decided to travel outside the perimeter. Since everything was flooded, the only route he could take was the main road. Later, the official response was that the Ontos was on a reconnaissance patrol. That explanation was ludicrous. You don't go on a recon patrol with a noisy Ontos driving down a major road.

It doesn't take a military strategist to guess what happened next. The slow, lumbering Ontos hit a large mine about 200 meters from the perimeter. The lightly armored Ontos was destroyed. We could hear the explosion from our house. Once again, the first person to reach the destruction was Doc Clopton.

Although our squad had been out all night on an ambush, we were quickly roused and dispatched to the accident scene. Our primary mission was to provide security for the corpsmen and rescue crew. As we approached the twisted and burning piece of now useless metal, Doc was frantically working on a badly burned Marine. Another Marine was being aided by a corpsman from the second platoon. A third Marine was ambulatory and stumbling around in a shocked daze. The fourth Marine wasn't as lucky. He was lying on a portable stretcher covered with a poncho. The only visible part of his body was his feet. They looked undamaged.

A medevac was ordered and our task switched from security to transportation. The two wounded Marines and the KIA had to be carried on stretchers to the LZ inside the company perimeter. Joe and I were closest to the dead Marine so we each grabbed an end. Joe took the front of the stretcher, I picked up the back. We headed toward the perimeter.

The road was slick with mud, but we made it inside the perimeter of the LZ without falling. During the entire hike I stared at the dead Marine's feet. The boots looked new, not tattered, scuffed and torn like mine. I surmised that the Marine was a new guy. I wondered what his face looked like. Was he burned or riddled with shrapnel? The dead Marine's arms had been strapped down so I couldn't even see his hands. I didn't know if he was a chuck dude or a splib.

The chopper was already at the LZ waiting for its cargo. The wounded-but-walking Marine was helped into the medevac first. Next, the two wounded were lifted on stretchers into the chopper. The last piece of cargo was our dead Marine.

A crewman of the chopper grabbed the front end of the stretcher from Joe. I continued to hold the back. The angle into the hold of the chopper was about forty-five degrees. As the crewman pulled and I pushed, a murky pink liquid of blood, urine and other body fluids that had collected in the bottom of the canvas stretcher poured out the bottom drenching my shirt and chest.

I didn't have another shirt to change into but it really didn't make any difference. The incessant rain would wash my shirt while I wore it.

The Mud

From mid-November until we left Dien Ban, it rained almost ceaselessly. Small dikes inside the perimeter connected the various defensive positions to the command post. Some of these slippery walkways were part of the permanent network of dikes connecting the various houses; others were temporary walkways. These Marine-constructed dikes used anything and everything available. Many were architecturally unique, a tribute to Marine Corps ingenuity. All trails or dikes eventually ended at the CP, which was like the hub of a bicycle wheel.

On this particular day, I decided to go to the far northeastern edge of the perimeter. The mortar pit was in that area, and some-one said that one of the mortar team was from Minnesota. I decided to look him up.

To get to the mortar pit, you followed a narrow network of dikes bordering the nearby village for 100 meters. Then, on a

Marine-made dike, you cut back in a southerly direction to where the mortars were placed. It didn't seem like a difficult journey, since it was all inside our secured perimeter.

As I was slipping and sliding along the permanent dike next to the village, I could see the mortar pit to my right. As a crow flies, it was less than seventy-five meters away. But to get to the mortars, my roundabout route would be about four hundred meters. I decided to take a short cut across the paddy that separated me from the mortars. The water in the paddy didn't look any deeper than any of the other paddies. And mud was mud—always sucking at your boots and trying to keep you from getting to your destination. I started across the paddy.

The first few yards weren't bad. The mud beneath the paddy water was barely over the top of my boots. I continued onward. The mud got deeper and my movement was severely slowed. Still I tried to move on. I was about twenty meters into the field when I realized that this wasn't your ordinary muddy paddy. Mud was up to my waist and I was immobile. I tried to turn back, but that movement only caused me to sink deeper into the muck.

I couldn't feel the bottom with my feet and I felt like Blackbeard sinking into the pit of quicksand. I had managed to keep my rifle out of the water and mud by holding it above my head with one arm. The more I tried to move, the deeper I sank. I was now treading mud that was armpit deep.

Two Marines were walking on the dike I had just left. I hollered for help. They realized the seriousness of my entrapment and quickly procured a long rope that they tossed in my direction. After several tries, I managed to catch the end of the rope. I wrapped the rope around my left arm and they started pulling. I didn't move an inch.

The power of the suction created by my submerged body was overwhelming: two Marines pulling on a rope couldn't break it. One Marine left and returned moments later with three additional pairs of arms. The five Marines pulled on the rope in unison, but still my body didn't budge. One of the Marines yelled, "Hold on! We'll get a trac."

Now my primary focus was to keep my head above the water. The paddy had been deceptive because the water above the mud level was only about a foot deep. While the mud pulled me down, I could drown in the foot of water on top that was already at my Adam's apple.

I could hear the amtrac grunting and spinning as it approached. Although the trac was very versatile and capable of crossing water and deep mud, it was not invulnerable. The mud that had me trapped could immobilize it. The trac stopped about ten meters away. A Marine on the top tossed me a cable with an attached shoulder harness.

"Slip this over your head and under your armpits," he instructed. "Make sure the cinch ring on the backside is secured. We'll get you out."

It took a considerable effort to get the harness under my arms. With all the mud pressure on my chest, I could barely breathe. I tried to complete the task with one hand since the other hand held my rifle. In my attempt to secure the harness, I dropped my rifle in the muddy water. This made me feel terrible. Above all, a Marine is responsible for keeping his rifle clean and in good working condition. Dropping your M-14 into a pit of mud does not fulfill that responsibility.

I struggled to get the harness over my head. I finally tightened the cinch ring in the back while the trac gunned its engine. I quickly reached down and retrieved my rifle just as the amtrac started slowly backing away. I could feel the pressure of the harness under my arms, but most of all, I felt the mud suction crushing my torso.

The powerful amtrac pulled and suddenly the suction broke and I was free. The trac continued to pull me through the water and mud until I reached the dike. A cheer went up from the bystanders who had been enjoying the show.

I decided to cancel my visit to the Minnesota guy in mortars.

The Communion

We had been slogging through the flooded terrain for over two days. It was a roving patrol where we combined a two-day search and destroy mission with a night ambush. The ambush would be crammed between two days of patrolling.

I had spent the night in an ambush, sitting in a foot of water. None of us had slept. Everyone was cold, wet and tired. It had rained all night and it was still coming down. It was morning, but the sun was invisible behind clouds that only a duck hunter would appreciate.

Lieutenant Sloat called the squad leaders together to plan the day. We met under what remained of the roof of a small, partially-destroyed pagoda. The piece of the roof that was left provided some protection from the driving rain.

I was dying for a cup of coffee. My canteen was full of water collected the night before. I had used the old banana leaf trick to direct rain into my canteen. I thought there was enough time to heat the water before everyone arrived for the briefing. An empty beans and frank's can functioned as my coffee pot and my cup. I crimped together the partially-removed top and bent it downward to make a usable handle. I placed a hunk of C-4 in the bottom of a small C-rat can that had been made into a bush stove. I lit the fuel, put the coffee pot on, and waited. In a matter of minutes, the water was boiling. I added the instant coffee and a couple packets of dry creamer before stirring it with the bow of my glasses.

Although C-rat coffee isn't exactly aromatic, a sweet-bitter bouquet rose with the steam. I took a sip. It was almost orgasmic. After a few swallows, I felt refreshed and rejuvenated. The rest of the squad leaders and the lieutenant joined me under the roof.

Lieutenant Sloat looked exhausted. I was sure that he hadn't slept either. I offered him a drink of my coffee. He thanked me as he accepted it. He wrapped both hands around the warm can and took a sip of the hot liquid. After several swallows, he gave it back to me. I took another sip and looked into his tired, puffy eyes. He looked much older than his twenty-three years.

His war was my war and the effects were visible. Ultimately, he was responsible for the entire platoon. He had to make life or death decisions for everyone, everyday–often without credible information. I would have walked point every day rather than trade places with Lieutenant Sloat.

I gave him the last swallow. The coffee was gone. I felt as if I had received communion.

Chapter 25
Operation Arcadia

Stiffs

It was November 18, 1966. We were going into the horseshoe, and we were going in a big way. Tanks, tracs, an Ontos group and five companies of Marines would participate in the operation. The horseshoe had always been a haven for VC and NVA advisors. This was one time when we believed the intelligence reports. Most of us had been on patrols and ambushes in and around the horseshoe and most had been hot. The village of Cam Hai, located in the middle of the horseshoe, was our objective.

According to intelligence, two VC platoons with mortars and elements of the 302nd Main Force Battalion were actively operating in the area. In addition, a VC recruit platoon armed with mortars and automatic weapons was supposedly using the horseshoe as a training area. The leper colony was located on the eastern edge of the horseshoe. According to reports, the VC were using it as a sanctuary. It seemed like years ago, instead of four months, when I first visited the leprosarium.

The horseshoe operation was a typical search and destroy mission. Phase I involved establishing four-man ambush positions at all exits to the area. This was done the night before and the first day using two rifle companies. The ambush positions were kept in place until the next day when the remaining three companies established a cordon around the villages of Cam Hai and Thanh

Thui. Once the cordon was in place, the Marines that had been in ambush positions regrouped and became a sweep force through the villages.

Hicks got himself a gook on operation Arcadia. He shot him from an ambush during Phase I. There wasn't anything unusual about the actual killing of the VC—it was how he looked when Hicks checked him out the next morning.

He shot the VC at about midnight, but we had to wait for daybreak to check the kill-zone of the ambush. Hicks walked down the trail to where the dead gook was splayed across the path. Suddenly we heard, "Jesus Christ, you guys ain't going to believe this. Come here quick!"

We walked to where Hicks was standing in amazement over the dead soldier. He continued to shake his head as he looked at the fallen foe. He wasn't looking at the face or the congealed blood covering the hole in the abdomen, he was staring at the groin.

"The gook died with a hard-on; I can't believe it. Look at the gook dick: deader than shit but pointing to the sky. I can't fuckin believe it."

Sure enough, there it was: a stiff, dead prick tilting to the left. Hicks had shot the VC in the lower abdomen and blood had somehow filled the penis tissue. It was the first time I had seen this phenomenon. Hicks found the anomaly more entertaining than the rest of us did.

I remembered Hicks telling me once that if you put bug juice on your dick, you would get an instant hard-on. With such a lack of entertainment in the field, I could imagine how he discovered that.

Corn Fields and Cane

An incident that happened during Operation Arcadia brought back a memory from my childhood.

I was four years old, and my family lived on the farm across from my grandfather's homestead in northwestern Minnesota. My grandparents were taking care of me while my parents shopped in Thief River Falls, fifty-five miles away. I was alone playing in my grandparents' yard when I decided to walk home.

Since I was only four years old, most of the details were told to me much later, except for the fear that I vividly remember.

Grandpa's house was about half a mile directly across from our house. The two dwellings were connected by a gravel driveway bordered by tall cornfields. Rather than take the road, I decided to walk home through the cornfields. The only thing I can remember was not being able to see anything but round corn stalks. Everything looked the same. I couldn't see either our house or my grandparent's house. I know I kept walking in circles in the forty-acre field. I remember, above all, the youthful panic and fear.

My father later told me that my grandfather spent over two hours searching for me in the field. He couldn't see me, and apparently I wasn't crying so he couldn't hear me either.

Sport, Grandpa's dog, was the hero. He located me in the field and led my anxious grandfather to me.

An incident on Operation Arcadia contained some of the same elements as my cornfield expedition. I had been squad leader for several weeks since Mac had been promoted to platoon sergeant. As squad leader, I had the authority to select the point man. Our squad was accompanied on this specific patrol by Staff Sergeant Patterson who had recently joined the company after a four-year assignment at the federal prison in Portsmouth. We also had an FNG, PFC Schilliman. I put the new guy on point. On the map, our route looked pretty easy, a simple movement from point A to point B.

The first thirty minutes of the patrol were pretty calm. We found a few caves and blew them up. I also found 8400 piasters hidden in a hollow tree. I had no idea how much it was worth. I later turned it over to Mac who in turn gave it to Lieutenant Sloat.

I was in the middle of the squad patrol. SSgt Patterson was in front of me, Hicks behind me. Joe felt bad that I didn't put him on point. Although he was one of our best point men, and knew the area, he also had two purple hearts. He had paid his dues. Joe didn't argue too much when I assigned Schilliman point.

The patrol had entered a large planting of sugar cane that was about twelve feet high, and every stalk was the same size. On the map, the field didn't look that big—at the most, it was two hundred meters square. A river and two man-made canals bordered it. Although we continued to move forward, I had a hunch that we were walking in circles. We had been in a two hundred square meter field much too long. I moved past SSgt. Patterson to Schilliman at point.

"What going on?" I asked.

"Can't keep a line. I take a compass reading and in thirty seconds I'm ninety degrees off." Schilliman was doing his best.

"Keep it up, but get us out of this goddamn bamboo or sugar cane or whatever it is," I said.

The patrol continued, but we were still moving in circles. We had been wandering around in the cane field for almost an hour. Finally, I decided to take point. I took a compass reading, and like

Schilliman said, in seconds I was ninety degrees off. I put the compass in my pocket and decided to move on gut instinct.

I charged forward followed by Hicks and SSgt. Patterson. Schilliman was right, there was nothing to take a compass reading on. Everything was the same color, same height and same diameter. I crashed through the identical stalks; they were like the corn stalks in my grandfather's field sixteen years ago.

After about ten minutes of cursing and thrashing, we broke out of the field into normal jungle. SSgt. Patterson was amazed at how I had managed to take control of the situation and get us out of the field. I didn't tell him that it was a frightened four-year-old who led the way out.

Female VC and The Kill Ratio

We captured the female cadre leader of the area early in the operation. She was surly, beautiful, arrogant and righteous.

Rather than have her bound and safely positioned in the middle of the squad, we decided to have her pay for her sins. We tied a rope around her neck and made her walk point, barefooted. She knew where the booby-traps were, and we would simply walk where she stepped. If she refused to walk down a trail, we avoided that trail. ARVN intelligence later confirmed that she was, in fact, the number one female VC operative in the region. Although ARVN intelligence seemed to be even worse than ours, we wanted to believe them this time.

Operation Arcadia was formally declared a success. Enemy losses were sixteen VC KIA's and fifteen captured VC. We also had captured large quantities of food, weapons, ammunition, and medical supplies.

We lost one KIA and suffered two WIA's. In addition, an amtrac was disabled when it hit a mine. Our overall losses were amazingly low when compared to recent actions.

I felt that the operation was successful, but my criterion for success was simple: nobody I knew got killed. In the short run, the capture of a few weapons and medical supplies may have disrupted the VC and altered immediate goals, but in the long run, it made little difference.

Chapter 26
Operation Trinidad

The leader for the second squad had been killed, so I was temporarily given command of his squad. I had become very attached to my personal floor space and the first squad, so I decided not to move to the second squad's quarters. I had been meritoriously promoted to corporal on December 1st. It felt good. I was now a non-commissioned officer with less than one year of Marine Corps service.

I had only led the second squad for a week when we were notified that we would be participating in Operation Trinidad. Delta Company had been designated as the sweeping force. Our ultimate goal was to drive the NVA and VC located in the Thanh Phong district toward the blocking force dug in along the Song La Tho River. As the surprised and fleeing enemy tried to cross the river, they would be picked off like swimming rats by the allied blocking force that had inconspicuously moved in the night before.

Of course, none of this happened quite like it was supposed to.

It was December 6, 1966, and Operation Trinidad was officially underway. I don't know why we were selected, but the second squad of the first platoon was chosen to walk point for our portion of the battalion-sized operation. Lieutenant Sloat was promoted to 1/1 Combined Action Company Commander shortly before the operation and was replaced by Lieutenant Fooser as Platoon

Commander. I had enormous respect for Lt. Sloat. I knew nothing about Lt. Fooser.

We left the Company compound on the morning of December 6th. Scotty, one of the second squad's fire-team leaders, took point. We were walking southwest down the formerly major road, Highway 4. We passed the spot where the Ontos hit the land mine several weeks earlier. The hole made by the exploding mine was filled with water. Other than that, there was little that distinguished that piece of road from any other.

Our orders were to continue in a southwestern direction on Highway 4, cross a branch of the Song Binh Long River, and stop when we reached the old railroad grade that crossed the highway.

We crossed the river without a problem, but some of the amtracs that carried our supplies had tough going. They were not planning to accompany us on the entire operation, but were scheduled to return to base camp when we reached our initial line of departure (LOD).

The river was about five feet deep so everything quickly became wet. Binoculars were a luxury in a Marine Corps platoon; we had only two pair. I had written my father and instructed him to buy and send me the best pair of binoculars in International Falls. They had arrived a week earlier and quickly proved their worth. The mistake I made on December 6th almost ruined my $39.95 pair of Bushnell's. While crossing the river, I kept my cigarettes and rifle dry, but I forgot about the binoculars hanging around my neck. Although they were the best Riley's Sport Shop had, they were not totally waterproof. I realized my mistake about half way across the river, but it was too late. Water had seeped through the lens seals. Instead of looking through clear glass, the inside of the lens was covered with water vapor.

I stopped the squad when we reached the abandoned railroad bed. Hicks was still my radioman, because my request to have him temporarily assigned to the second squad had been granted. Communication between units in a large and multi-faceted operation is essential. You have to know and trust your radioman.

The long column of Marines stopped when we hit the abandoned railroad bed. We sat and waited. After several hours of waiting we were notified that we would spend the night on the road. We doubled up for night security positions waiting for daybreak. The rain started at 1500 hours and continued all night. Since we were encamped on the roadbed, there weren't any trees to support temporary shelters. When not on watch, we curled up inside our ponchos and slept. The only upside to sleep deprivation, is that you can sleep anywhere, anytime.

In the morning we got the word to walk "on-line" which meant in a lateral line and move north. We would sweep several large villages and many smaller hamlets, most of which were surrounded by large rice paddies. The rice in the paddies looked healthy with fat, plump heads.

Our squad was on the western edge of the 2000-meter on-line assault. Lieutenant Fooser was obsessed with keeping the assault line straight. The muck in the paddies was over our boots, the water knee-high. Walking was difficult and trying to stay on-line was next to impossible. We splashed onward without taking any enemy fire.

At this stage of an action, the average Marine knew nothing about the objectives or goals of the operation. Our personal goal was to complete the operation without getting killed. Our secondary goal was to complete the operation without someone we knew getting killed. Nobody agonized over the geopolitical ramifications of a communist South Vietnam. The only thing we agonized over was trying to keep our cigarettes dry.

We were almost midway between the road we had left and our second LOD. The villages we had walked through had all been empty. This was not a good sign. I had been slogging through the paddies about ten meters behind my partially on-line squad when a Marine from the third squad, directly to my right, started firing his M-14. The guy firing was PFC Hardy, a black Marine who had been with the Company since before Hastings.

He was staggering backward and firing his weapon into the water. I moved as quickly as I could toward him, still unsure what he was shooting at. When I reached him, he was frantically trying to put a fresh magazine in his weapon. His eyes were wide open in white terror.

Hardy was a good Marine. Before being drafted by the Corps, he had been the leader of a successful soul band in South Los Angeles. Now, he was shaking uncontrollably. I glanced down and saw what was causing his distress—a ten–foot poisonous water snake was twisting in agony fifteen feet in front of him. Hardy said the snake had started at him without provocation. He had done what any other Marine would have done—kill the snake before it got to him. It didn't seem to be dead, but we bypassed it and continued northward.

We received no fire during our sweep toward the second LOD, but we heard sporadic shots to our left. The secondary LOD was a large dike on the southern edge of a 1000-meter square rice paddy. When we reached the dike we were ordered to hold up. Our 3000-meter trek had been physically taxing, so we welcomed the chance to rest and have a smoke.

It was only 1600 hours, and the sun had broken through the thick monsoon clouds. We were on the extreme left flank, next to an elevated, but unusable, railroad bed. Five hundred meters north, a railroad bridge that had been operational fifteen years earlier, was a mass of twisted rails pointing toward the clouds. We set in for the night. We would not have the luxury of bamboo saplings to support temporary shelters from our ponchos.

It was still daylight, so I tried to use my foggy binoculars to check out the tree line that would be our destination in the morning. Even though the water had diminished the quality of the picture, I was able to zero in on the tree line 1000 meters away. I was astounded. Enemy troops were moving in what appeared to be a trench line. Not only could I clearly see them, I could see what they were doing. They were busily employed in setting up mortar positions and machine gun placements.

I felt good about what I saw: we knew their positions. In the morning, we could easily call in artillery and air strikes. They were dead meat, but they didn't know it.

Not unexpectedly, it rained all night. After a cold breakfast of a can of beans and weenies and a cup of instant C-rat coffee, we were ready to rock and roll. The artillery and air strikes would soon start kicking ass on the enemy troops in the far tree line.

We waited. We waited some more. No air strikes. No artillery. We didn't panic. We knew that the chain of command was complicated in operations like this. It would come.

It didn't. We got the word to start an on-line assault across the 1000-meter paddy.

This was insane. We had seen the NVA setting-up positions the day before. This was suicide. Who was making these decisions? We were walking into disaster! We felt like WWI troops ordered to charge a fortified trench. Where were the air strikes? What about artillery?

The order was, "Move out!"

We moved out.

Lieutenant Fooser instructed us to cross the paddy in an echelon right – one of the assault formations every Marine learns in AIT. It isn't much different from an on-line assault, except the radioman and grenadier (if you have one) and the squad leader are positioned about ten meters behind the squad.

Everyone was scared shitless. We knew that the enemy had a day to establish mortar and machine gun positions. With no artillery or air strikes to drive them out, they were still there.

We trudged through the mud and water trying to fashion something that resembled an echelon right. We made it to the middle of the massive paddy without receiving any enemy fire. Maybe they had left during the night? We were trying desperately to put a positive spin on our situation. In the middle of the paddy, at coordinate BT 995595, my squad became the target.

We heard the thump of the mortars first, and then the .50 caliber machine guns opened up. Two guns were positioned atop the abandoned railroad grade. RPG's were landing randomly around us. We were in the water with nothing to hide behind—exposed and vulnerable. Two months earlier, we had caught a squad of VC in the middle of a rice paddy without cover. We had annihilated them. Today the roles were reversed.

Two mortar rounds and several rifle grenades landed in the middle of my squad. The NVA had a day to set up their mortars and the middle of the rice paddy had been accurately calibrated. The .50 caliber guns on the railroad bed continued firing. We were being cut apart.

The first barrage of mortars and rifle grenades took a horrendous toll on my squad. I could see at least five wounded Marines flailing in the water. Several looked seriously wounded and two of them appeared unconscious.

My first concern was that the wounded would drown in the two-feet deep water. I moved toward the fallen Marines, while the .50 caliber gun continued to fire at us, one shot at a time. The enemy gunners were not wasting ammunition—they were being deliberate and exacting with each shot. When the large caliber slug hit the water around us, a mini geyser of paddy water erupted. I tried to drag the wounded to different positions to make it more difficult for the gunner to zero in on a specific target.

Those of us on the western edge of the assault line had taken the brunt of the enemy attack. I could see the Marines on my right moving toward the tree line, our objective. My squad had been left alone and unprotected in the middle of the paddy, without a corpsman, and with five casualties.

I wiped some moisture off my neck and chin and saw that it was blood. I could also see my bloody knee, exposed through the ripped utility trousers. The front of my left thigh was throbbing, although no blood was visible. The only damage was to the extra loaded magazine that I carried in the left cargo pocket of my utilities. It was bent and dented, unusable. Apparently, it had taken the impact of a large piece of shrapnel. It probably saved my leg.

I moved between the two seriously injured, unconscious Marines, frantically trying to keep their heads above water. I tried to prop them up with their backpacks. The other three wounded Marines were conscious, so at least I didn't have to worry about them drowning. One, however, was bleeding profusely. I had used all available battle dressings and patched up the wounds as best I could with what I had.

As the rest of the company assaulted the tree line, I spotted the two downed choppers about three hundred meters to my right front. One was a medevac chopper; the other was a dual rotor Chinook that had been brought in to retrieve the downed medevac. Before we started our on-line assault across the paddy, we had witnessed the downing of the Chinook. It was hovering two hundred feet above the crash site, when it too, was hit. It spun in slow motion as it plunged downward into the mud and water.

We were now the only element of the assault force left in the paddy. I knew that the rest of the assault force had made it to the tree line and, hopefully, had secured it. Hicks was frantically trying to contact someone, anyone. The fucking radio wasn't working again.

I moved from wounded Marine to wounded Marine. Now, three were unconscious. After about thirty minutes, a corpsman from the second platoon finally made his way back to our position. By this time, the .50 caliber rounds and mortars had stopped. The tree line apparently had been secured.

"Has a medevac been called?" I yelled.

"Yes, one's been called, but they're worried about the LZ. Two choppers have been shot down trying to land in this paddy today."

My response was emotional, "They've *got* to get one in here! I've got three guys in tough shape. Five total that need to get out."

"Shit, I know. I don't have anything to say about what goes or comes. We got a bad situation, but I'm fucking helpless. Only thing I can do is call for them. If they come or not is out of my control."

I knew the corpsman was right. He didn't have the power to direct anything. If he had that authority, a medevac would be on the way. I certainly didn't hold him responsible.

"What happened on the other end?" I asked.

"Not much, only one casualty—Hardy got killed. Took a .50 caliber slug right between the eyes. Other than that, resistance was light."

Hardy was dead. I couldn't believe it. He had been terrified by the water snake, but an NVA bullet got him instead. Shit! Good guy, Hardy. Good Marine.

Finally a medevac landed between the downed choppers and us. Why couldn't they land closer to us? It would be a challenge to get the wounded to the chopper since there were only three Marines and an exhausted corpsman physically capable of carrying the wounded. Carrying, dragging and dropping, we managed to get them to the chopper and load them.

The medevac would only take the wounded. It didn't have room for Hardy. We were assured that another chopper would return for Hardy's body.

We had to carry Hardy in a poncho to the tree line. He was a fairly big guy, and we took turns carrying his body until we reached the NVA trenches where we would spend the night. They were better fortified than anything we had spent a night in except for the crematorium. We would sleep tonight where the enemy had slept the night before. They were gone—either dead or hiding somewhere else.

The night in the NVA trench was not a good experience. None of us felt comfortable with Hardy lying next to us. It just didn't seem right. His eyes were open and nobody had the courage to close them. His body had fallen out of the poncho several times on the way to the tree line. We felt terrible. We knew he was dead, and whether he fell out of the poncho or not really didn't mean shit, but we still felt bad. We felt like we weren't taking proper care of his body even though we were trying our damndest.

We moved north the next morning, but we didn't move far. A unit from the 26th Marines ran into some bad shit. They were probably fighting the troops that had trapped us in the paddy. We only moved about 500 meters before we were told to set into night defensive positions. Hardy was still with us.

My jungle utility trousers were once again ripped. Since we didn't wear underwear, my dick was visible to anyone who bothered to look, but that number was probably small. We all had concerns much greater than someone's exposed dick. Apparently, Lieutenant Fooser didn't feel the same way.

We were scheduled to get our first re-supply chopper in three days. Not only would the chopper bring in mail, C-rats and supplies, but it would also take Hardy to Graves Registration. The rumor was that the chopper was also bringing in a CBS news crew with Dan Rather. We felt honored by his rumored visit.

It was a hot LZ. The chopper carrying the CBS crew came under intense fire as it landed. We had set up a security perimeter around the LZ, but because of the canopied jungle, we couldn't see where the firing was coming from. When the chopper was above the trees, it took intense fire but landed safely. The supplies were dropped, we loaded Hardy, and the chopper left with the CBS news crew safely aboard. Nobody had seen Dan Rather.

In addition to mail, ammunition and C-rats, a bundle of jungle utility trousers were aboard the chopper. Lieutenant Fooser grabbed one and headed for my squad.

"Tornes, get over here!"

I responded immediately. "Yes, Sir. What do you want, Sir?"

"Here, take these, I'm tired of looking at your dick."

He tossed me a pair of new jungle utility trousers. Like the ripped pair I was wearing, they were size small for waists 26 to 29 inches. I had never seen a larger size distributed in the field. I was sure they made them, but they never got down to our level.

I thanked him for the trousers, and returned to my squad. Actually, I didn't have a squad anymore. There were just three of us left. Since our number was so low, we were told to join Corporal Brown's squad.

The rest of the operation was routine. We searched the abandoned huts. Those that had been used as gun emplacements were torched. When a certain kind of bamboo burns, it pops like fireworks or gunshots. Those who experience this for the first time are understandably apprehensive—they think they are taking fire.

We made it to the Song La Tho River, where the main blocking force had been placed. I heard later that the majority of enemy troops had escaped before the blocking force was in place. The few that had not were killed.

We crossed the river after being informed that an amtrac detachment from 1/26 would bring us back to base. It was undoubtedly the best news we had heard for six days. After an hour's wait, a convoy of tracs arrived and we clambered aboard and headed for home.

The next day the scorecard for Operation Trinidad was released:

USMC   KIA   1

            WIA   20

ENEMY   KIA   32

            KIA probable   10

            WIA probable   7

The only Marine KIA on the operation had been Hardy. The majority of the WIA's had been on the western end of the sweep force. My squad had six of the entire operation's WIA count. My wounds were superficial, but I would still get a Purple Heart. Hardy would get the same Purple Heart, but he was dead. Hardy was older than most of us; he would have been twenty-five years old on December 19th. His wife would receive a $10,000 government life insurance check and a posthumous Purple Heart. The insurance amount hadn't changed since WWII. I remember Dad saying he had a $10,000 government life insurance policy during the war. It could buy the farm in 1943, but not today.

Doc said he heard I had been nominated for the Bronze Star for my efforts to keep the wounded alive while under fire during Operation Trinidad. I never heard any more about it. I didn't receive the medal and it didn't matter. I had done what any Marine would have done in similar circumstances.

Rumors of a Christmas truce spread through the company. The recent history of multi-lateral truces was not very good. Marine patrols were instructed not to fire on enemy forces unless they were fired upon first. Generally that's what happened anyway, so a directive allowing only retaliatory fire seemed pointless.

I was back with the first squad and functioning as squad leader. Technically, my promotion to corporal was probationary until January 1st, but my pay increase became effective December 1st.

The increase in my monthly check was less than $50. My base pay was now $155 a month. When you added the $75 combat pay and the $45 overseas pay, my total monthly gross was $275. That broke down to $68.75 a week and for a twenty-four hour workday, about forty cents an hour. Not too bad. I was moving up the ladder.

I felt at home back with the first squad and the Marines who shared my war. In mid December, Mac was awarded the Bronze Star. It wasn't awarded for any specific heroic act, but rather for an entire tour of heroic and often overlooked actions. He had been a pillar of stability in a fluid and uncertain environment.

Neither Operation Trinidad nor Operation Arcadia will ever be listed in a Marine Corps textbook of exemplary military operations. On the other hand, both operations were successful because the loss of Marines was minimal. More enemy munitions and equipment were captured on Arcadia, but more permanent enemy fortifications were destroyed during Trinidad.

Both operations were cooperative efforts between American and ARVN forces and involved Marine companies from several battalions. A common thread between both operations was that neither had an element of surprise. It was obvious that the NVA and VC forces knew in advance the general operational objectives of both actions. We never knew for sure but we all suspected that certain ARVN or PF forces shared what they knew about the operations with the enemy.

Chapter 27
Dien Ban Memories

In the course of a person's life, there are occurrences that become permanently imbedded in the memory. During my six weeks at Dien Ban, several such indelible events took place.

Around and Around

Shortly before Christmas, a sergeant major from the commandant's office arrived at Delta Company's field headquarters. His primary purpose was to grade our company's combat-readiness and effectiveness. In order to fairly evaluate us, he was to accompany us on one of our routine search and destroy patrols. My squad was selected for the patrol that Captain Kelly had plotted.

When Lieutenant Fooser briefed me, I couldn't believe what I heard. First of all, it was a roving night patrol. Second, it was longer than a routine patrol. And finally, it sent our undermanned squad, with the sergeant major, into the middle of an area that everyone knew was an NVA stronghold. Captain Kelly appeared to be trying to impress the sergeant major with the length and danger of the patrol. In the process, he was probably going to kill the sergeant major. The patrol was suicide.

I decided to poll the members of my squad to see what their opinions were. After a brief discussion, everyone agreed that it would be a reckless risk to follow the pre-assigned route of the patrol. The squad members unanimously approved an alternative plan.

We left the perimeter at 2200 hours and moved down the trail in a westerly direction toward the first checkpoint. After reaching it, we called in our position and trekked onward. The second checkpoint was about five hundred meters south. To get there we had to cross a huge rice paddy with thigh-deep mud. Our progress was slow but deliberate. We called in our second position and moved toward the third.

Because of booby-traps, we walked through the paddy mud instead of on the trail. This, of course, required twice as much energy. Everyone was tired, but relieved that we hadn't taken any fire. At 0100 we reached our last checkpoint and changed direction once again. We headed back to camp. It had been an unremarkable patrol. We had encountered no enemy, triggered no booby-traps, and gone nowhere.

Rather than go on a suicide mission and endanger the sergeant major, we had re-designed the patrol route. We were never farther than five hundred meters from the perimeter. We had hiked to a point three hundred meters away and from there we continued to walk in large circles. At the end of three hours, everyone was disoriented, especially our guest. The middle-aged sergeant major was almost incoherent from exhaustion and oblivious to where we were. His safety was our main concern, and he would never know just how far we went to protect him.

At 0130 we notified Delta One's radioman that we were entering the perimeter. We dropped the bleary-eyed sergeant major off at the schoolhouse before returning to our position. After several hours of sleep, we were once again ready to serve the Corps.

The entire squad was concerned that our bogus patrol would be discovered, and this concern intensified the next day when I got word to report to the platoon commander. As I walked through the mud toward the company HQ, I was mentally rehearsing what I would say if the legitimacy of last night's patrol were challenged.

The captain, the lieutenant and the still weary-looking sergeant major were gazing at a map as I entered the building. Not a good sign. Lieutenant Fooser looked up from the map.

"Tornes, sergeant major said you did an admirable job leading last night's patrol." The lieutenant smiled as he congratulated me. Captain Kelly said nothing as he continued to look at the map.

"Thank you Sir," I answered. "It was a pretty basic patrol. Didn't take any fire or anything."

I returned to the squad with the good news: our deception had been successful.

Did You Get Hit?

Joe was on point and I took the position immediately behind him as the patrol moved out.

It was another ordinary patrol. We took fire, returned fire, called in artillery, and moved on. We were hit several times during our three-hour outing, and I sensed a tension in Joe. He had five months left on his tour. This was supposed to be his safe time. You seemed more susceptible at two points—early on in your tour and then later, when you were short.

We had to cross the Song Vinh Dien River and traverse a large flooded rice paddy before we hit the main road back to camp. I passed word back to hold up. Everyone dropped to a one knee down position. I walked to Joe at the head of the patrol.

"Joe, we gotta talk."

"What's wrong?"

"You've got to get out of the field. You're all fucked-up and jittery. Not good, Joe. You could get the big one the way you're wandering around. You've got to get out of the field."

"Yeah, I know," Joe apologized. "Can't seem to keep it all together. My mind's wandering. I don't know what's wrong." He stared off in the distance—feeling stupid, I could tell.

"I've got a plan. A plan that will get you out of this place alive and in one piece."

"What's that?" Joe's interest was obvious.

"We'll find the right spot and wound you, a real minor wound, but still a purple heart, then you'll be out of here. You want to try?"

"Yeah, I suppose it would be okay. What'll you use?"

"First we find a place where you can protect your body–like a big tree or a ravine. Then you lie down and stick up your leg and foot. I take a grenade, pull the pin, and throw it about twenty-five meters away. The grenade blows-up, one or two small pieces of shrapnel hit your leg and you're outta here."

"Sounds okay to me," Joe said.

"Can't tell anybody; we'd be fucking court-martialed," I cautioned.

"Yeah, I know."

I gave the word to move out and the patrol continued. Joe wasn't looking for booby-traps or VC, he was searching for the perfect spot to get wounded.

Joe's hand went up and he motioned me forward. We had crossed the river and were on an east-west trail. As I approached Joe, I saw why he had stopped. About ten meters in front of him a large tree lay across the trail. The tree had a diameter of at least thirty inches and would be a very adequate protective shield.

"Okay Joe, let's get it over with and get you back to Brooklyn," I said, as I positioned him behind the tree. The rest of the patrol was strung out to our rear and out of sight.

Joe was on his side with the calf and foot of his left leg above the tree trunk. I pulled the pin of a grenade and heaved it down the trail before joining Joe next to the tree. The grenade exploded and thousands of small pieces of wire shrapnel peppered the kill zone.

"Joe, did you get hit?"

"Don't know. Don't feel anything."

"You had to get hit–shrapnel was flying everywhere! Get your leg up here. Let me look at it," I said.

We knew the rest of the patrol would respond to the explosion by advancing to the front of the column. We had little time to examine Joe's leg.

By now, we were both standing and I had pulled Joe's trouser leg up. I searched in vain for any sign of shrapnel. I found none.

"Jesus Christ," I muttered. "We can't even hit ourselves when we're trying to."

Although what we tried to do, and failed at, was basically the same act that the chickenshit corpsman had done when he put a .45 slug through the top of his foot, it felt totally different. Joe had been in the field for eight months and had two purple hearts. The corpsman had been in the field for less than a day. He tried to avoid combat by shooting himself. I was trying to save Joe's life. It had been my idea, not Joe's. With two purple hearts, Joe's luck could be used up. I didn't want him to tempt fate and try for three. Our actions were easy to rationalize.

Langley was the first to our position.

"What happened? Heard an explosion."

"Nothing big," I said. Gooks had a grenade rigged with a trip-wire, but the grenade was too far away. We didn't get hit."

Joe took point for the short walk back to the company area. He would have to wait for his third Purple Heart.

Missing a Toe

During the month of December, our platoon received several replacements. They were assigned as needed with the most under-manned squads getting priority. The first squad received only one replacement during December—a tall skinny PFC from one of the New England states. He was with us so briefly, that I'm not sure I ever knew his name.

It was the first patrol for the new guy. We began by crossing the river, which meant we started out wet. Early in the patrol, we took several sniper rounds. We didn't bother to return fire. We just kept walking. It was the ultimate insult to the sniper.

The route of our patrol was a sweeping arc ending up back where we started. We were on the back half of the arc when we were hit by heavy machine gun fire. This attack wasn't ignored. We responded in a big way. The initial fire had pinned the rear element of the patrol behind a dike where they continued to receive the brunt of the attack. Someone behind the dike was call-ing, "Corpsman up!" I wondered who had been hit. I knew it wasn't Joe. He was next to me.

I plotted the coordinates, and had Hicks call for an arty mission. Almost immediately, I heard the whistling of the 105's heading for their target. The first volley landed exactly where I wanted it. A second volley followed. The machine gun stopped. Maybe we got it.

The patrol regrouped to assess damage. We had taken one WIA, the new guy. He had been trapped behind the dike by the initial machine gun fire. His wound was minor but unusual. One of the machine gun slugs had cleanly blown off the little toe of his right foot. The bleeding was minimal, and Doc had the foot bandaged by the time I got to them.

"Hey, Buddy. You're going home. This is the million-dollar wound," Doc said to the wounded Marine.

"Do we need a medevac Doc," I asked?

"Naw. It really isn't too bad. We're not far from base and he can walk on his heel. Why don't you see if you can find a branch or something he can use as a crutch?" Doc suggested.

Someone found a piece of wood for a crutch, and the patrol moved on with the new guy hobbling along on his heel. When we got to the company area, an amtrac took him back to battalion headquarters. The doctors at BAS would patch him up and ship him out. He would soon be out of combat and out of the Corps.

Everything happened as expected. The new guy was taken to BAS. The doctors cleaned and re-bandaged his toe and assigned him a bed in the ward. He was scheduled to go to NSA later that day. From there, he would be on his way home.

But the plan didn't play out. He died. He was lying on his cot in the small ward with the million-dollar wound, and he died. Apparently, neither the corpsmen nor the doctors noticed that he was slipping into shock. So he died—killed by a missing little toe.

The squad reacted to his death with amazement rather than sadness or grief.

Grapes of Wrath

John Steinbeck's visit to the platoon was a non-event for many. I was surprised by the large number of Marines who had no idea who he was. Apparently, they hadn't read *The Grapes of Wrath* or *Of Mice And Men* in high school English.

The platoon commanders knew who John Steinbeck was and you could tell they felt honored by his visit. Captain Kelly spent the most time with our guest. He even arranged a special patrol that would include Steinbeck, and, of course, himself. Nobody could figure out why the Captain seemed to be sucking up to Steinbeck until we found out he was on assignment for *Newsday*. Captain Kelly probably figured that if Steinbeck wrote something favorable about him, his promotional opportunities would improve.

Several months later, Floyd Patterson, the former heavyweight boxing champion, visited the battalion. Everyone knew who he was.

Roving Night Patrols

During our six-week assignment at Dien Ban, I did something that I still question. I know others did the same thing, but I still wonder if it was right.

Our squad had been assigned a roving night patrol, not an ambush. Instead of staying in one place waiting for the enemy, we would be on the move and subject to all the dangers of a day patrol with the added peril that we couldn't see. We had been assigned to circle the outer edge of the perimeter looking for unusual movements and situations.

We had almost completed the circuit around the outer perimeter when we approached a hut that was barely outside the concertina wire. We heard people talking inside the hooch. We were surprised because they were talking in English. Before going in, I announced our presence and our desire to enter. I was shocked by what I saw.

A squad-sized patrol was scattered around on the earthen floor of the hut. Some were sleeping; some were awake either bullshitting or smoking cigarettes.

"Who the fuck are you guys?" I asked.

"Hey, Man, who the fuck do you think we are? Ho Chi Minh's personal guard." The comment was followed by a round of loud laughter.

"You're not supposed to be at this co-ordinate," I said, still unsure what I had walked into.

"Get real, Man. What do you think this is? We're not going out on the night patrol we've been assigned. It's fuckin suicide. We don't have a corpsman, our radio works about half the time, and the area we were supposed to go into is crawling with NVA. Do you think we're fuckin stupid? Would you go under those conditions?"

What he said made sense, but it still wasn't right.

"You won't report us to the Big Guy, will you?"

The reference was to Captain Kelly. I didn't respond, just left the hut. The hooch they were in was less than 200 meters from where Captain Kelly was sleeping.

A week or so later, I was faced with a similar scenario. My squad had been assigned an all-night ambush about 4000 meters from base. To get to the ambush site, we would have to cross a major river and several raging streams. Our ultimate destination was a crossroads located near the villages of Tay Dang Ban (1) and Bac Dong Bai.

The area was an NVA and VC stronghold. I would not have a corpsman assigned to the patrol. There were too few corpsmen to handle all the patrols and ambushes, and the ones we had were working overtime.

I remember the night like it was yesterday. The rain was almost horizontal, driven by an unusually strong easterly wind. Nobody looked excited about the assignment. We would be nearly five miles away without a corpsman. If we took a casualty, the chances of getting a medevac into the area were almost zero because of the weather. I had a decision to make and it wouldn't be easy. If I hadn't stumbled across the patrol holed-up in a hooch the week before, it wouldn't have been an issue. We would go.

This was an agonizing decision to make. It challenged the core of Marine values and training. I would be violating a direct order, and a court-martial could be the consequence. I compromised. I went halfway, placing our ambush on a trail near the village of Dong Van Song. We were midway between the CP and our designated ambush position. It was still a good ambush, but closer to the CP if something happened.

Not having a corpsman bothered me more than anything else. At least from our halfway position, we could carry any casualty to the company command post. Nobody disagreed with my decision. The night was quiet and nothing came down the trail.

I was certain that any smart NVA or VC was sleeping in a dry hut that night. Only stupid Americans would spend the night watching a trail that wouldn't be used until morning.

Christmas and New Years

It was the first Christmas in my life with a temperature above freezing. A year ago the temperature had been thirty-four degrees below zero when the Greyhound bus left International Falls, Minnesota.

We were on a six-man ambush. We had set up an L-shaped configuration with two teams. I was with Wilson and Hicks. Langley, Sage and Joe made up the other team. Wilson was the only one in our threesome who had a working watch, so it was passed from man to man during the night.

The night sky was almost cloudless with Christmas stars twinkling overhead. You rarely saw the stars during the monsoons. Usually, it rained all night and the cloud cover was heavy. Tonight was different. I thought about home and my family.

Christmas eves were always the same in a positive way. Grandma and Grandpa Ostgarden would come to our house. Dad would cut a tree from the woods behind the house and Mom would decorate it with the same lights and bulbs she used every year. Under the tree there would be eight little piles of wrapped gifts that my sisters had sorted and stacked.

Everything we ate for dinner was white. The main entrées were lutefisk and roast pork and, of course, there would be mashed potatoes, gravy and Mom's delicious, homemade lefse. For vegetables, we would have a creamy cole slaw and creamed peas. Homemade white bread was always on the table next to the freshly churned butter. Desserts were less predictable. We would either get pumpkin pie with whipped cream or rice pudding covered with sugar and cream.

I would kill for a meal like that now.

During dinner, my sisters and I had difficulty focusing on the meal. Instead, we thought about our pile of gifts in the next room. Dad seemed to take his time eating, and we couldn't leave the table until everyone was done and he excused us. Sometimes he would add to our agony by insisting that we wash the dishes before opening gifts. That was too much to take. Mom usually came to our rescue saying she would clean up later.

My hour was over. I gave Wilson his watch back when I woke him. I quickly fell asleep on the wet ground. Two hours later, the ambush was over and we walked back to camp.

Our squad hadn't gone giftless this year. Ara Parseghian, Sage's uncle who was the head football coach at Notre Dame, sent a huge box of goodies. Sage shared his gift with the rest of us. We ate the cookies, fruitcake and candy in minutes. We saved nothing for tomorrow.

Chapter 28
Animation and Insubordination

On January 2, 1967, we turned over our company patrol base to Alpha Company who had just finished a two month assignment at the Military Police Battalion in Da Nang. Their new assignment would be considerably different from running sweeps through dogpatch looking for Marines in skivvie houses.

We moved back to 1/1 Battalion Headquarters. This was luxury—cold beer, warm chow, and movies at night. There was even a mini-PX with a barbershop and a gift shop that was run by Vietnamese with Lt. Col. Bell's consent.

The only films I remember seeing were reruns of the TV hit series, *Combat*, and cartoons. We had fun jeering and screaming insults at the *Combat* actors as they fought their entertaining war. The cartoons were an insult. We were adults and Marines. I didn't care for cartoons when I was a kid, and I sure as hell didn't care for them now.

As usual, nobody knew exactly how long we were going to stay at battalion. The old rumor of an "Okinawan Float Phase" resurfaced. We also heard that we would provide perimeter security for the Air Base in Da Nang. Both options were acceptable, and neither would probably ever happen.

I had been insulated from racial issues most of my life. When I joined the Corps, everyone was treated the same. In boot camp everyone was equally abused. In ITR and Staging Battalion we all seemed to be on the same team. We had the same primary goal—staying alive.

The Corps was a microcosm of America. I had trained with Blacks, Asian Americans, American Indians, Hispanics, Peruvians, Canadians, Jews, Gentiles, WASPs, and rednecks. Race had not seemed to be an issue, but it was.

In the field and in combat, an unusual camaraderie flourishes. You depend on your fellow Marines, and they depend on you. Skin color, religion or education has no effect on what you do or do not do for each other. On the other hand, when you are assigned to the rear or are in a non-combative status, this feeling of dependency weakens. You tend to fraternize with those Marines who share similar traits—race, educational level or comparable upbringing.

Groups of homogeneous Marines were most visible at the Enlisted Men's Club. Blacks would be together, talking and listening to soul music on a portable phonograph. In another section of the club, Hispanic Marines would congregate, drink beer and bullshit in Spanish. Several tables would be packed with good ol' boys from the South who would listen to country western. The enlisted Marines who had college degrees would be off to the side discussing issues that didn't interest the rest of us. Headquarters' Marines drank with other Headquarters' Marines. Motor Transport Marines socialized with other Motor T guys. The ultra-religious Marines weren't even at the club; they were back in their tents studying the Bible.

To me, it seemed simple—you tended to seek out and socialize with those most like yourself. But in reality, it wasn't that simple.

Shortly after arriving at battalion, our platoon received replacements for the Marines we had lost during the previous month. My squad got two. Both were black, had been busted to private, and were coming from the brig in Da Nang.

Private Alvin Jones was the bigger of the two. Jones was from Washington D.C., at least six-foot-six and must have weighed in at two-eighty. According to Jones, he was considered a real mean dude back on the streets in D.C. His arrogant, tough-guy, jive-ridden attitude didn't sit well with the squad.

Before going to the brig, Jones had been assigned to a rear unit in Da Nang. He hadn't spent a day in the field, but talked like a cross between Audie Murphy and Mohammad Ali. We didn't have to wait long to find out how tough he really was.

It was Jones' third day in the field when he faced hostile fire for the first time. Our platoon-sized patrol had come under heavy small arms and rifle grenade fire as we swept through the village of Cuo Lu. The initial attack had taken a heavy toll: two WIA's and one KIA. The multiple cries for "Corpsman up!" coupled with an intense volume of incoming small arms fire wasn't anything like the streets of D.C. Jones froze. He wouldn't or couldn't move. He had a death grip on his M-14, but it wasn't firing.

"Jones, you got to get to cover!" I was screaming in his ear. His face was blank and without emotion. He didn't respond to my shouting. There we were in the thick of the fire and this FNG wouldn't move.

"Jones, you stupid Fuck! You want to get killed, it's okay with me, but I ain't gonna die here with you!"

Something clicked in Jones' head. His eyes came alive. He had been jump-started. We both ran for cover and found it in a nearby drainage ditch.

The transformation was immediate. I had heard about battlefield religious conversions, but this wasn't religion. Jones became a courageous and productive field Marine. He was accepted by the squad and became one of us.

Unfortunately, he didn't last long in the field. A week later, he took two rounds in his thigh. His femur was shattered and he almost bled to death before we got him out. He probably got a medical discharge from the Corps and a disability rating. He may have returned to the streets of D.C., but now he really *was* tough, not just jive-talk tough.

My second black replacement, Private Steven Fortnier, presented a more ominous challenge. Although he was technically assigned to the weapons platoon, he was our machine gunner. Unlike Jones' ebony black color, Fortnier's skin was light brown, almost dark tan. His features were more Caucasian than black, but he was black and proud of it. Unlike Jones, Fortnier had been in the field with 2/1. The rumor was that he had served time in the brig for assaulting an officer.

Private Fortnier was from Detroit. You could see the loathing in his eyes. It was hard for me to understand. I hadn't done anything to him that could have caused his hatred. I finally figured it out. He didn't hate me, personally—he just hated *all* Whites.

The first couple of patrols with Fortnier were without incident. On our third action, we were the designated blocking force for a joint Marine/ARVN sweep of Phong Ho. I had nothing but negative feelings about Phong Ho. Our platoon, as well as the battalion, had suffered horrendous casualties every time we ventured there.

Our orders were to set up blocking positions along the southern edge of the village. As squad leader, it was my responsibility to designate where each individual position would be. All were now in place with the exception of the machine gun. I called for Fortnier. He didn't respond. I called again. Still no response. I walked to where he was standing and said, "Didn't you hear me calling for you? We have to get your gun set in."

Fortnier looked up. His eyes were pure rancor as he started speaking. "Listen here, Mother Fucker, nobody tell me what to do or when to do it – specially some white, mother-fuckin' corporal. *Nobody* tell me what to do!"

I could handle his verbal insubordination, but what he had done with the M-60 gun was a different story. He was holding his gun with both hands when I first approached him. While calling me a white mother-fucker, he pointed the gun at my chest. His finger was on the trigger as his hostile eyes glared at mine. He moved the muzzle of the gun closer and upward to a position three inches from my neck. He said nothing as we continued to stare each other down.

"Just take your gun and set it up on that old bunker hill," I said, pointing to a sand pile thirty meters away.

He dropped the muzzle of his gun and slowly gathered his gear together. PFC Ledesma, another new guy who had been assigned to Fortnier's team, helped in the move. I turned and walked away.

Never before had I been threatened by a fellow Marine. The incident destroyed my idealistic perception of Marine Corps solidarity and trust. I was shaken, but I tried to hide it. I fooled everybody but Joe. He had watched the confrontation from his position twenty meters away and was headed toward me.

"Gar, what the fuck was going on between you and the black gunner?"

"Son-of-a-bitch threatened me with the M-60. Said he wasn't taking orders from any white, mother fucking corporal. Thought he was going to kill me, Joe. Fucking gun was 'this' close to my neck."

"What are ya gonna do," Joe asked?

"Not going to do anything yet. But tomorrow I'll go to the lieutenant. Bad enough having every other gook in the country wanting to kill your ass, but when your own guys want to waste you—that's too much. Fucking unbelievable."

I had one request of Joe.

"If we get into some shit today, and everyone starts shooting – keep an eye on Fortnier. If you see him swing the M-60 toward my position, shoot the motherfucker because he's going to try to kill me."

"No problem, Gar, I'll cover your back. He won't get you first." Joe's answer to my request had been without hesitation.

During the mayhem of a typical firefight, nobody really knows everything that's going on. Bullets are usually flying in all directions, grenades and rockets are exploding all around, chopper gunships are often overhead, and calls for "Corpsman up" are the rule. In all the confusion, it would be very easy to shoot one of your comrades without detection.

The next day, I went to the platoon sergeant and the lieutenant. I told them what had happened, omitting, of course, the contingency plan Joe and I had agreed on. Fortnier was transferred out of our platoon immediately. I didn't hear where he went, and I didn't care. I just didn't want him attached to my squad.

Dysentery and Discourse

The re-supply amtrac brought C-rats, ammo, water and, best of all, mail. I received two letters, one from Mom and Dad and one from Andrea, my pen pal from a southern college. Although her letter was generic and not a bit romantic, I read it twice. Wilson also received a letter from his infatuated southern belle. He was holding the letter in one hand as he shook his head.

"Hey, Wilson, what'd your love-struck honey say this time?"

We had continued to compare our letters since the beginning. His gal pal initiated romantic gush whereas mine described sorority events.

"She shit-canned me, Gary," Wilson answered. "I finally told her I was black and that ended it. Look at this: it has only three lines. She says, 'I hope you understand. But I can't write to you again. Do not write to me.' I wonder if she'll get back together with the fiancé she dumped?"

I wasn't surprised. I had been the one who persuaded Wilson to continue the correspondence. I guessed what would happen when he eventually told her he was black, but I wanted him to continue to receive letters as long as he could.

We continued to run patrols and ambushes out of the battalion area. During Operation Arcadia, I contracted amoebic dysentery and so did a lot of other Marines.

It rained each night and everyone's dysentery worsened. There were times when a patrol would have to stop every few minutes to let someone take a shit.

The severe stomach cramps doubled you over, and your asshole was raw from overuse. Sometimes, when you were set in a night ambush and couldn't move, you would just shit in your trousers. You were wet anyway, and a little more liquid made little difference. The rain and water you laid in would wash your trousers before you got back to base.

Hicks was promoted to lance corporal, and reassigned to the platoon commander. His primary responsibility was to monitor and operate the lieutenant's radio. His promotion probably saved his life in that he wouldn't have to go out on squad-sized patrols and ambushes anymore.

Kent Knapp was my new radioman. I had met him when he was the company clerk and liked him. Although still a PFC, Kent had been with the company three months. He was a twenty-three-year-old, college-educated, enlisted Marine. Because of his education and ability to write, he had been the administrative and personnel clerk for Delta Company. He had been relatively safe in his position, but he wanted to be in the field.

Like Lieutenant Sloat, Kent was from California. He had graduated from the University of California, Santa Barbara. His pleasant manner and confident maturity made him a popular addition to the squad.

Not only was Kent easy to talk to, he discussed issues that weren't normally the topic of conversation among field Marines. He had the ability to ask questions that forced you to put some thought into your answer. You were required to support and defend what you said. You couldn't simply answer, "Fuckin A." I was surprised by my answers. They made me sound smarter and better educated than I really was. We all felt good around Kent.

The first half of January was about the same as the first half of December except that we now had hot chow, cold beer and a dry place to sleep every third night. Our squad's tent was directly across from the chow hall. The food was hot, greasy, plentiful and good. We usually managed to get at least one chow hall meal a day.

Our mission remained the same—conduct daily patrols, nightly ambushes and an occasional battalion operation. During this time, we participated in Operation Shasta I and II. Both operations were marginally successful, killing more of the enemy than they killed of us.

Delta's tactical area of responsibility included old haunts as well as new territory. The horseshoe was still a hotspot, as were the hamlets of Lai Nghi, Co Luu and Trem Tu. We had forty-five casualties during the first two weeks of the New Year. That was an attrition rate of about twenty-five percent, slightly higher than the previous month.

I was changing. The man I had been six months earlier was now a stranger who I would never see again. I had seen a similar metamorphosis happen to others. Now it was happening to me.

In my opinion, there are four distinct phases of a combat tour. The first is the "don't know shit" phase. You are totally overwhelmed by all that's happening. You know nothing. Everything seems like mass confusion. You seldom see the enemy. It is hot, wet and miserable. You don't know anyone. You feel lost and alone. You plod along on patrols, scared and anxious, not knowing what to expect. The length of this phase depends upon how much action your unit sees—the more action, the shorter the phase. It is during this time that you have the best chance of becoming a casualty.

I call the second phase, "I'd-give-my-left-nut-for-a-job-in-the-rear." You've been in action, maybe killed a few gooks, saw fellow Marines get killed or maimed, lived on C-rats and slept on the ground for months. You've lost weight and are perpetually tired. You dread patrols and ambushes. The war seems like a waste. It also seems obvious we'll never win. A basic mathematical calculation predicts that there ain't no way you're going to make it for nine or ten more months. You'd take almost any job in the rear that would increase your odds of survival except one in Graves Registration.

The third phase is "I-don't-give-a-shit." You have more or less accepted your fate. You're not going to get a job in the rear and you still have more than half your tour left. If you're going to get killed, you're going to get killed. You often act with reckless abandon—or maybe it's confidence. You've been tested and you've passed. You don't have to prove anything to anyone, including yourself. You've become fatalistic. You know the odds don't favor you, but you don't give a shit. Statistically, I believe that this is the safest phase.

The last phase is "made-it-this-far-maybe-I-can-make-it-the-whole-way." It typically starts around the tenth month. You've seen a lot of Marines killed or maimed, but you've made it so far. Maybe you'll be lucky and make it out in one piece. You become overly cautious, you move more tentatively when patrolling. Frequently, you daydream about home and family. You become easily distracted and less aware of your surroundings. This phase is second only to the "don't-know-shit" phase for mortality.

I had been in phase three since late October. I didn't give a shit.

January 16, 1967

After eating a meal of fried meat, instant potatoes, corn and bread, Kent and I walked back to our tent to have our after dinner cigarette. His cot was next to mine. We would lie in opposite directions so we could see each other as we talked. I lit a Salem. Kent lit a Kent.

"Know what Gary, I'm kind of special," Kent said. I knew there was going to be a punch line.

"How's that?"

"How many people do you know that always have a print of their full name with them at all times. I'm talking civilian life, not in the Corps."

"What do you mean?"

"When I was back in the States going to college, I smoked KENT cigarettes and wore KNAPP shoes. Kind of cool, huh?"

"Yeah, it is. There aren't too many names that you would be able to do that with, especially both names. I knew a kid back home whose name was Lucky Elsworth. No shit! Lucky was his real first-name, not a nickname. But his last name would have to be Strike to duplicate your feat."

"What were the final results from Operation Shasta I?"

If Kent had still been in his previous position, he would have known the details of the operation. As the primary administrative assistant for the company, he knew everything. Now he was just an uninformed field grunt like the rest of us.

"Some good, some bad," I answered. "The first phase wasn't that great. We killed seventeen VC/NVA. Some of the enemy dead had letters and mail on them from North Vietnam. I heard we took eleven casualties. Only three KIA's though."

"What about Shasta II?"

"You remember the shit we took on that, with the mortars and all those booby-traps? I think sixteen guys were hit by mines. Couldn't get any tanks or tracs into the area cause of all those canals and swamps. What a piss-poor place to pick a fight. Killed a pile of gooks though. Think there were like twenty-four confirmed enemy KIA and about thirteen or so probables. The CO of Charlie got wounded along with his radioman."

Kent was silent while he lit another cigarette. Finally he spoke. "You know, although it is much harder—both physically and mentally—to be in the field, I still prefer it to what I did before. I never really felt like a Marine. I was an office pogue—filing, processing and ordering. All paperwork. Marines are trained to fight and the guys doing the fighting are at the top in terms of respect. A lot of people thought I was nuts to volunteer for the field, but it is right for me. I feel like I am finally contributing something."

Although I had never had the opportunity to be assigned to a rear area support position, I thought I knew how he felt. I reflected back to the frat-boy-looking military personnel I had seen on the ride to China Beach. In my heart, I knew that they were contributing to the war effort, but it still wasn't the same as being in the mud, shooting and being shot at.

It was 2200 hours and we had been talking for over three hours. We were scheduled to leave at 0300 the next morning to set up a platoon-sized blocking force along a river bordering the southern edge of Co Luu (2). We wanted to be in position before the sweeping element of the operation started moving south from Binh Minh (1). The area being swept was about two grid-squares in size and heavily populated with civilians. Intelligence reported that a reinforced company of VC were based in the area. As usual, we doubted the accuracy of their reports.

Although we were both tired, Kent and I continued to talk. He was a good listener. He never interrupted and let you ramble on, even when you didn't know what you were trying to say. When he spoke, everyone listened. With his education, intelligence and leadership qualities, he could be successful at anything. He had already turned down requests to go to OCS and become a Marine Corps officer.

"Are you religious, Gary?" Kent's question caught me by surprise.

"I don't know what you mean by religious," I answered. "I was raised Lutheran, went to Sunday school and all that. So I guess I'm religious. Don't know if I buy all that heaven and hell stuff though. Sounds kind of like a fairy tale. What about all the people that existed before Christ? Would they go to hell? Or maybe they'd get some special deal. You hear where in heaven you reunite with your family. What if you didn't like them on earth and hadn't talked to them in years? What would you talk about in heaven? As for all that burning and eternal suffering in hell, I think it's a crock. What if you met a Cong in heaven that you had shot—would he like you?"

Kent responded to my babbling about heaven and hell by saying, "I believe in fate, Gary. I don't really know who sets the dates or monitors the schedule, but I believe everyone's death is predestined. I don't think we have the power or ability to change our personal date with destiny. You can be in the wrong place at the wrong time, or the right place at the right time, but whether you die or survive is predetermined. Remember that guy that died when he got his toe shot off? He shouldn't have died. Christ, you lose more blood getting a tooth pulled than he lost. He still died. He was destined to die. Then that poor bastard in the amtrac that burned after it got blown-up by a mine. Remember him? He lost a leg, an arm and both eyes and still lived. He wasn't supposed to die. He was destined to live."

Everyone else in the tent was already sleeping. We quickly joined them. Three hours later, we were awake once again.

January 17, 1967

The first platoon walked through the zigzagging trail that led us through the tanglefoot and concertina wire encircling the battalion perimeter. My squad was the point for the platoon. It was Langley's turn on point for us. Our destination was about 4000 meters away, the Suoi Co Luu. I think Suoi meant stream or creek in Vietnamese. I knew that Song was river, and our destination wasn't as big as a river. Langley was followed by Heatley, I was behind Heatley and Kent was behind me. Everyone else followed in single file.

It was midnight dark, and almost impossible to see the person in front of you. We tried to keep at least fifteen meters apart for safety reasons, but at night, it was impossible to keep that distance of separation. You tried to stay as far away from the Marine in front of you as you could and still maintain visual contact. After a time, everyone would start to bunch up and the word would have to be passed along the column to spread out.

We were bunching up, and I was as guilty as anyone. I told Heatley to try to stay farther away from Langley. I turned to tell Kent to pass the word back to spread out. Since Kent was my radioman, he was only five meters away.

In the darkness, I could barely make out Kent's profile.

"Kent, pass the word back to spread out. We're getting too close together."

"Okay" he answered.

My head didn't make it back to a front-facing position when I felt the explosion.

The next few hours were spent in various stages of unconsciousness. I think I remember certain things but am not sure.

Maybe it was the dreaming of an unconscious brain, or maybe it was real. I think I remember someone looking in my eyes. I think I remember telling myself to get up, but I couldn't. I think I briefly regained consciousness in the medevac chopper. Somewhere in my mind, I remember knowing that Kent was there, too, next to me.

The table was cold, and I was partially conscious. I couldn't hear or see, but I felt the cold stainless steel on my back. People were cutting off my clothes. I could feel the hands. Then the lights went out.

Chapter 29
An Early Ticket To Life

Heaven was great. The angel walking toward me had hair to her shoulders—thick blonde hair. The skin-tight sweater accentuated her protruding breasts. Her mini-skirt was one of the shortest I'd ever seen. Even her white go-go boots were beautiful. She couldn't be one of the angels they talk about in the Bible—they had wings and flew around on clouds. I wished I could see her better. My eyes weren't focusing and everything was fuzzy. I hoped she wouldn't leave. She was getting closer to me, but someone else was with her. Her companion couldn't be an angel—it was some guy wearing starched utilities.

I don't know how long I was unconscious, sedated, or both. When I woke up, I was in a ward of NSA, the Naval Hospital in Da Nang. The wards were a connected network of Quonset huts. My neck was sore and the buzzing in my head sounded like a fire alarm that couldn't be turned off. I was in a real bed, with real sheets and a pillow. The guy in the bed next to me resembled a mummy. His entire body seemed to be one big bandage. He wasn't awake.

A corpsman sat on my bed and took my temperature and pulse. He said something, but only a few words made it through the roaring in my ears and head. I fell asleep and woke up later, how much later I don't know. I only know that when I woke up, the bed next to me had a guy whose face was visible. I could hear people talking on my other side.

I tried to piece together what I knew or thought had happened. I realized that Kent had stepped on some sort of mine. I didn't know if he was alive. I also didn't know if anyone else had been injured by the blast. I hoped not. My left ear was packed with cotton and covered with a gauze pad. I knew my head, ears and neck had been injured, but that's all I knew. I hadn't talked to a doctor since I woke up. I didn't even know how long I had been there.

February 13, 1967

I stayed in the hospital until February 11th. Someone told me that Kent had been killed. I thought back to the long discussion we had the night before his death. Kent's predestined date with fate was over. Someone also said Nancy Sinatra had visited the hospital during my stay. She had been the angel walking down the aisle. I have loved her ever since.

During my hospital stay, two specialists—an audiologist and neurologist—subjected me to multiple tests. They said that the trauma caused by the concussion of the mine had destroyed nerves in my inner ear and head. My ear had been draining since the explosion. The constant buzzing in my head and ears hadn't stopped. I was told it would be permanent.

Both specialists were amazed my head hadn't exploded. Kent had detonated a fifty-pound shape charge fifteen feet from where I was standing. The doctors said that an explosion that large would dangerously alter the surrounding atmospheric pressure. Consequently, the pressure in my head would be greater than the outside pressure. This should have caused my head to blow up. Being a bull-headed Norwegian saved my life.

The mine had been built to disable a tank. Kent had detonated it by stepping on it. Usually, those types of mines wouldn't detonate if stepped on by a person. Three of us had walked over the mine without setting it off, but Kent had. There was some speculation that the additional weight of Kent's radio had been enough to trigger the mine.

I caught a ride to the Battalion HQ the day before I was scheduled to fly to Clark Air Force Base in the Philippines. I wanted to pick up my personal effects and seabag and say hello/goodbye to the guys. It had been nearly a month since I had seen them.

The platoon was in the field so there was no chance to say goodbye.

The company had a new 1st sergeant. A new guy, another college-grad draftee, had already filled Kent's old position. Neither of them knew me. To them, I was just another Marine returning to his old unit to gather up some personal gear.

I was a stranger in my own unit. I had been with the battalion for over six months, but at that moment, I felt totally alone. Everyone I knew or cared about was gone. They were dead, back home or in the field.

I started for the battalion administrative office where I was supposed to catch a ride to the air base. My flight to Clark was the next morning, and I would spend tonight in Da Nang's transit barracks.

As I walked by Delta Company's supply tent, I spotted a friendly face—someone I had shared my personal battlefield with. It was Sanchez, the only Protestant Hispanic I ever met. He was from Chicago, in his early twenties, and had been in a Marine Corps Reserve unit. His mistake had been missing several Reserve meetings and the punishment was activation and assignment.

"Que paso, chinga?" Sanchez greeted me with a firm handshake and a smile. Someone unfamiliar with Spanish Marine Corps slang might have taken offense to his greeting. Literally it was, "What's happening, Fucker?"

"Nada, gordo puta," I answered. My Spanish was limited to what I had picked up from Hispanic Marines. My response could be roughly translated as, "Nothing, you big cunt" (or whore—I never really knew which).

"What the hell you doing in the rear," I asked?

"Man, they finally gave me a skating job—cold beer, warm chow. What more could you ask for? Plus, no fucking gook is trying to kill my ass, Man."

Sanchez had more than paid his dues. He had spent time in both the second and third squad and, without question, had been the platoon's best point. We had been on countless patrols and operations together. We also had been involved in something that neither of us was proud of, but this was war, and we had done it. Later someone said we had violated the Geneva Convention. We didn't know or much give a shit what was in the Geneva Convention. My memory of what Sanchez and I had done was as vivid as if it had happened yesterday, instead of five months ago.

Mac had lent me to the second squad for a week. We were all undermanned, but they had two guys on R&R and didn't have enough troops for a patrol. I wasn't happy about going to a different squad, but it was early in my tour, and I didn't complain. I joined Sanchez and the rest of the squad.

Sanchez was on point. Both of us had been lucky because point men typically didn't last long in the field. Sanchez was a fearless Marine, with probably more personal kills than any platoon member. The patrol was nothing special—a normal three to four hour walk through the jungle.

We were moving down a trail on the edge of Phong Ho (2) when an armed VC fired two shots at us. The VC then made his fatal mistake. After firing and missing, he turned and ran directly away from Sanchez on the trail. That was his last mistake. Sanchez crumpled him on the trail with a single M-14 shot.

Cautiously, we moved toward the twisted body of the dead gook. He was on his back with his leg turned sideways. He had died immediately. The rifle slug had blown away most of his neck.

Sanchez bent over and retrieved the .30 caliber carbine trapped under the torso. He had his war trophy. I can't remember whose idea it was, but we decided to give the gooks a taste of their own medicine. We would leave the body where it fell, but would booby-trap the corpse with a grenade.

Sanchez pulled the pin but held the spoon of an M-26. With one hand, I pushed the body on its side while my other hand dug a small hole in the sand. Sanchez carefully laid the grenade, spoon up, in the hole. As he continued to depress the spoon, I pushed the VC's shoulder blade downward until it smothered the spoon, then we quickly ran for cover. We wanted to be sure that the weight of the body continued to depress the spoon of the grenade. Nothing happened. The body didn't explode. Our booby-trapped gook was in place.

After warning the rest of the patrol to leave the body alone, we continued moving toward Phong Ho. Both of us knew what would happen. The VC took care of their dead. Like the Marine Corps, they didn't leave their dead to rot in some rice paddy. Someone would return to retrieve and bury the dead body. When they moved the body, the grenade's spoon would disengage and it would explode leaving more than one dead gook lying on the trail. We didn't have to wait long. About five minutes and three hundred meters later, we heard the explosion. It was followed by screams and cries. We didn't know who had been hit, but at the least, it was a confirmed Viet Cong sympathizer.

I spent a few minutes bullshitting with Sanchez before I headed for the main gate where I would catch a ride to the air base. I had my seabag, but no weapon. When I was medevaced, my M-14 stayed behind. Someone else was probably already carrying it.

I left Vietnam in a C-130 retrofitted to transport non-ambulatory Marines. Inside, the fuselage was lined with folding, removable webbed cots for the wounded. Everyone was required to be strapped to the gurney-like beds during flight. Most of the Marines on the plane were severely wounded. Containers of IV liquids hung on hooks above them feeding the plastic tubes stuck in their arms. Although I could walk, I still had to be strapped to a cot for the flight. I was embarrassed by my seemingly minor wound. I felt like a fraud. I was receiving the same treatment that they were and I was okay.

I wasn't able to see the vanishing landmass of Vietnam from my gurney on the C-130. I remembered the first time I had seen the country from the deck of the USS *Gordon* almost eight months ago and in a different life.

The bottles of IV liquids suspended above the users swung like lonely chandeliers when the plane throttled up for take-off. Now they were swinging again. We must be landing. I had kept my eyes closed for most of the trip, still uncomfortable with my comparatively minor wounds. The IV users had been sacrificed; I had just been used. Some of them would probably die. Others would spend their lives as paraplegics. I probably wouldn't see any more combat. My wound had given me an early ticket to life. I felt like I didn't deserve it, but I took it.

Chapter 30
Treatment and Okinawa

Valentines Day, 1967

I arrived in the Philippines on February 14, 1967, Valentine's Day. The lumbering C-130 landed on the tarmac of Clark Air Force Base, taxied for a distance, and then stopped, dropping the rear-loading door. Almost immediately, the fuselage filled with medics, intent on getting the cargo off as quickly as possible.

The medics carried me off the plane on my removable gurney. I shut my eyes. I couldn't stand to look at anyone. Maybe they would think I was unconscious.

Once I was off the plane, I pleaded with one of the medics to let me walk to the bus where I was to ride with ambulatory Marines. He argued a bit before finally conceding to my plea. I didn't want to be carried one foot farther on a stretcher. Several buses were lined up to transport us to Clark's main medical complex. Those seriously wounded or nearly dead were checked into the hospital. The ambulatory Marines were taken to transit barracks.

My stay in the Philippines was a brief three days. I saw another group of specialists, was subjected to more tests, and experienced my happiest moment in eight months. I called home.

The phone was on the outside wall of the entryway to the out-patient clinic. It was a standard, Ma-Bell-issued civilian pay phone. I noticed it when I checked in and asked the receptionist if it was a real phone. She said it was, and that it could be used to call the States if I called collect. Luckily, I didn't need a dime to get an overseas operator—I was broke.

My hand trembled with anticipation as I placed the call. I will never forget that phone number: Atlas 55-806. My mother answered the phone. I heard her ecstatic shriek as the operator asked her, "Would you accept a collect call from Gary Tornes?" Mom continued her elated squealing without saying, "Yes." The operator repeated her request. Mom finally said, "Yes! Yes!"

I hadn't spoken to anyone in my family since last July. My letters were always sanitized and I never told them what was really happening. They thought my duties were routine and safe. Then, within six weeks, they received two telegrams saying that I had been wounded in action. The County Sheriff delivered the first notification. Staff Sergeant Geronimo hand carried the second. He was the Marine recruiter from Duluth who had persuaded me to join the Corps fourteen months earlier.

I can't remember how long we talked, but it didn't seem long enough. Dad was working, and my sisters were in school so I talked only to Mom. I told her I was fine and wouldn't have to go back to Vietnam. That made her happy. I also said that I had checked into the early release program for college-bound Marines. If approved, I could get released from active duty in August. That too, made her happy. She said everyone was fine and that Minnesota was having one of the coldest and snowiest winters on record. I told her it was about ninety in the Philippines, but sunny and clear.

I knew the call was costing a fortune, so I said I had to go. She started crying. I told her I loved her and would be home in a few months. She was still crying as I reluctantly hung up the receiver.

Although I felt sad hanging up, the conversation left me invigorated and refreshed. The call had reestablished a link to my previous life. The possibility of life after war seemed almost certain. I had moved from phase three into phase four.

I left Clark Air Force Base for Okinawa on a C-130 similar to the one I arrived on. The difference between the planes was that one carried wounded Marines, and the other transported military equipment and a few healthy Marines. I was one of those.

Okinawa

Twenty-two years earlier, the island had been the site of one of the bloodiest battles in Marine Corps history. On April 20, 1945, U.S. Marines successfully secured the northern part of the island. Army forces would continue to fight for weeks in the southern part of the island. On May 24, 1945, Marines entered Naha City. At that time, it was the largest Japanese city to fall to American forces.

I landed at Kadena Air Base, the second largest air base in the Pacific. My initial destination was Camp Kuwae, a Marine Corps/Army medical facility. I gave my medical records to the receptionist. I was scheduled to see the doctor tomorrow. I would spend tonight in an outpatient-housing unit adjacent to the hospital.

My private room was actually a tastefully furnished efficiency apartment. This was the first time in over a year that I would sleep in a private room. Whether it had been in a barracks, hospital ward or fighting hole, I had slept next to another Marine for twelve months. The little apartment had a couch, recliner and a TV. It even had a private bathroom with shower. I felt like a king in his palace.

Before going to bed, I decided to explore the hospital's recreation center. The primary attraction of the rec hall was its large, well-stocked library. The magazine section had current editions of all popular periodicals. I hadn't read a magazine for almost a year so I decided to catch up on the news. I grabbed a pile of Saturday Evening Posts and started paging through them. After an hour of looking through magazines, I moved to the military history section. It was by far the largest and most impressive section in the library. Thousands of military-related books lined the shelves. One caught my eye: *Congressional Medal of Honor Recipients of the United States.*

The book had a mini biography of everyone who had received the medal and was organized chronologically by war. Vietnam hadn't yet been added. I went to the Korean War section and looked for the name Rosser. I found it: Corporal Ronald E. Rosser.

Rosser had been telling the truth. His brother had been with the 38th Infantry Regiment in Korea and was awarded the medal for his actions on July 7, 1952. After reading what he had done to receive the medal, I felt very average. I put the book back, and left the library, feeling guilty because I hadn't believed Rosser.

The two brothers shared the same genes and, in my opinion, both were heroes. I knew in my heart that under similar circumstances, Rosser would have done exactly what his brother had.

It was too quiet. I tossed and turned in the double bed for an hour before falling asleep. The next morning I felt great. I had forgotten what it felt like to sleep alone, undisturbed and in a soft double bed. I took a warm shower, dressed and walked to the hospital mess hall for breakfast. The food was plentiful, well prepared, and attractively presented. From the mess hall I walked to the hospital for my appointment.

Three doctors spent most of the morning probing, inspecting and testing. Their conclusion was the same as it had been in Da Nang and the Philippines—there wasn't much that could be done. I was told that the nerve damage in my head, neck and ears was permanent. I had lost 75% of the hearing in my left ear and 25% in my right ear. The loud buzzing noise in my head and ears was tinnitus. It, too, would stay with me for life. They gave me my medical file with instructions to give it to the doctor at Camp Hansen.

With my seabag on one shoulder and my records under an arm, I caught a military transit bus for Camp Hansen. The ride there took us through the Okinawan countryside. Most military facilities were on my left, with many small villages and farms to my right. America's military presence was everywhere. The road was teeming with military trucks, jeeps and pick-ups. Sprinkled between the military green were small Japanese-made cars.

Most of the villages and small farms looked clean, well maintained and prosperous. Television antennas poked upward from many of the homes. Although both were Asian countries, the contrast between Japan and Vietnam couldn't have been greater.

Camp Hansen

I could see the military base on my left. To my right were the storefronts and vendors of Kin Village. The little town was immediately outside the main gate of the base. It obviously had some attraction for the large number of civilian-dressed Marines strolling the streets.

The bus dropped me off at Administrative Headquarters where I gave my personnel and medical file to a lance corporal. After a cursory review of my records, he assigned me to Casual Company. He gave me a mimeographed map of the base, directions to my new barracks, and told me I could take any bunk that was open. He also warned me to be careful with valuables since the lockers didn't have locks. I thanked him, threw my sea bag over my shoulder and headed for my new home.

The term "Casual Company" is a Marine Corps misnomer. It is neither casual nor a company. Rather, it is a holding tank for transients, misfits and miscreants. It is an artificially-created, constantly-changing unit. The Marines stay only until they get reassigned, retired, or incarcerated.

Your time in the unit was normally too short to have assigned duties or establish lasting relationships. Sometimes you were lucky and you met someone you knew. More often, the only thing you had in common with others in the unit was that you were all Marines. You don't need to be combat-bonded to drink and carouse, and we did plenty of that. With twenty-cent beer and a combo haircut/hand-job at two bucks, a little money went a long way.

The transient barracks were stark and noisy. Ambience was absent. Nobody stayed long enough to care how it looked. Blacks bunked near other Blacks, Whites were with Whites, and Hispanics went both ways. There was always music playing—soul, country, rock and roll—at the same time, all the time.

I bunked near the door, a black dude on one side and a redneck on the other. I was between the battle of the bands. One played Percy Sledge's "When a Man Loves a Woman," the other, Buck Owens and the Buckaroos. Each tried to drown the other out.

The only valuable personal effects I had were the Viet Cong Flag I had found the day I killed the young girl and the Purple Heart General Walt pinned on me. I decided to send both home rather than haul them around in my seabag.

The non-commissioned officer in charge (NCOIC) of Casual Company helped me wrap them for mailing. I addressed the package to my parents and put it in my locker. Lunch was being served at the mess hall, so I decided to eat before taking the parcel to the Base Post Office. I finished an unmemorable lunch and headed back to my spartan quarters.

As I walked into the barracks, several black Marines were grouped near the bed of my black bunk-mate. Percy Sledge was still wailing; the redneck was gone. As I approached my bunk, the group of black Marines moved to the far side of the barracks. Nothing struck me as unusual. I was the interloper, disrupting their soul brother talk.

I dug through my seabag, looking for the roll of seven-cent stamps. Surely, I would have enough stamps to mail my package home. I opened the unlocked door of my locker. Nothing was on the top shelf. Maybe I had looked in the wrong locker. But it wasn't. The few civilian clothes I had bought were hanging from the locker's hooks. My payroll records had caught up with me and I once again had money in my pocket. But my flag and medal were gone.

My heart dropped. Some son-of-a-bitch had stolen my Purple Heart and flag. If I had a weapon, and knew who had done it, I would have put a bullet in his head without hesitation. I looked at the Blacks in the far corner. Their backs were toward me. Well aware of the recent racial murders and beatings on base, I nevertheless stormed toward them.

"Any you guys see anybody going through my locker?" The inflection in my voice made the question sound like an accusation.

"Fuck no, Man. You accusin us a stealin some a yo mutha fuckin shit?" Their answer was a challenge.

"Some bastard stole my fucking Purple Heart and a VC flag. If I find out who did it—I'll kill the son-of-a-bitch!" I was shaking with anger as I indirectly accused and threatened them. They stared at me with defiant hatred—the same look that had been in Fortnier's eyes when he pointed the muzzle of his M60 at my throat. I knew they were guilty, but had no proof. I used my head and walked back to my bunk before starting something I would surely regret.

Sitting on my bunk, head in my hands, I felt like fucking crying. I was proud of my Purple Heart and war trophy. Both were irreplaceable. I could get another medal, but it wouldn't be the same. It wouldn't be the one General Walt pinned on my chest. The flag could never be replaced. I felt angry, sick, and lower than whale shit.

My two months in Casual Company were a major contrast to the previous eight months. Instead of constant activity, we had little to do. Rather than not getting enough sleep, beer and food, we got too much. Other than a few assignments such as night shift duty non-commissioned officer in charge (DNCOIC) for the company, I was usually bored. I spent some time in the base library, reading and looking at college catalogs, but most of the day was spent lying on my bunk, reading and eating. In the evening, that changed.

A number of us would go into Kin Village, buy several quarts of Japanese sloe gin, hop in a skosh cab and head for Naha. The ride took about thirty minutes. By the time we arrived, the sloe gin was gone and the night was just starting.

There were three categories of bars that catered to American servicemen. At the top of the hierarchy were the clubs that had good bands, pricey drinks, and bar girls that would only dance with you. On the second tier were establishments that had good juke-boxes, cheap drinks and bar girls that would do anything for a price. At the bottom of the pyramid were the bars that catered to black servicemen. Here, the jukebox played only soul music, the drinks were slightly overpriced, and the bar girls were on the retirement circuit.

The low point of my last visit to Naha was losing my Zippo lighter. We had been drinking in the Bar Wings for most of the night. It was late, and none of us had overnight liberty. Curfew was fast approaching as we staggered from the bar to hail a skosh cab. In the rush to leave, I left my lighter on the table. It had been a gift from a friend and I treasured it. It was gold plated with my initials embossed across one side. Although it was only a lighter, I felt like I had abandoned a friend. It had been in my pocket for almost eight months.

Unlike Naha, Kin Village was directly outside Camp Hansen's main gate. Not only was it closer to base, but it had other advantages: we didn't have to take a cab, the action was more concentrated, and some of the brothels had contests and offered payday specials. The most famous was the climax-in-two-minutes special.

This brothel had an extremely talented and aggressive female employee. If you could last longer than two minutes, your ride would be free. On payday, a long line would form outside her room.

False, bravado laughter and macho mutterings resonated down the hallway. Any possible embarrassment or self-consciousness had already been extinguished by ten beers. The pressure to perform—and to perform slowly—was intense. Everyone who entered the door would be timed not only by an attendant in the room, but also by those still in line. Few ever won the prize, but it was a marketing success for the brothel.

There was more to Kin Village than brothels. Many bars and lounges lined the few streets. Steam baths and massage parlors were sprinkled between the bars. At least four pawn shops flourished, one of which probably had my Purple Heart and VC flag for sale. Several barber shops where only haircuts were available somehow managed to survive. Food could be bought from the many street vendors or in a sit-down restaurant. The best shrimp fried rice I had ever eaten was served in an eight-table sidewalk cafe.

All Marines going to Vietnam and coming back were processed through Camp Hansen. The Marines wandering the streets had made it through their tour alive or they had their tour just ahead of them. Either way they would party, and Kin Village offered what they wanted. If you had survived, you would celebrate life. If you were going over, you would try to get one last drunk and piece of ass. With the massive build-up of troops expected to continue, Kin Village was looking at an economic boom.

Since no one really knew what to do with me or where to reassign me, I ended up staying in Casual Company longer than most. I was designated one of the rotating DNCOIC's. One of the perks that came with the appointment was a new place to sleep. I gladly left the noisy confines of the transit barracks and moved to a private cubicle in the permanent NCO quarters. The walls of the cubicle didn't extend to the ceiling, but the living area was comfortable and private.

Usually I would work the twelve-hour night shift from midnight until noon of the following day. I would then have two days off before working another night shift. I welcomed the opportunity to do something. I had become bored and broke. Too much free time without any structure takes its toll. My duties were quite basic. I was responsible for keeping a semblance of military order among the members of Casual Company. If fights broke out in the barracks, I would investigate and call the MP's. If someone showed up at the gate, drunk and disorderly, I would pick him up with the jeep at my disposal and put him to bed. If the Marine at the gate had overstayed his liberty, I would make a report and send it to the company commander of Casual Company.

Some of the Marines in Casual Company were awaiting orders to go back to the States to be discharged from the Corps. Most of these would receive medical discharges for physical injuries received in combat; others had mental or emotional disabilities. It was the latter group that gave me the most trouble.

Hardly a night passed without an incident involving an emotionally disturbed Marine. I would get a frantic call from one of the barracks asking for help. The message was usually, "Get someone over here at once, we got this guy that's going fucking crazy on us." I would run to the barracks with a straitjacket and try to subdue the guy. Usually I needed help from some of the other barrack's residents to get the crazy guy into a straitjacket. I would then call the MP's who would take the guy to the mental ward of the base medical facility.

The majority of night duty was boring. I spent most of my time looking at books and magazines in the small reading room near my desk. It was here that I decided what college I would attend and what my major would be.

The reading room had a large selection of college catalogs and other career-related information. I wanted to attend college after the service, but I didn't know where I wanted to go or what I wanted to study. I narrowed my choices to three in Minnesota: Bemidji

State College, University of Minnesota--Duluth, and St. Cloud State College.

My selection process was not objective. The basis for choosing St. Cloud State College was that Connie, a girl I knew in grade school and junior high, attended that school. Although we had only seen each other twice since high school, she had written me a couple of times in Vietnam. In my heart I knew that it was nothing more than a high school crush, but it was something. Maybe I would bump into her in on campus and my adolescent infatuation would develop into something more. Although scenarios like that usually only happen in the movies, my decision had been made. I would apply for an early out and attend St. Cloud State College in the fall.

Next I had to decide what I wanted to study. I paged through the St. Cloud State College catalog, searching for a course curriculum that appealed to me. I didn't like much of what I saw. My math skills were below average; I didn't like the liberal arts; only jocks and idiots majored in business; sociology and psychology were a crock of shit. I wanted to study something I enjoyed, not necessarily something that would provide future employment opportunities. After looking at all the offerings, I finally found something that I kind of liked—geography. I liked to travel and I liked the thought of studying exotic countries. I decided to become a geography major at St. Cloud State College in Minnesota.

I sent the college an application along with a letter describing my situation. I told them that time was of the essence. To be considered for an early out, you had to be accepted by an accredited college. In less than two weeks, I received notification that I had been accepted. Now I had to start saving money.

My two months in Okinawa had depleted my savings. I had blown the money I had been carrying on the books while in Vietnam. In some ways I'd been on an extended R & R. Now I had to get serious about both earning and saving some cash. For months I had fantasized about buying a red Mustang if I made it back alive. Now it looked as if I would make it back, but I was almost broke. I gave it a lot of thought and came to the conclusion that the only place I could and would save any money was Vietnam. I decided to go back.

The day after receiving my acceptance letter from college, I went to see the commanding officer of Casual Company. Even though I had a permanent non-combative profile, the war needed bodies. Surely there would be something I could do in Nam. I would volunteer to go back on one condition—that I would be assigned to my old battalion and my old company.

The major who was the commanding officer of Casual Company looked at me like I was crazy.

"Are you sure you want to go back to Nam?" he asked.

"Yes, Sir. I believe I can still contribute."

"You're sure?"

"Yes, Sir. But only if I can go back to my old unit."

"That won't be a problem. Although you're on medical profile, there are still things you can do in battalion. Get your stuff together. You'll have to go through an overseas physical before you leave. I'll get your assignment approved. You leave the day after tomorrow."

"Thank you, Sir."

Back Again

It was April 11, 1967—two days before I would leave, once again, for Vietnam. I was ready. This time I knew what to expect. Although the chance to earn and save more money was my primary reason for returning, I also felt guilty. I had the million dollar wound, and those still in my squad and platoon didn't. Their days and nights were much different from mine. While they were trying to stay awake in a wet night ambush, I was drinking cold beer, eating hot chow and sleeping in a private cubicle. The only hand-to-hand combat I had experienced in the last two months was wrestling a mentally fucked-up Marine to the floor. I was returning not only for the money but also to diminish my guilt. To reflect more clearly on the decision I had made, I decided to go the Enlisted Men's club and have a few beers.

Camp Hansen's EM Club would have made money in Las Vegas. It had two main bars, a large dance floor and a stage where live bands performed on weekends. Its special feature was the hundreds of slot machines lining the walls. The machines always seemed to be busy and I am sure they provided a healthy profit for the club. I bought a beer and sat down in front of a nickel machine. I had only lost a dollar or so when I heard someone behind me say, "Hey, Gar! What are you doing here?"

I turned around and couldn't believe what I saw—Joe "Hardcore" Cullens, beer in hand and a smile on his face.

"Joe! What are you doing here? You finally get number three?"

"Yeah, I got it, Gar. Got nailed by some shrapnel from a gook rifle grenade. They're sending me to Gitmo on some security detail for my last few months. What about you? The squad has been wondering what happened."

"Been here almost two months. Heading back to Nam the day after tomorrow."

"What! You crazy Fuck! What do you want to go back for?"

Four hours and ten beers later we left the club. I had explained to Joe my reasons for going back. He still thought I was crazy. We reminisced about some of our good times and some of the bad. Joe told me that after Kent had detonated the anti-tank mine, the rest of the patrol had to walk by my body and Wilson cried. In a strange way, hearing that made me feel good.

Our farewell handshake was long and firm. We had been through a lot together.

The next morning I reported as ordered for my overseas physical. Two thousand Marines stood in formation on the concrete "grinder" near the middle of the base. Something was wrong. We were here to take our overseas physical, but the setting wasn't right. A stage with a podium was located at the front edge of the large troop formation. After a few minutes, a full bird colonel grabbed the microphone on the podium and started talking.

"You men are all going to Vietnam. Your government and the Marine Corps appreciate what you're doing. You are here today to take your overseas physical. Only those who pass will continue on to Vietnam. Please raise your right arm, lock your elbow and point to the sky."

It was an unusual order, but two thousand arms were soon pointing upward toward the sky.

The colonel continued. "Make a fist and extend only your index finger toward the sky."

We once again complied.

"Now contract your finger. Now extend. Now contract. Extend. Contract. Drop your arm to your side. You have all passed your overseas physical."

The quick-witted Marines started laughing. Others looked around bewildered by what had happened. Soon everyone realized that our overseas physical was Marine Corps humor at its best. For most Marines, their right index finger is also their trigger finger. We had all been able to extend and contract that finger; therefore, we could pull the trigger of a rifle. We were overseas fit, ready for combat. Laughter was everywhere.

"You're not dismissed yet." The Colonel said as he brought the microphone to his mouth.

"All those who have been in Vietnam raise your hands."

I followed his order and raised my arm with about a hundred others.

"You Marines are dismissed. We don't want your blood. The rest of you, fall in behind the ambulances."

To the right of the colonel, groups of corpsmen were busily setting up collection points. Each blood collection point had an ambulance parked next to it. If you hadn't been to Vietnam, you would "donate" your blood to the cause. The blood collection process took hours. Those who didn't have to donate went back to their barracks and packed.

Chapter 31
Vietnam II

My return to Nam was much smoother than the first time. The flight on the chartered 707 from Kadena Air Base to Da Nang Air Base was short. The attractive, civilian stewardess who served beverages was mentally raped by everyone on board. This time I knew the drill and what to expect. The cabin was thick with cigarette smoke and edgy laughter.

As we left the plane and climbed down the stairs of the moveable walkway, I heard several comments regarding the heat. For those not acclimatized, it was a shock to walk from an air-conditioned cabin into the sweltering, breath-robbing heat of South Vietnam. For me, the temperature was hot, but not unbearable.

I felt almost at home and knew where to go. I caught a ride to regimental headquarters where I quickly found a convoy going to 1st Battalion Headquarters. It was a re-supply convoy, so I jumped in the cab of one of the six-bys. I was riding shotgun without a weapon.

The truck was driven by a lance corporal who spent most of the trip telling me how often his truck was hit by enemy fire. I listened to his combat tales without saying much. Since I was still wearing my starched utilities along with shined jungle boots, he probably thought I was an FNG. As I looked at him, I realized that many Marines without an Infantry MOS had inferiority complexes.

They felt like non-contributors. It wasn't their fault. The truck drove through the gate of 1st Battalion Headquarters. I was home.

Delta Company: Revisited

I reported to Delta Company with new orders in hand. It had been two months since my last visit. At that time, Sanchez had been the only familiar face. This time, even Sanchez was gone. He had finished his tour and had rotated back to the States. The men in the company tent were all strangers. The new 1st sergeant greeted me with a friendly handshake. He was a WWII veteran who had been with the company for only a month but had paid his dues in two previous wars. He seemed to approve that I was voluntarily returning to the field. He introduced me to his administrative clerk, an academic-looking corporal. I wondered where Kent's replacement had gone. I doubted whether he had volunteered for a field assignment like Kent had.

Top told me which tent I would bunk in and said all platoons were either at outlying patrol bases or on an operation with 3/1. He assured me I would be kept busy and attached to the company until I rotated back to CONUS. I thanked him, and lugged my seabag to my assigned tent.

My first job at Delta Company was to supervise the construction of a prisoner holding area. Someone in S-2 had drawn a rough plan on a piece of paper of what they thought the finished product should look like. It was not drawn to scale nor were there any specs for materials. My labor force consisted of Marines on light duty, Marines waiting to be sent to the brig and several who had been determined mentally unfit for combat duty.

I had a plan, a labor force, a pile of wood and miles of barbed wire. My hardest task was motivating the labor force. The monsoons were over and the suffocating heat had returned with a vengeance. Although my labor force changed daily, we managed to build a perimeter of metal posts and barbed wire. We also built a barbed wire-covered, wood-framed swinging gate. The outside of the barbed wire fence was encircled with concertina wire. When we were done, the prisoner compound looked like it was surrounded by a giant slinky. In the middle of the holding area we constructed temporary quarters with timbers and sand bags. When we finished, even my workforce of malcontents was proud of what we had accomplished.

I had been attached to Delta Company for five weeks when I got the word to report to Top. It wasn't an unusual request because we frequently collaborated on my daily assignments. I removed my cover as I entered his office.

"Corporal Tornes, do I have a deal for you!" Top's grin suggested that I would be pleased by what he had to say.

"What's that, Top?"

"There's an opening at the EM Club for an assistant manager." His grin became wider. "What do you think? You want it? If you take it, you will have to transfer to H&S Company, but hell, you only have two months left in Nam. Another side benefit of the job, you get paid $1.25 an hour for each hour you work. Can't beat being paid to sell beer to thirsty Marines!"

I couldn't believe what I was hearing. I would be able to save enough money for a Mustang and college. Assuming I got paid for eight hours a day, seven days a week, I should clear $300 a month. With two months to go, I could bank an additional $600. When I added that to my normal monthly pay, I could save close to $1500 by the time I left.

The EM Club

The Enlisted Men's (EM) Club was located on the western edge of the base, fifty meters from the perimeter's protective sand berm. Directly across the outer edge of the concertina wire was the supposedly government friendly village of Triem Trung.

The club was built on a foundation of treated timber posts. It had a wooden floor, screened walls and a tin pitched roof with the sheets of roofing extended to partially protect the interior from rain and sun.

Inside the club, rattan tables and chairs were crammed together. An old, well-used 33 RPM phonograph with a pile of records sat on a shelf at one end of the building. Behind the bar was a small addition that housed three, large, lift-top coolers and us. Corporal Elsworth, the Club Manager, slept on one side of the addition, I on the other. A conveniently located piss tube was outside our back door. Behind the club, two padlocked metal reefers protected the battalion's beer supply. There were more keys to the battalion armory than to the beer reefers. We had the only key.

As managers of the EM Club, our duties were limited but quite specific. Our primary responsibility was to ensure that the correct amount of beer and soda got loaded onto the amtracs that re-supplied field troops.

Our secondary duty was to keep the club open from 1400 hours until 2000 hours. During that time we were the club's bartenders selling cold beer for fifteen cents a can and offering a sympathetic ear for personal problems and war stories. We probably gave away and drank as much beer as we sold. After closing at 2000 hours we were expected to sweep and clean the club.

An additional task was to order the battalion's beer and pick it up at the large naval depot in Da Nang.

Although we were located in the middle of enemy-infested real estate, I felt relatively safe. The base was hit by sporadic small arms fire, but the rounds sailed harmlessly overhead. The sand berm protected us. We were mortared several times during my two months at the club, but fortunately the rounds didn't hit the club. The only times I was exposed to hostile small arms fire were during my weekly beer runs to Da Nang.

Often, the beer run would consist of just the driver of the flatbed truck and me. The road to Da Nang was full of military vehicles, tanks and tracs, and that gave me a sense of security—false or otherwise. Trips to the beer depot were typically uneventful, though several times we had to turn around because the bridge across the Song Vinh Dien River had been blown up. But usually the trip was enjoyable, and the few sniper rounds were considered a nuisance rather than a crisis.

Since transferring to H&S Company, I had become acquainted with a whole new category of field Marines. They were almost—but not quite—in the rear-with-the-beer. Some volunteered for field duty weekly, but their requests were always denied. Apparently it was harder to get someone who could type and file than hump and shoot.

One guy I got to know well was Red, a tall, lanky and very athletic lance corporal. He distributed all incoming mail and collected and bagged the outgoing mail. Red was a combat zone mail clerk who would have rather been walking point. His constant pleas for an MOS change were ignored and his requests for a field assignment denied. Since he was a friend, Red's happy hour at the club lasted all night.

The hardest part of my job was when old friends from the first platoon came into the club. Usually, they were working out of an outlying patrol base and didn't have the opportunity to visit the club, but when they visited battalion, the club was their first stop. We didn't have a two-beer quota so they would pound back as many beers as they could during these brief respites.

Everyone from the old platoon was friendly. I would reminisce with the "short ones" about old times and old battles. We would laugh, slap each other on the back and have multiple toasts to "getting the fuck out of here." But it wasn't like it used to be. I had the skating job and they faced death daily. I felt unbelievable guilt. Although I enjoyed talking to them, I dreaded their visits.

The favorite 33 LP among all types of music fans was a record by Eric Burdon and the Animals. I liked the entire LP, but one song was everyone's favorite, "We Gotta Get Out Of This Place." That song was played so much, the grooves actually wore out. At the chorus, the entire club would join the refrain, "*We gotta get out of this place, if it's the last thing we e-v-v-ver do*" and this would echo across the entire battalion area.

I applied for an early out and sent my request along with my acceptance letter from St. Cloud State College to the appropriate senior officer. I think that was the Commanding General of the 1st Marines. I soon received a letter denying my request. That decision was probably made by some office pogue. I was furious, but I couldn't appeal the decision because there wasn't enough time.

Since I couldn't get an early release, I wouldn't be starting college until January 1968. Consequently, after very little thought, I decided to extend my tour for three months. Not only would I make more money with my club pay, but I would also avoid some make-work assignment for my last three months in the Corps. But most of all, I wouldn't have to put up with the chickenshit requirements that went along with a stateside assignment.

In contrast to my early out application, this request was promptly, verbally approved. My orders would have to be officially changed to show a rotation date of November 6th instead of August 6th. This would take time as the paperwork had to make its way through appropriate levels of command.

"Tornes, you want to ride with me into Hoi An and get some booze?"

In the Marine Corps, field Enlisted Men's Clubs serve only beer. Officers had hard liquor in their clubs, but if you were enlisted, you only drank beer. Beer was my drink of choice, so the lack of booze didn't bother me. Corporal Elsworth, on the other hand, liked straight bourbon and his stash was low.

Elsworth's source for whiskey was either the small Special Forces club or the West German Humanitarian Compound. Both were located in Hoi An, one of the largest cities in I Corps that had a real downtown with two-story buildings.

"Yeah, I'll go," I answered.

"Maybe we can get a little gook 'poon tang' while we're there," Elsworth added. "A guy in H&S gave me directions to a skivvie house on main street. Said the girls were pretty decent."

The ride into Hoi An took fifteen minutes. When we reached the edge of the city, the traffic on the road increased tenfold. The narrow city streets were teaming with ARVN military vehicles, motorbikes driven by young Vietnamese males, bicycles and thousands of pedestrians.

Elsworth honked the horn continuously as he maneuvered his way through the crowded network of streets. He brought the vehicle to a stop in front of a blue and white masonry building. A limp black, red and gold flag was hanging from a pole in front of the entrance. I assumed it was the West German flag.

"Stay here while I'm gone. Will only be a minute. You want me to get you some booze or something?"

"Nah, beer's fine for me."

In less than ten minutes he returned and we continued with the second phase of the operation—finding the skivvie house. Elsworth seemed to know Hoi An quite well and we were soon parked in front of a two-story dwelling. This time, both of us got out.

Elsworth led the way as we entered the building. Inside, we found the remnants of what was once a four-star hotel. The interior was an example of negligent disrepair. Paint was peeling, the chandelier was gone and more than half the marble tiles covering the floor were either broken or missing. I imagined that in the heyday of French occupation, this hotel was a hotspot.

A forty-something-year-old mamasan came down the stairway to meet us.

Elsworth greeted her, "Mamasan, you get numba one boom-boom girl, okay?"

The woman started rattling on in rapid-fire Vietnamese. Elsworth repeated his request.

"You get us numba-one boom-boom girl. OK? Five bucks!"

The woman answered, "Ten bucks."

"OK, OK. You get the fucking boom-boom girl." Elsworth was getting pissed.

"Marine. You come." The mamasan motioned for us to follow her upstairs.

We were both armed and cautious. We had heard enough stories about Marines being lured to their death by the promise of a piece-of-ass. We carefully followed her up the stairs.

"Numba one boom-boom girl," the mamasan pointed to a small room with a bamboo bed almost as big as the room. In the middle of the bed sat the numba one boom-boom girl. Actually, she wasn't too bad, except that all the pretty young women seemed to be VC sympathizers. She looked suspicious but still sensual. Elsworth told me to guard the door as he handed the mamasan a ten dollar bill. The woman took the money and went back down the stairs. Elsworth dropped his utilities to his ankles and mounted the bored-looking teenager.

I am not a voyeur, but my position guarding the door forced me to become one. The scene could have been out of an X-rated Twilight Zone episode. Elsworth is pouring the coals to this gal, huffing and humping away, his trousers around his boots, while she's chewing bubble gum and blowing these big pink bubbles. But that's not all she was doing. She had a flyswatter in one hand, and while Elsworth was busy porking her, she swatted flies. I wasn't looking for love or romance, but this was too much. When Elsworth finished, I declined my opportunity for seconds.

On the way back to the battalion, I had a great time needling Elsworth about his bubblegum-blowing, fly-swatting boom-boom girl.

Time seemed to be dragging and work at the club became routine. I started taking the cold beer, soft cot and electric fan for granted. It's amazing how easily you can settle into your own comfort and forget why you are doing what you do. All personnel in battalion and regimental headquarters are there for one purpose: to support the men in the field who are doing the fighting. I understood how those who were never in the action could forget, but how could I?

I was starting to have doubts about the decision I had made to extend my tour. It was already mid-July, and if I hadn't extended, I would be going home in three weeks. The supposedly chicken-shit spit-and-polish of stateside duty didn't sound that bad anymore. I had screwed up. Nobody had forced me to extend. It was my choice and I would have to live with the consequences.

Red and I were into the cold Budweiser. I kept a stash of Bud in one of the coolers for special occasions. This was one. I was crying in my beer over the stupid decision I had made to extend my tour. Red had been listening to me whine for at least four Buds when he suddenly snapped to attention.

"Gary, I got a plan that might help you out."

"What's that?" I was interested.

"Have you received your new orders from regiment yet?"

"No, not yet."

"Maybe I can intercept the orders before they get to the XO. Then we can shit-can them. Nobody will ever find out. Everything is fucked-up anyway, and the last thing they'd be worried about would be the extension orders for some corporal."

"How do you plan on pulling it off?"

"Easy. Part of my job is to deliver all the incoming mail where it's supposed to go. The XO is responsible for signing all orders, so before I deliver his mail, I'll look through it for your new orders. When I find your orders, I'll pull them out. Fucking XO never sees it. We shit-can them and you go home in August."

"Let's try it! Have another Bud on me."

Several days later Red approached me as I was loading pallets of beer into the outside reefer.

"I got it!"

"No shit!" I knew what he was referring to without asking.

"Came in today. Slick as shit. Just slid that sheet of paper out of the XO's pile before giving him the rest of his mail."

"Let me see it."

He reached beneath his utility shirt and pulled out the orders. There they were, approved, and in my hand.

"We can't tell a fucking soul, Gary. If we got caught doing this, we would be looking at Portsmouth—you know, breaking big rocks into little rocks."

"I know. I know, I said. Not a word to anybody. Let's celebrate. Got a cold case of Bud in the cooler."

Three Times And You're Out

I said my good-byes at battalion earlier in the day. Although Elsworth was a decent Marine, I wasn't close to him. I shook Red's hand and thanked him for what he had done. I said farewell to Top.

Now I could relax. The wheels of the 707 had been retracted and the plane was in a powerful climb. The Nam legend of a lone sniper shooting a departing Marine in the head as his jet takes off for the world did not happen. It was bullshit, of course, but you couldn't truly relax until your plane was safely away from the war.

The plane landed at Kadena Air Base in Okinawa where a bus transported us to Camp Hansen. We had our orders processed, were assigned bunks in Casual Company barracks, and given liberty until 0200 hours the next morning. Three other homeward-bound Marines and I decided to visit Naha.

We jumped into a skosh cab, each with a bottle of sloe gin in hand, and headed south. Naha was bigger and less crowded than Kin Village, and it was cheaper. Because of the large influx of Marines processed through Camp Hansen, prices had climbed. A haircut/hand-job combo was now three dollars.

By the time we got half way to Naha, we stopped worrying about being killed in a car accident. The driver acted like he wanted to commit hara-kari with his car, but the powerful sloe gin had eliminated our fear.

We made the tour, hitting class bars as well as the dives. All were fun. Before grabbing a cab back to Camp Hansen, I suggested we visit the Bar Wings, one of my old favorites. By this time, everyone thought I was the best of guides. Approval was unanimous.

The Bar Wings hadn't changed. We were drunk but not disorderly. Our four beer order arrived quickly. The Japanese were efficient, orderly and obsessively clean. We toasted our imminent return to the world many times. The only other subject of our toasts was all the sexy round-eyes that would be waiting for us when we returned home.

I told the story of losing my lighter at the Bar Wings four months ago. One of the group said maybe they still had it. I assured him that it would be long gone. He said I should ask anyway.

"Hey, Cocktail-Waitress-San." I waved one of the bargirl-waitresses to our table.

"Hi dozo," she said as she stood next to the table. Her face was at our level—God, she was short. I asked her if they had a lost and found box of lighters. She was unsure of what I wanted.

"Wanna go boom-boom?" one of the group asked, spreading his legs and opening his arms.

"Shut the fuck up, this is a class place." More pissed-off than embarrassed, I picked up a lighter from the table and flicked it several times to illustrate what I meant.

"You wait, I talk Mamasan," she answered, as she went behind the bar to confer with the sixty-year old matriarch. The older woman walked into a room behind the bar and returned with a large cardboard box. The waitress brought the box to our table and set it in front of me.

"You look, if find, you take," she said.

Apparently, I wasn't the only one who left his lighter behind: the box was filled with hundreds of abandoned Zippos. We dumped the contents of the box on the table, divided the pile into four somewhat equal piles, and started looking.

We had been sorting through our piles for several minutes without success when one of the guys said, "Is this it?"

He handed me his find. It was my lighter. I couldn't believe it. They had kept my lost lighter for four months. They could have sold or pawned it for five bucks, but they hadn't. I added honesty to my list of Japanese characteristics.

Most of us slept during the cab ride back to the base. We had all been able to sleep in a foot of cold, muddy paddy water. Sleeping in a miniature cab driven by a suicidal Okinawan driver was easy.

After breakfast the next morning, everyone received a departure briefing. The $1400 in ten-dollar travelers checks I bought two days earlier was safely tucked under the inside of my tee shirt. This represented my total net worth. My previous experience with theft in Casual Company barracks made me cautious. I slept with my traveler's checks safely tucked in my undershorts.

The staff sergeant warned us not to try to smuggle any contraband back to the States. The list of prohibited items seemed so obvious, it was ridiculous. Then he escorted our group into a large Quonset hut displaying items that had been confiscated from wannabe smugglers. It was unbelievable what Marines had tried to smuggle out of Vietnam in their sea bags: grenades, drugs, .45 pistols, M-14's, C-4, ammunition of all kinds, LAAW's, and unbelievably, a 60mm mortar tube, with base and live rounds.

There were several large trash containers by the door. We were told that we could deposit any contraband we may have in our sea bags in the trash cans. If we did it now, nothing would happen to us. We would receive blind amnesty, and continue on to the States. On the other hand, if they caught us with any illegal item after we left the Quonset, we would be court-martialed and incarcerated in Okinawa.

I had nothing illegal, but other Marines were frantically digging through their packed sea bags. I could hear the clank of items being dropped into the trash containers as we filed out of the hut.

Buses transported us to Kadena Air Base where we were grouped together by flight manifest. We would be flying in C-130's to Yokosuka Naval Base, then board a commercial jet for our eleven-hour trip to Travis Air Force Base in California.

The flight was short. Once at Yokusuka, our wait was minimal before boarding a military chartered World Airways 707 for California. I fell asleep immediately and was awakened for breakfast somewhere between Japan and Hawaii by a cute, Caucasian stewardess.

Our jet differed from the normal commercial 707 in two ways—it had no windows, and all the seats faced backward. It was probably made to haul cargo but retrofitted to transport military personnel. I guessed that the backward facing seats were for safety reasons.

The behavior of the troops going home was subdued. Maybe it was because most of us had gargantuan hangovers or maybe we were reflecting on the past year and how lucky we were to be flying home alive. The only thing that hadn't moderated was the smoking. It seemed like everyone smoked. Thick, stagnant layers of gray smoke floated above the seats.

Without windows, it was difficult to tell what time of the day it was. The gold Omega wristwatch that I purchased at the battalion PX before leaving was still on Okinawa time. The star sapphire ring on my finger had a story of its own.

I was working in the battalion EM Club when I bought the ring. The seller was Private Grimsrud, an overweight, puffy-faced malingerer. He was an FNG who hid in a dumpster rather than accompany his squad on his first scheduled patrol. Such behavior was extremely rare in the Corps, and his fall to the bottom caste was immediate. Although he was a draftee, it made no difference. Most Marine Corps draftees served honorably.

Grimsrud was going to have some time in the Da Nang brig to reflect on his actions. It was about noon, and still two hours before we opened the club when he knocked on the back door. He didn't look like a Marine. He looked anxious and pathetic.

"Hey, Man, I'm goin to the brig and I don't have any money. I'll need some money in the brig. Wanna buy my ring? My fiancé in

Bangkok gave it to me—genuine black star sapphire and fourteen carat gold." His voice was nasal and whiny. I disliked him immediately.

"Let me see the ring," I said. It was an order, not a request.

I examined the ring and it looked authentic. The star sapphire was perfect, the six surrounding zircons brilliant.

"How much?" I asked.

"Twenty dollars," he answered.

"Fuck you!"

"Ten bucks."

"Still too much. Five bucks," I countered.

"Jesus Christ, you're trying to rape me cause you know I'm goin' to the brig," he whined.

"Five bucks and five beers, final offer," I said.

"OK. Here's the fucking ring, gimme the money and beer. You fucked me good."

"Who's going to the brig, and who isn't? You want to sell the ring or not, Asshole," I said as I turned to walk away.

"No, no—take the ring, gimme the money and beer and I'll go." By now he was almost crying.

The ring was authentic.

Another Breakfast

The stewardess woke me again for breakfast—my second since leaving Okinawa. By now, everyone had lost track of what part of the day our windowless plane was in. We knew we would pass through many time zones and cross the International Date Line on the flight, but we weren't sure if we gained or lost a day. The easiest way to determine how long you'd been flying was by the number of cigarettes you had smoked. I was on my second pack of Salems.

The final time I was awakened was when the pilot announced our approach to Travis Air Force Base, northwest of San Francisco. When the 707's wheels hit the tarmac, a spontaneous cheer erupted. While taxiing to a stop, the pilot informed us that it was 0300 hours, Wednesday, August 9th, 1967.

We felt like bears coming out of hibernation as we stumbled, half asleep, through the cabin door and down the portable steps. When I went from the last step to the ground, nothing extraordinary happened. I didn't feel like Columbus or General Doolittle. I didn't kiss the earth. Our welcoming committee consisted of five blue air force buses and a six-by truck. We climbed into the buses and our seabags went into the six-by.

By August 1967, the personnel processing center at Travis was experienced and efficient, and we were on our way to San Francisco International Airport in less than an hour. The bus was quiet during the ninety-minute ride to the airport. Everyone slept.

At 0600 I stumbled to the ticket counter of Western Airlines. Since I was paying for my own ticket, I could save fifty percent by flying military standby. The downside to flying standby was the possibility of being bumped by a full fare traveler. Nevertheless, the ticket agent confirmed me from San Francisco to Minneapolis with a plane change in Chicago. My flight was scheduled to leave in an hour.

The only event on the flight to Chicago was another breakfast, served somewhere over Nebraska. In Chicago, I had to run through the airport to get to my departure gate on time. Although the flight was short, I got another breakfast. It was my fourth since Okinawa. I wanted a cheeseburger and fries.

Chapter 32
No Homecoming Parade

Wold Chamberlin Airport in Minneapolis seemed small compared to the airports I had flown into during the last year, but size didn't matter because I was home. Almost. I still had to buy a Ford Mustang and drive the 290 miles north to International Falls.

I collected my seabag at the baggage claim area and changed into civilian clothes in the bathroom. I was proud of my uniform, but had forgotten what it felt like to be a civilian. Most likely, I fooled no one with my PX clothes, military haircut and a tan that only extended exposure to tropical sun can produce. I walked outside to get a cab.

The driver took my seabag and stowed it in the trunk. I jumped in the front seat.

"Where to?" he asked.

"Take me to a Ford dealership on the north side of Minneapolis," I answered.

"Which one?"

"Hell, I don't know, I'm not from here. Just take me to a Ford dealership on the northside." It was an order—I was the customer; I was in charge.

Minneapolis seemed small. The cabbie drove through the city, turned left on Broadway and dropped me off in front of the large blue and white sign of Market Ford.

I expect I looked strange, standing in the middle of a used car lot, an over-sized seabag at my side and a bewildered look on my face.

"Can I help you?" The approaching salesman almost shouted, talking much louder than he had to.

"Yeah, I'd like to buy a Mustang."

Negotiations had started.

Home

I bought a candy apple red Ford Mustang from Market Ford. It was a seller's market; I had one to pick from. I didn't negotiate or even look under the hood. The hardest part of the purchase was signing ninety ten-dollar traveler's checks. They financed the remaining $900.

My Mustang handled like a sports car as I drove north through the lake country. I had forgotten how beautiful the north woods looked in the summer. I was driving more slowly and cautiously than normal. I was still in phase four, and the last thing I needed was to be killed in a car accident on my way home. I was shorter than short; I didn't even cast a shadow.

The house looked like it had eighteen months ago. Nasturtiums bloomed in the small flowerbeds that flanked the steps. Dad's garden was jungle green and the yard freshly mowed. I opened the unlocked door and walked inside. No one was home.

The smell of our house was still the same—a pleasant, slightly sweet aroma that was welcoming and comforting. I walked slowly through the house remembering the good times and the bad. What I used to consider bad, wasn't bad anymore.

As I left the house not knowing where to go, a car pulled into the driveway. It was one of my mother's friends who lived two houses away. She greeted me and told me Mom was at a Women's Circle meeting at church.

I drove around the block where the church was for the second time. Groups of middle-aged women were exiting the church. I hoped to spot Mom. Then I saw her leaving several women and heading toward Dad's red Chevrolet. I pulled up next to her parked car and rolled the window down.

"Hey, Lady, do you want a ride?"

She turned, looked toward my car, then bent over to look in the window of the low riding Mustang.

She stared at me for a few moments before she realized who was in the car. "Gary! Gary!" she shrieked. It was a squeal of disbelief and joy. I jumped out of the car and we embraced in the middle of the street.

I was reunited with my sisters later that evening. They were glad to see me, but eyed me warily. They might have been young, but they were intuitive. Dad got home from work at 11:30 PM. You could see the relief in his eyes as he gave me an extended handshake and a pat on the back.

Mom made Sandy, my oldest sister, vacate my old room and I moved in. Before I fell into a paralyzing sleep, I felt a glow of security and serenity envelope my entire body. I hadn't felt like that for almost two years. I was in my home, in my own bed, and with my family. I was dead tired, but very much alive.

Other than the immeasurable joy of reuniting with my family, my homecoming was barren. Few of my old friends were around. Most had either left or were preparing to leave for college. Some were working in the paper mill for the summer. The few I bumped into at the bars were with girlfriends and involved in their own lives.

During my three-week leave, I can't remember being asked a meaningful question about Vietnam. It was almost as if the war didn't exist. I ran into a few former friends but our lives could not have been more different during the last two years. A huge abyss separated us. I was home, but I felt alone.

I was somewhat of a minor celebrity in town. My first employer, *The Falls Daily Journal,* had printed several articles about my service in Vietnam. After I was wounded the second time, they ran a front-page article complete with picture. They also had an article describing my Valentine's Day call to Mom from the Philippines. Another shorter piece, also with a picture, described my treatment and short assignment in Okinawa. Because of my fifteen minutes of fame, the Rotary Club asked me to speak at their weekly luncheon.

I had never done well in speech and had no idea what I would say, but nonetheless, I accepted the invitation.

The luncheon was in a private room at the Rex Hotel. As I looked around the room at the senior leaders of the community, I speculated that most—who were in their late 50's or 60's—had been too old to have served in WWII. After the meal, I was introduced by the current president.

I hadn't prepared a speech and was shooting from the hip. I gave them what little I knew about the geography of the country, and more specifically, the area I fought in. There were several questions which I answered and received polite applause. Then came a final question, "Corporal, I hear that there is a lot of corruption among the political, military and business leaders in Vietnam. What are your comments on that?"

I thought for a minute before answering.

"Well, the corruption is probably worse there than here in the States, but not much."

The audience was silent. They politely thanked me for speaking and dismissed me. Their meeting continued.

I didn't want to admit it, but in some ways, I wanted to return to duty. I yearned to be with those like me—combat veterans who shared a common bond and secrets. Those who never served would never comprehend.

I Can Now Vote And Drink

My twenty-first birthday was literally a world apart from my twentieth. Last year, on August 17th, Joe had given me his ration of two beers for a birthday present. Later in the day, I was shot at. That night a swarm of mosquitos feasted on me as I sat in the jungle waiting to kill a Cong.

This year, I was dressed in a suit, eating a sixteen ounce T-bone, drinking a cold Grain Belt, and looking at serene blue water from a resort dining room table. I had taken my parents to Rainy Lake Lodge for dinner. Neither had been there before.

I felt lucky to be able to spend my birthday with the two most important people in my world. I ordered another legal beer before leaving. Dad had driven because the back seat of the Mustang was too cramped for his long legs.

Short Timer

I left Minnesota for Camp Pendleton nine days after my birthday. I stopped to visit my grandmother and aunt before driving to St. Cloud, where I would start college on January 4, 1968. I wanted to look the town over and check out the school. This would be my first exposure to an academic environment since high school, and I was apprehensive about how I would perform.

After cruising the streets near the college, and visiting the Student Union for a cup of coffee, my apprehension disappeared. If the students I observed were my classroom competition, I was confident I would succeed.

I drove south from St. Cloud toward Minneapolis and briefly considered visiting several high school friends who were attending Macalester College.

Last year, while home on boot leave, I had spent two days with them. During my visit, they had been friendly but reserved. I don't know whether they were intimidated by my military status or felt superior because they were in school and I wasn't, but a void existed.

Throughout my short visit, we spent most of our time at a nearby college watering hole drinking beer. In addition to cheap draft beer, they made exceptional pizza and the jukebox was free. For the duration of my visit, our meals were beer and pizza, then more beer.

I was obviously an oddity in the crowded college hangout. Even without my uniform, my military status was obvious: whitewall haircut, farmer tan and cheap PX clothes. My friends told their friends that I was in the Marine Corps. They, in turn, told their friends. After my second visit, everyone in the bar seemed to know who and what I was.

At that time in my life, I was physically stronger and in better shape than I ever had been or ever would be. One afternoon, a jock from the football team came over to our table, boisterous and slightly drunk. He was apparently trying to validate his manhood by challenging me to arm-wrestle.

"Hear you're in the Marine Corps." He said with a slur in his speech.

"Yeah, I am," I answered.

"Pretty tough, is it?" the inflection in his voice dripped sarcasm.

"Yeah, it's pretty demanding," I answered. The guy was starting to irritate me.

"Wanna arm-wrestle?" he asked. He sounded like an over-confident jock, pissing me off a little more.

"Not really," I answered. "I'm just here for a day or two visiting some old friends. Nice bar."

"Why don't you wanna arm-wrestle—afraid of embarrassing the Marines?"

"Fuck you, Jack, let's go." I accepted the asshole's challenge and assumed the position: elbow on the table, forearm and hand at ninety degrees.

He spun a chair around, placing his right arm parallel to mine. Our left hands were locked in a power grip under our right biceps. We maneuvered for an advantageous right-hand grip. Someone from the table held our clasped hands before yelling, "Go!"

The back of his right hand hit the table in seconds. He had been surprisingly easy to beat.

"Didn't have a good grip," he said. "Let's do it again."

"Nah, once is enough," I answered.

"What, you afraid to try it again?" he countered, almost whining.

"Let's go," I said.

The second time was quicker than the first. He made some excuse about having a pulled muscle but wanted to try it again. I declined. I was done. I didn't want to beat this prick again and totally humiliate him. If he was the strongest lineman on the Macalester football team, I could understand why they only won two games the previous year.

As the Mustang approached the suburbs of Minneapolis, I decided against a return visit to Macalester.

Camp Pendleton

Route 66 went through the heart of Oklahoma. Just outside a little town called Perry, I heard the siren, pulled the Mustang over and cursed myself for not seeing him. The highway patrolman ambled over to my window.

"You're a little pedal-heavy for these parts, Son. Let's see your license."

As I pulled my wallet out to retrieve my license, he put his head down and looked in, then smiled. "Where you headed, Marine?"

"Camp Pendleton, Sir."

"I spent four years in the Corps, myself. You back from Nam?"

"Yes, Sir."

He talked for a while about how it was in the "old Corps" and then gave me a warning ticket.

The old adage, "Once a Marine, always a Marine" was true. It saved me ten bucks.

The Mustang made it across seven states, the Rocky Mountains and the Mohave Desert with no mechanical problems. On the stretch of Route 66 from Needles to Barstow, cars with raised hoods and billowing steam littered the roadside.

I spent the night in a cheap Barstow motel room with a broken air-conditioner. The night was uncomfortably hot. It felt as hot as any night I had spent in Vietnam.

The next morning the heat was still almost unbearable. I opened all the car windows as I sped down Route 66 toward Camp Pendleton. Even the wind that hit my extended arm at 75 MPH felt oven hot.

Tuesday, September 5th was my first day of duty. The Marine Corps seemed to have a tough time finding meaningful tasks for returning combat veterans with few months left on their enlistments. Those with more time remaining received more worthwhile assignments. Marines like me, with less than three months left, were given make-work, menial jobs. For some it was a demeaning and inglorious end to their tour of duty. Many didn't mind—we were counting the days until we would be released. We still felt the Marine Corps bond, but were looking forward to civilian life.

I was assigned to be the assistant manager for the base's VIP quarters. My duties were primarily to oversee the civilian janitorial employees who kept the unit clean and presentable. It was not what I had trained to do, but with only three months left, I didn't mind. A drill instructor once said, "You can stand on your head in shit for three months." He was right. The three months passed, but much too slowly.

I reconnected with my old friend, John Williams, who rotated back to the States a few days after me. John was an anomaly—a

Marine grunt who spent his entire tour in the field without being wounded.

John's job was about as challenging and fulfilling as mine. Our daily highlight was a five mile run after work. After running and showering, we would go to the NCO club for happy hour to replace all the fluids we lost while running. Four pitchers of beer later, we would grab a hamburger and fries at the canteen and go to bed. Our routine varied only on weekends when we would pile into the Mustang and head for John's parents' home in Santa Monica.

Some of our old pre-Vietnam crew had reunited. Out of the group, only John and I had an 0311 (Rifleman) MOS, and that is where the real bond was. You understood each other without words. All you could think about in Vietnam was getting out of there, but now that you're home, you're unsure what to do. You feel older than everyone else. The skills you've learned aren't marketable. There is the absence of exhilaration at just staying alive. You don't miss the terror, but you miss the rush, the trigger-fast reflexes that kept you alive, the absolute power in killing to preserve yourself and your squad.

No one was really interested in what you did over there. You felt like Vietnam was all just a fast food meal—once it's finished, you throw everything away—no silverware or plates or cups to wash, no memories. You couldn't think about all this too long. You knew if you did, you'd be in serious trouble.

The female bartenders working the cabanas on Santa Monica Beach still ignored us, as did the bikini-clad girls. We didn't care. We felt superior to everyone on the beach. We laughed inwardly at the guys roller skating and lifting weights. We tried to imagine their smooth, tanned bodies dodging bullets in a leech-infested rice paddy. They still needed to validate their manhood and courage. We didn't. They were trying to impress; we had no need for that. Although most were our age or older, they seemed like narcissistic children performing for themselves.

The weekends at John's were enjoyable, but different from before. It would take years to fully comprehend what had happened to us. Some of us would never understand the life-altering consequences of our experience. Some would never admit that the war had changed them. Others would blame the war for every bad decision they made or subsequent misfortune they experienced.

The three months passed. I was concerned about how I would perform at college. I bought several vocabulary study guides, because I was ashamed of my rough, Marine DI vocabulary.

VIP Visit

Something major was happening at the base. Camp Pendleton was abuzz with rumors, and unbelievable levels of security were in place. It was November 9, 1967, the day before the greatest annual celebration in the Corps—the birthday of the Marine Corps. All entrances to the large base had been closed. Marines and dependents on the outside were not allowed to enter and those of us inside were not allowed to leave. The rumor was that a VIP was going to visit the base for the birthday bash.

A large birthday cake sat on a table straddling the fifty-yard line of the football field. The stands were packed and Marines stood ten deep behind a rope security barricade. A receiving party of generals and other senior officers stood at attention near the cake. The Marine Band was on the field, ready to play when ordered. A massive communications complex had been set up behind one of the bleachers. Snipers, with scoped rifles were positioned on top of several barracks overlooking the football field.

Suddenly, a group of five Marine helicopters appeared over the field. The formation included two CH-46 choppers and three Huey gunships. The Hueys circled the field as if it was an enemy target. The need for such extreme security was hard to understand. This was a military base, not the UC campus at Berkeley.

The first CH-46 landed on the LZ near the middle of the field. Several minutes passed before passengers started disembarking. I was one of the ten-deep standing-room-only Marines with a poor view. I saw someone in a suit walk out of the chopper, then I saw him. He was easy to spot—tall, silver hair, with a leader's posture. The Marine Band started playing Hail to The Chief. They played for just seconds before stopping. The president walked only a few yards on the red carpet before disappearing. Then the second CH-46 landed with the real president. Although never officially confirmed, the first president had been a body double, a decoy.

Secretary of Defense Robert McNamara and a group of dignitaries I didn't recognize accompanied President Johnson. The public address system wasn't working, but I pretty much knew what he was saying without hearing it. He thanked us for our sacrifice and reiterated our commitment to support South Vietnam against the Communist North. He praised the Marine Corps and called us the premier fighting force in the world.

I have no idea what McNamara said. I didn't care. I didn't like him. His hair style was particularly irritating. He looked like a banker who enjoyed denying loans to struggling farmers.

My last two weeks in the Corps seemed like an eternity. I had been at the NCO club all evening. I had drunk my way through happy hour and was now paying full price. Several of us, including John, were sitting around a table talking about the war.

The intensity of combat in Vietnam continued to escalate. We all had been in combat and were thankful to be home alive. But inside, many of us felt guilty that we were home while thousands of others were still fighting our war. Everyone had left except me. I was sitting by myself. Sitting and drinking.

At about 2200 hours, I made an alcohol-induced decision. I would extend my Marine Corps enlistment and return to Vietnam. Although I was on a medical profile and could not serve in a field combat role, I could still contribute. The more beer I drank, the better the plan seemed. I decided to call home and run my idea by Dad.

I called home, talked to Mom for a while, and asked to talk to Dad. Mom asked me if I had been drinking. I told her I'd had a couple of beers. Dad came to the phone. He never talked long on the phone. That night was probably the longest phone conversation of his life and it lasted about five minutes. He told me I had done my duty and that another year wouldn't make me a better man. He also said that extending would probably kill my mother. He ended our conversation by saying, "Go to bed, get a good night's sleep, and call me tomorrow. We love you, Son." I followed his advice, and when I woke up the next morning, my idea to extend didn't seem like that great a plan. I didn't call him back. Dad knew what my decision would be.

Homeward Bound

On December 8, 1967, I was released from active duty. I received my *DD214* that said I was being released for the "Convenience of the Government." I had no idea what my career path would be, but on line 23b, it said that my Related Civilian Occupational Classification was *Proof Director, Small Arms (firearms)*. I didn't know what a Proof Director, Small Arms was, but apparently the government thought I was qualified. The Marine next to me in line said a Proof Director was the guy who tested all the rifles and pistols before a manufacturer sold the weapons to dealers. If that was true, I felt qualified.

I said my good byes to a very small and special group of friends. My farewells to John and Arturo were the hardest.

The guard at the Camp Pendleton main gate waved me through for the last time. I felt excited but unsure. I was twenty-one-years-old with the rest of my life to live. I pointed the Mustang east and headed for Minnesota.

Much of Route 66 is desolate and empty—an excellent environment for thinking. I reflected on the past and uncertainly anticipated the future.

The mood of the country was changing. When I enlisted in the Marine Corps, victory in Vietnam seemed certain. When I was released, losing seemed very possible. It wasn't like WWII when everyone was behind the war and losing was not an option. Nevertheless, I was proud of my service. Even if we ended up losing the war, I had won my personal battles.

My thoughts drifted back to August when I returned from Vietnam and landed at Travis Air Force Base. Our paperwork was efficiently processed and we were whisked under the cover of darkness to San Francisco International Airport. There weren't any bands or parades to welcome us back. I hadn't expected any, but I felt like I was sneaking back into my own country. I felt guilty about changing into civilian clothes in the bathroom at the Minneapolis Airport.

After experiencing the mental and physical rigors of combat, much seemed immaterial and unnecessary. For me, the stateside military assignments seemed meaningless, and civilian life lacked excitement. The exhilaration of total personal power was gone, but I had the unique self-confidence that combat survival produces. My priorities had changed and I would never be the person I once was. I would be better.

It was December 9th and I was seventy-five miles from the Minnesota border. I would miss deer hunting season this year. I was a month too late. I didn't care. I no longer needed a trophy.

Epilogue

My job requires frequent trips to Washington, D.C. For the last fourteen years, I have made it a point to visit the Vietnam Memorial whenever I am in town. It has become a personal pilgrimage. I feel that I owe it to the heroes whose names are inscribed there. Ten years ago, I would walk from my downtown hotel to the Wall and back. Now, I take a cab and walk back.

On December 9, 2003, I visited the Wall. Several days earlier, Washington D.C. had been hit by an early snowstorm, and the temperature was in the low 30's. As a result of the inclement weather, there were few visitors. I took my time walking down the black slate walkway that fronts the Wall, stopping periodically to look at a grouping of names. I had no plan. I wasn't looking for a particular name; I was just walking and reflecting.

I stopped and noticed that I was in front of panel 10E. I looked at the names on the wall starting from the bottom to the top. Near the top of the panel I spotted the name, **Larry Glover**. This certainly couldn't be the same Larry Glover who had been with Delta Company and was killed by a booby-trapped 60mm mortar round. Several Larry Glovers were probably killed during the war. Nevertheless, I noted the panel and line where his name appeared and continued my walk to the end of the wall.

To satisfy my curiosity, I looked up Larry Glover at one of the locator indexes on the sidewalk. "USMC, panel 10, line 124, killed in action September 20, 1966." It *was* the Glover I knew. It was Wilson's friend.

Once again I had been in the right place at the right time. Why had I stopped at panel 10? Why did my eyes fall on the name Larry Glover? (It is difficult to find a name on the Wall even when you know the panel and row number.) The answer is simple: luck. It is the same reason I am alive and so many other fine combat soldiers are dead.

Semper Fi,

Gary L. Tornes

In Memory of

PFC PATRICK J. CONNORS

Killed in action, August 30, 1966

PFC GARY E. ROSSER

Killed in action, September 20, 1966

PFC KENTON D. KNAPP

Killed in action, January 17, 1967

and

Sgt. JAMES "MAC" McGOUGIN

Died, July 2001

Heroes of:

Delta Company, 1st Squad, 1st Platoon

1st Battalion, 1st Marine Regiment

First Marine Division

Glossary

ACTUAL: The Unit Commander. Used to distinguish the commander from the radioman when the call sign was used.

AIT: Advanced Infantry Training. This is the second phase of boot camp.

AK-47: Standard assault rifle of the NVA – usually Russian or Chinese made.

AMTRAC, TRAC: An amphibious tractor, mounted with a machine gun and capable of traversing water barriers.

ARTY: Slang for artillery.

ARVN: Army of the Republic of Vietnam (South Vietnam). The term was commonly used to refer to both the individual soldiers and the South Vietnamese Army itself.

AWOL: Absent without leave.

BAS: Battalion Aid Station

BATTERY: A U.S. battery consists of six artillery guns.

BLOOPER: Nickname for the M-79 grenade launcher, a 40-millimeter, shoulder-fired launcher with an effective range of 400 meters.

BRONZE STAR: Forth highest U.S. combat award.

C-4: Plastic explosive, carried in one-pound bars. Often used for cooking as well as detonating.

C-130: A cargo aircraft. Hercules.

CH-34: The smallest of the troop and cargo carrying helicopters used by the Marines. Sea Horse.

CH-46: Medium lift helicopter. Sea Knight.

CH-54: Heavy lift helicopter. Sea Stallion.

CHOPPERS: Helicopters.

CHUCK DUDE: A term originated by black Marines to refer to whites.

CLAYMORE: Directional, command-detonated, anti-personnel mine.

CLICK: Slang for kilometer

CO: Commanding Officer.

CONCERTINA: Large rolls of barbed wire used in this configuration for perimeter security defense.

CORPSMAN/(DOC): Enlisted navy medical personnel assigned to Marine field units.

COUNTY FAIR: A keystone of the U.S. attempt to pacify the population of South Vietnam, County Fairs were "cordon and search" operations designed to separate the VC from their population bases.

COVER: Marines call hats "covers" and the army calls them "caps."

CP: Command post. Units platoon–sized and larger established command posts, usually temporary, to coordinate the activities from a central point.

C-RATS: C-rations, provided to the field in cartons of twelve boxes. Boxes contained food such as ham and chopped eggs, beans and franks, chicken and noodles, pound cake, instant coffee; cigarettes, toilet paper, matches, etc.

DI-DI: Vietnamese for "to run". American's used it to order Vietnamese to "get away".

DMZ: Demiliterized zone. The zone centered on the Ben Hai River that separated North and South Vietnam during the war.

DUNG LAI: Vietnamese for "Stop !".

E-TOOL: Entrenching tool. A small folding shovel used for digging fighting holes or filling sandbags.

EMBARK: To load aboard.

F-4: Fighter–attack aircraft. Phantom.

FIRE FOR EFFECT: Command given supporting arms when the forward observer is satisfied that they are registered on the target. Usually preceded by the firing of spotter rounds to zero-in on the target. In critical situations, firing for effect would be requested without spotter rounds.

FNG: Fucking New Guy

FOUR HOLER: Field toilet facility.

FREE FIRE ZONE: In Vietnam, an area supposedly cleared of noncombatants and anyone remaining in the designated area could be regarded as the enemy and fired upon.

GOOK: Derogatory slang for any Oriental; also, dink, slope, slant.

GRENADIER: A Marine who carried the M79 grenade launcher as his primary weapon.

GRUNT: Any ground-pounding infantry man.

GUNNY/GUNNERY SERGEANT: This is a rank, a pay grade (E-7), and the senior operational NCO of a rifle company.

GUNSHIP: An armed UH-1E (Huey) used to provide support for ground troops.

HOOCH: Any dwelling, whether temporary, as in a Marine poncho hooch, or reasonably permanent, as in a Vietnamese villager's home.

HQ: headquarters

ITR: Infantry training regiment. Where all enlisted Marines received advanced infantry skills after they finished recruit training or boot camp.

K-BAR: A Marine Corps fighting knife initially issued in WWII.

KIA: Killed in action.

LAAW: Light anti-tank assault weapon. A shoulder-fired, 66-millimeter, single use rocket, disposable after used once.

LAI DAY: Vietnamese for "Come here!"

LIFER: A career military person. Often used derogatorily.

LOD: Line of departure.

LP: Listening post. A small group of men stationed outside the lines or perimeter at night who listened for enemy movement or approach.

LST: Landing ship tank. Flat-bottomed naval vessel that could land tanks, troops and other materials directly on the beach.

LZ: Landing zone. Any place where helicopters were called upon to land.

M-14: A 7.62 millimeter, semi-automatic/automatic military rifle. Standard issue for all Marines in Vietnam until early 1967. Replaced by M-16.

MEDEVAC: To medically evacuate a casualty. Priority medevacs were seriously wounded. Emergency medevacs were those near death. Routine medevacs were walking wounded or dead.

MOS: Military occupational specialty.

MPC: Military Payment Currency; issued in denominations from 5 cents to 10 dollars.

NAPALM: Canisters containing 125 gallons of jellied gasoline. Would ignite on impact when dropped from planes and spread a torrent of flame through hundreds of yards of jungle that fragmentation bombs could not penetrate.

NCOIC: Noncommissioned officer in charge.

NSA: Naval Support Activity; naval hospital in Da Nang.

NUMBER ONE: The very best.

NUMBER TEN: The very worst.

NVA: North Vietnamese Army or more properly called the Peoples Army of Vietnam. NVA, like ARVN, its counterpart in the south, was used to refer to individual soldiers as well as the army itself.

OP: Observation post or outpost. A post manned by small groups of men to observe and report on enemy movement.

POGUE: A Marine assigned to an office job in the rear.

PROBE: An attempt by an attacking force to learn something about the defending force by sending small units in exploratory attacks against the enemy lines.

PURPLE HEART: Medal awarded for wounds received in combat action- ranks immediately behind the Bronze Star in importance.

R & R: Rest and recuperation. A five day vacation to places, such as Hong Kong, Taipai, Hawaii, Bankok or Australia. You were granted one R&R during your 13-month tour.

RPG: Rocket-Propelled Grenade; a shoulder-fired rocket launcher used by the NVA and VC against tanks, personnel, and low flying helicopters.

SHORT: One whose tour in Vietnam is almost over.

SIX-BY: Two-and-a-half or five-ton truck that has six drive wheels.

SKATE: A task or assignment that required little effort or pain.

SPIDER TRAP: A small, well-camouflaged hole that can be used by a sol- dier to conceal himself from the enemy.

SPLIB: A term originated by black Marines to refer to other blacks.

TANGLEFOOT: A way of configuring barbed wire at ankle-deep height.

TAOR: Tactical Area of Responsibility – the area for which a particular base, unit, or squadron was responsible.

TOP: Informal form of address used for enlisted men above the rank of gunnery sergeant.

UTILITIES: The Marine field uniform. In the army, they are referred to as "fatigues".

VC: Viet Cong. Communist guerrillas.

VCS: Viet Cong Sympathizers.

VILLE: French word for town.

XO: Executive Officer – number two officer of a battalion unit or larger.

WHITE PHOSPHORUS: A very hot incendiary round fired by several weapons. Used for adjusting onto targets, marking targets, incendiary effects and smoke.

WIA: Wounded in Action.

Index